THE
OSAMA
BIN
LADEN
FILES

Letters and Documents Discovered
by SEAL Team Six During Their Raid
on bin Laden's Compound

**INCLUDES AN INTRODUCTION AND IN-DEPTH
ANALYSIS BY THE COMBATING
TERRORISM CENTER**

Skyhorse Publishing

Visit our website at www.skyhorsepublishing.com.

10 9 8 7 6 5 4 3 2 1

Library of Congress Cataloging-in-Publication Data is available on request.

ISBN: 978-1-62087-382-3

Printed in the United States of America

CONTENTS

DESCRIPTION OF THE ABBOTTABAD DOCUMENTS PROVIDED TO THE CTC

This document provides a general description of the 17 declassified documents captured in the Abbottabad raid and released to the Combating Terrorism Center (CTC). For additional context please see the documents themselves and/or the CTC's report "Letters from Abbottabad: Bin Ladin Sidelined?" released in conjunction with this summary.

The 17 documents consist of electronic letters or draft letters, totaling 175 pages in the original Arabic and 197 pages in the English translation. The earliest letter is dated September 2006 and the latest April 2011. These internal al-Qa`ida communications were authored by several leaders, including Usama bin Ladin, `Atiyya `Abd al-Rahman, Abu Yahya al-Libi and the American Adam Gadahn, as well as several unknown individuals who were either affiliated with the group or wrote to offer it advice. Other recognizable personalities who feature in the letters either as authors, recipients or points of conversation include Mukhtar Abu al-Zubayr, leader of the Somali militant group Harakat al-Shabab al-Mujahidin; Nasir al-Wuhayshi (Abu Basir), leader of the Yemen-based al-Qa`ida in the Arabian Peninsula (AQAP); Anwar al-`Awlaqi; and Hakimullah Mahsud, leader of Tehrik-e-Taliban Pakistan (TTP). Some of the letters are incomplete and/or are missing their dates, and not all of the letters explicitly attribute their author(s) and/or indicate to whom they are addressed. Given that they are all electronic documents either saved on thumb drives, memory cards or the hard drive of Bin Ladin's computer, except for the letters addressed to Bin Ladin, it cannot be ascertained whether any of these letters actually reached their intended destinations.

SOCOM-2012-0000003

This letter was authored by Usama bin Ladin and addressed to Shaykh Mahmud (`Atiyya Abdul Rahman) on 27 August 2010. Mahmud is specifically directed to tell "Basir," who is Nasir al-Wuhayshi (Abu Basir), the leader of al-Qa`ida in the Arabian Peninsula, to remain in his role (presumably in response to a request from Abu Basir that Anwar al-`Awlaqi take his position), and for him to send "us a detailed and lengthy" version of al-`Awlaqi's resume. `Atiyya is also told to ask Basir and Anwar al-`Awlaqi for their "vision in detail about the situation" in Yemen. References are also made in the letter to the 2010 floods in Pakistan, a letter from Bin Ladin's son Khalid to `Abd al-Latif, al-Qa`ida's media plan for the 9/11 anniversary, and the need for the "brothers coming from Iran" to be placed in safe locations.

SOCOM-2012-0000004

This document is a letter authored by the American al-Qa`ida spokesman Adam Gadahn to an unknown recipient and was written in late January 2011. In the first part of the document Gadahn provides strategic advice regarding al-Qa`ida's media plans for the tenth anniversary of 9/11. The letter is in essence a response to many of the requests/queries that Bin Ladin makes in his letter to `Atiyya dated October 2010 (SOCOM-2012-0000015), particularly those concerning a media strategy for the ten-year anniversary of 9/11. In other parts of the document Gadahn incisively criticizes the tactics and targeting calculus of the Islamic State of Iraq (AQI/ISI) and the Pakistani Taliban (TTP); he strongly advocates for al-Qa`ida to publicly dissociate itself from both groups. The document concludes with a draft statement, which provides a candid assessment of these issues.

SOCOM-2012-0000005

This document is a letter dated 7 August 2010 from "Zamarai" (Usama bin Ladin) to Mukhtar Abu al-Zubayr, the leader of the Somali militant group Harakat al-Shabab al-Mujahidin, which merged with al-Qa`ida after Bin Ladin's death. The document is a response to a letter Bin Ladin received from al-Zubayr in which he requested formal unity with al-Qa`ida and either consulted Bin Ladin on the question of declaring an Islamic state in Somalia or informed him that he was about to declare one. In Bin Ladin's response, he politely declines al-Shabab's request for formal unity with al-Qa`ida.

SOCOM-2012-0000006

This document is a letter believed to have been composed in December 2010 and its content relates to SOCOM-2012-0000005. The letter is addressed to Azmarai, perhaps a typo or misspelling of the nickname Zamarai (a nickname or *kunya* for Bin Ladin). While the identity of the author is unclear, the familiar tone and implicit critique of Bin Ladin's policy vis-a-vis al-Shabab suggest that this is from a high ranking personality, possibly Ayman al-Zawahiri. Referring to "our friend's letter" and the perspective of the "brothers…[who might have been] too concerned about inflating the size and growth of al-Qa`ida," the author of the document urges the receiver to "reconsider your opinion not to declare the accession [i.e. formal merger] of the brothers of Somalia…" This is clearly a reference to al-Qa`ida's potential merger with al-Shabab and suggests that al-Qa`ida's relationship with the "affiliates" is a subject of internal debate. If indeed the author of the letter is Ayman al-Zawahiri this could be an indication of a major fissure over a key strategic question at the pinnacle of the organization (for different interpretations of this letter, see Appendix of "Letters from Abbottabad").

SOCOM-2012-0000007

This letter is authored by Mahmud al-Hasan (`Atiyya) and Abu Yahya al-Libi and addressed to the *amir* of Tehrik-e-Taliban Pakistan (TTP), Hakimullah Mahsud. It is dated 3 December 2010 and is sharply critical of the ideology and tactics of the TTP. The letter makes it clear that al-Qa`ida's senior leaders had serious concerns about the TTP's trajectory inside Pakistan, and the impact the group's misguided operations might have on al-Qa`ida and other militant groups in the region. The authors identify several errors committed by the group, specifically Hakimullah Mahsud's arrogation of privileges and positions beyond what was appropriate as the TTP's *amir*; the TTP's use of indiscriminate violence and killing of Muslim civilians; and the group's use of kidnapping. `Atiyya and al-Libi also take issue with Mahsud labeling al-Qa`ida members as "guests" and the attempts made by other groups (presumably the TTP) to siphon off al-Qa`ida members. The authors threaten that if actions are not taken to correct these mistakes, "we shall be forced to take public and firm legal steps from our side."

SOCOM-2012-0000008

This letter was originally an exchange between Jaysh al-Islam and `Atiyya that was forwarded first to a certain `Abd al-Hamid (and presumably to Bin Ladin later). The gist of Jaysh al-Islam's letter makes it known that the group is in need of financial assistance "to support jihad," and that the group is seeking `Atiyya's legal advice on three matters: 1) the permissibility of accepting financial assistance from other militant Palestinian groups (e.g., Fatah and Palestinian Islamic Jihad); 2) the permissibility of investing funds in the stock market in support of jihad; and 3) the permissibility of striking or killing drug traffickers in order to use their money, and even drugs, to lure their enemies who could in turn be used by Jaysh al-Islam as double-agents. `Atiyya's response, written sometime between 24 October 2006 and 22 November 2006, is cordial but distant, responding to the questions but refraining from giving any strategic advice.

SOCOM-2012-0000009

This document is part of a longer letter which was not released to the CTC. It is not clear who authored the letter or to whom it was addressed. It discusses the potential need to change the name of "Qa`idat al-Jihad." The author is of the view that the abridging of the name "al-Qa`ida" has "lessened Muslims' feelings that we belong to them." The author is further concerned that since the name "al-Qa`ida" lacks religious connotations, it has allowed the United States to launch a war on "al-Qa`ida" without offending Muslims. The author proposed a list of new names that capture Islamic theological themes: *Ta'ifat al-tawhid wa-al-jihad* (Monotheism and Jihad Group), *Jama`at wahdat al-Muslimin* (Muslim Unity Group), *Hizb tawhid al-Umma al-Islamiyya* (Islamic Nation Unification Party) and *Jama`at tahrir al-aqsa* (Al-Aqsa Liberation Group).

SOCOM-2012-0000010

This letter is authored by "Abu `Abdallah" (Usama bin Ladin), addressed to "Shaykh Mahmud" (`Atiyya) and dated 26 April 2011 – a week before bin Ladin's death. In it, Bin Ladin outlines his response to the "Arab Spring," proposing two different strategies. The first strategy pertains to the Arab World and entails "inciting people who have not yet revolted and exhort[ing] them to rebel against the rulers (*khuruj 'ala al-hukkam*)"; the second strategy concerns Afghanistan and it entails continuing to evoke the obligation of jihad there. The letter also makes

4

reference to a wide variety of topics including: the scarcity of communications from Iraq, "the brothers coming from Iran," and hostages held by "our brothers in the Islamic Maghreb" and in Somalia. The document also briefly discusses Bin Ladin's sons, his courier, Shaykh Abu Muhammad (Ayman al-Zawahiri), and other individuals of interest.

SOCOM-2012-0000011

This letter, dated 28 March 2007, is addressed to a legal scholar by the name of Hafiz Sultan, and it is authored by someone who is of Egyptian origin. The author makes it explicit that he was alarmed by al-Qaʿida in Iraq's conduct and he urges Sultan to write to that group's leaders to correct their ways. The author also asks for legal guidance on the use of chlorine gas, which he appears not to support. A reference is also made to "the brothers in Lebanon" and the need to arrange "to have one of their representatives visit us in the near future." A message from the "brothers in Algeria" is also included.

SOCOM-2012-0000012

This letter dated 11 June 2009 was written by ʿAtiyya to the "honorable shaykh." It is possible that it was addressed to Usama bin Ladin, but it may have been addressed to another senior leader. The majority of the letter provides details on the release of detained jihadi "brothers" and their families from Iran and an indication that more are expected to be released, including Bin Ladin's family. It seems that their release was partially in response to covert operations by al-Qaʿida against Iran and its interests.

SOCOM-2012-0000013

This is a draft that formed the basis of a publicly available document, part four in a series of statements that Ayman al-Zawahiri released in response to the "Arab Spring." Through the document one can observe al-Qaʿida's editing process (reflected in the editor's comments highlighted in green and in a bold font). While it is not clear if Bin Ladin himself did the editing, whoever did so has solid grammatical foundations and prefers a more self-effacing writing style than al-Zawahiri. The edits were not included in al-Zawahiri's final speech which was released in a video on 4 March 2011 on jihadi forums. Of the 12 proposed corrections only one appears in al-Zawahiri's speech.

SOCOM-2012-0000014

This document consists of two letters addressed to "Abu `Abd-al-Rahman," almost certainly `Atiyya `Abd al-Rahman. It was sent by an operative who knows `Atiyya and is a religious student with ties to the senior shaykhs and clerics in Saudi Arabia. While the letters are not dated, their contents suggest they were composed soon after January 2007; they read very much like an intelligence assessment, designed to provide `Atiyya with some perspective on how al-Qa`ida generally, and the Islamic State of Iraq (ISI) more specifically, are perceived amongst Saudi scholars of varying degrees of prominence. The author provides `Atiyya with brief summaries of private meetings the author had with certain scholars, with the clear intent of evaluating the level of support that al-Qa`ida enjoys from some relatively prominent members of the Saudi religious establishment.

SOCOM-2012-0000015

This document is a letter dated 21 October 2010 from Bin Ladin to "Shaykh Mahmud" (`Atiyya). The letter is primarily focused on issues in the Afghanistan/Pakistan region. In the letter Bin Ladin specifically comments on: the security situation in Waziristan and the need to relocate al-Qa`ida members from the region; counter surveillance issues associated with the movement of his son Hamza within Pakistan; the appointment of `Atiyya's three deputies; various al-Sahab videos and the media plan for the tenth anniversary of 9/11; the release of an Afghan prisoner held by al-Qa`ida; and the trial of Faisal Shahzad. Ayman al-Zawahiri, Abu Yahya al-Libi, Saif al-`Adl, and Adam Gadahn are also mentioned in the document.

SOCOM-2012-0000016

This document is a letter addressed to "Abu Basir" (Nasir al-Wuhayshi, leader of al-Qa`ida in the Arabian Peninsula - AQAP) from an unidentified author, most likely Usama bin Ladin and/or `Atiyya. The letter is in part a response to specific requests for guidance from AQAP's leadership. The author specifically advises AQAP to focus on targeting the United States, not the Yemeni government or security forces. The author also discusses media strategy and the importance of AQAP's relations with Yemen's tribes.

SOCOM-2012-0000017

This document is a series of paragraphs, some of which match the content found in SOCOM-2012-0000016. This document was likely written by the author of that document. This letter discusses strategy, the need for al-Qa`ida to remain focused on targeting the United States (or even against U.S. targets in South Africa where other "brothers" are not active), the importance of tribal relations in a variety of different countries, and media activity.

SOCOM-2012-0000018

This document is a letter addressed to Usama bin Ladin from "a loving brother whom you know and who knows you" and dated 14 September 2006. The author is critical of Bin Ladin for focusing al- Qa`ida's operations on "Islamic countries in general and the Arabian Peninsula in particular." He enumerates the numerous negative consequences of engaging in jihad inside Saudi Arabia, and informs Bin Ladin that people are now repulsed by the technical term "jihad" and even forbidden to use it in lectures. The author strongly advised Bin Ladin to change his policies.

SOCOM-2012-0000019

This document is a long letter authored by Usama bin Ladin after the death of Sheikh Sa'id (Mustafa Abu'l-Yazid) in late May 2010 and it is addressed to "Shaykh Mahmud" (`Atiyya) who he designates as Sa'id's successor. Bin Ladin's letter is concerned with the mistakes committed by regional jihadi groups, which have resulted in the unnecessary deaths of thousands of Muslim civilians. Bin Ladin indicates that he would like to start a "new phase" so that the jihadis could regain the trust of Muslims. He directs `Atiyya to prepare a memorandum to centralize, in the hands of AQC, the media campaign and operations of regional jihadi groups. Considerable space is devoted to a discussion about Yemen, external operations and Bin Ladin's plans for his son Hamza. This document includes an additional letter that Bin Ladin forwards to `Atiyya authored by Shaykh Yunis, presumably Yunis al-Mauritani, consisting of a new operational plan that al- Qa`ida should consider adopting.

The following 17 documents
are reprinted exactly as they
were released by the
Combating Terrorism Center
at West Point

In the name of God, Most Gracious, Most Merciful

Praise be to God, Lord of the universe, and peace and prayers be upon our Prophet Muhammad, his family, and all of his companions

Now then...

To the noble brother, Shaykh Mahmud, may God protect him
Peace be upon you, God's Mercy and Blessings

I hope you receive this message of mine while you, your family, children, and all of the brothers are in good health.

So,

- With regard to what you had mentioned in a previous message, that some brothers may go to Iran as part of a plan to protect the brother, thus I see that Iran is not suitable. Also, when choosing the areas where the brothers will be inside Pakistan it's necessary to take into consideration that they are not areas that encountered floods or may encounter them in the future.

- With regard to the brothers coming from Iran, thus I see, at this stage, that they be at safe locations outside the areas being attacked.

- Regarding what's related to Pakistan, thus I didn't take a look at the report you mentioned. However, the opinion in general is to be concerned with calming things down and focusing efforts on the Americans.

- With regard to what pertains to appointing the brothers in the administrative positions, thus I see that they pledge an allegiance that would include some points, which would protect the work and its secrets. Therefore, I hope that you all deliberate concerning the matter and inform me of your opinion, and amongst the proposed points, for example:

1- Listening, obedience, and Jihad so as to bring back the Caliphate.

2- Protect operational secrets.

3- Protect the work he is going to be responsible for, and provide advice to the leadership.

- Regarding what brother Basir mentioned relating to Anwar al-'Awlaqi, it would be excellent if you inform him, on my behalf in a private message to him, to remain in his position where he is qualified and capable of running the matter in Yemen.

Therefore, he shall continue, by the blessings of God, as he has the characteristics that makes him capable of that. Additionally, the presence of some of the characteristics by our brother Anwar al-'Awlaqi is a good thing, in order to serve Jihad, and how excellent would it be if he gives us a chance to be introduced to him more.

- Also, I hope that he be informed of us still needing more information from the battlefield in Yemen, so that it is feasible for us, with the help of God, to make the most appropriate decision to either escalate or calm down. And with regard to informing us of the situations by them, thus I hope that brother Basir writes me his vision in detail about the situations and also asks brother Anwar al-'Awlaqi to write his vision in detail in a separate message, as well as brother Abu-Sufyan Sa'id al-Shahri, to send his vision in detail and separate.

How excellent would it be if you ask brother Basir to send us the resume, in detail and lengthy, of brother Anwar al-'Awlaqi, as well as the facts he relied on when recommending him, while informing him that his recommendation is considered. However, we would like to be reassured more. For example, we here become reassured of the people when they go to the line and get examined there.

Also, I hope that brother Basir be informed that the media appearance is his task, and in general, they should reduce the appearance during this period unless necessary, and if necessity calls for one of the brothers to issue a speech, thus Basir should review it before it's broadcasted in the media. It shall be pointed out, whereas you didn't point out, that the speech of

brother Sa'id al-Shahri that was issued about the apprehension
of one of the sisters in Saudi was not appropriate at the time.

With regard to what you mentioned in a previous message,
regarding your opinion to reduce the correspondence, thus we are
concerned with the security aspect, yet I have a tape for the
nation that includes instigation of the people of Iraq and
preaching to the Awakenings to return to the Mujahidin. I am
going to send it, God willing, the next time, thus you can
arrange with the courier to have the card that's going to
contain this statement delivered to the media section directly,
and if a necessary matter develops, we are going to attach to
you a message that will be sent to you by the media section.

- Attached with this message is a visual statement to the
American people that I hope a copy of it be given to the
International Al Jazeera and the Arab Al Jazeera. I also hope
for it to be translated (voice over) to English and to be
delivered to the Al Jazeera channel prior to the anniversary of
9/11, to be broadcasted during it. Also, two copies of it are
attached, one of which is recorded and the other written.

- We sent you, along with the messages that preceded this, a
statement regarding the floods of Pakistan. Its broadcasting to
media was delayed, thus perhaps it's for a good reason. However,
in any case, I had attached the content of this card to this
message.

- Note: Please broadcast the flood statement before the American
People statement, as the American People statement to be during
the anniversary of 9/11.

- Attached is a message from my son Khalid to brother 'Abd-al-
Latif, and a message to the brothers in the media section.

In conclusion, I ask God, the Glorified and Almighty, to protect
you and to make you successful towards what He loves and is
satisfied with, and the last of our prayers is praise be to God,
Lord of the Universe, and peace and prayers be upon our Prophet
Muhammad, his family, and all of his companions.

Peace be upon you, God's Mercy and Blessings

Thursday

17 Ramadan 1431 Hijri (TN: 27 August 2010)

(TN: End of translation)

13

Full Translation begins:

In the name of God the merciful the compassionate

1- Evaluating the material of the speech and the benefit of the Shaykh's appearance in the present stage:

As for the material of the speech, it is fine and not specified on the midterm elections, but is good for publishing in any time, God knows best. But I have a warning about what was mentioned of a statement by (a previous president of yours) who is the person? If what is meant is what was referred to (Benjamin Franklin), who was mentioned by Shaykh Ayman in one of his statements, we should remind that (Benjamin Franklin) was not a president, but a "statesman" and one of the founders of the United States and its Constitution. I have not heard about what is quoted from him, but from Shaykh Ayman. I do not know the source of the story, or its popularity amongst the Americans. But such a mistake may be used to slander the Shaykh, and accuse him of talking about something he does not master (politics). The evidence is his mixing between the presidents and non-presidents. Although plenty of the Americans may also think that (Franklin) a president, because of his picture on the currency that usually carries the photos of the presidents. But this mistake is not usually committed by those talking in politics, analyzing and discussing. It is a common mistake among general people and not between specialists.

All of this, if the one desired is -"the previous president" (Benjamin Franklin). If another person was intended, then there is no need for my previous words.

As for the benefit of exposing the Shaykh at this stage, we should look at this matter from all angles. We should also consider the following points:

- Irrespective of the passing of the mid-term elections, the timing now is very suitable for the Shaykh to show with this speech. This is because all the political talk in America is about the economy, forgetting or ignoring the war and its role in weakening the economy. Just as what a Pakistani journalist residing in America has said, that the press conference held by Obama after the midterm elections, all the questions were on the bad economy, and the means to get out of the crisis. Nevertheless not one of the journalists dared to embarrass Obama

by questioning him about the influence on the American budget
and the national economy of spending the billions yearly on the
two wars of Afghanistan and Iraq.

- It is all right if the Shaykh appeared now, then appeared in
the 10th anniversary of the attacks of Manhattan and Washington.
Every exposure of him, as long as it is not daily or semi-
weekly, should have an influence. The repetition of his
exposure, irrespective of the vicious campaign that is waged
against al-Qa'ida, everywhere, is by itself something that
attracts attention.

- We should not forget that there are millions of admirers of
the Shaykh in the Islamic world, who are eager for his
appearance to ensure his health and that he is well. Those
should be targeted in our speeches and messages, before the
Americans and Europeans, who do not listen to or evaluate what
is being said.

- We should also not forget the Mujahidin brothers in the
fronts, who are passing through crucial times and facing
disaster after disaster. They also will be happy to see the
Shaykh again; his appearance will raise their morale with the
help of God. I would think that it is suitable for the Shaykh to
address a video speech to the Mujahidin in all the arenas,
consoling, urging them to endure, confirming their steps and
guiding them. The message that he sent when Shaykh Sa'id -may
God bless his soul- was strong and influential, so may God
reward him well. Many people do not read, and even if they read,
they are more influenced by visuals.

The bottom line, since there is no security precaution from
having a video appearance, and there is no error or something in
the speech which may need reconsideration, and as long as the
Shaykh is satisfied to publish it after the elections -being
silent is a sign of acceptance- I see that it is produced with
no hesitation or delay, and God knows best.

2- The Issue of preparing for the Tenth Anniversary, and how it
will be marketed in the Media, and How to Exploit the Media in
General:

As far as the American channel that could be used to deliver our
messages, whether on the tenth anniversary or before or after,
in my personal opinion there are no distinct differences between

the channels from the standpoint of professionalism and neutrality. It is all as the Shaykh has stated (close to professionalism and neutrality) it has not and will not reach the perfect professionalism and neutrality, only if God wants that.

From the professional point of view, they are all on one level-except (Fox News) channel which falls into the abyss as you know, and lacks neutrality too.

As for the neutrality of CNN in English, it seems to be in cooperation with the government more than the others (except Fox News of course). Its Arabic version brings good and detailed reports about al-Sahab releases, with a lot of quotations from the original text. That means they copy directly from the releases or its gist. It is not like what other channels and sites do, copying from news agencies like Reuters, AP and others.

I used to think that MSNBC channel may be good and neutral a bit, but is has lately fired two of the most famous journalists -Keith Olberman and Octavia Nasser the Lebanese – because they released some statements that were open for argument (The Lebanese had praised a Shia Imam Muhammad Husayn Fadlallah after his death and called him "One of the marvels of Hizballah" it seems she is a Shia.)

CBS channel was mentioned by the Shaykh, I see that it is like the other channels, but it has a famous program (60 Minutes) that has some popularity and a good reputation for its long broadcasting time. Only God knows the reality, as I am not really in a position to do so.

ABC channel is all right; actually it could be one of the best channels, as far as we are concerned. It is interested in al-Qa'ida issues, particularly the journalist Brian Ross, who is specialized in terrorism. The channel is still proud for its interview with the Shaykh. It also broadcasted excerpts from a speech of mine on the fourth anniversary, it also published most of that text on its site on the internet.

In conclusion, we can say that there is no single channel that we could rely on for our messages. I may ignore them, and even the channel that broadcast them, probably it would distort them somehow. This is accomplished by bringing analysts and experts that would interpret its meaning in the way they want it to be. Or they may ignore the message and conduct a smearing of the individuals, to the end of the list of what you know about their cunning methods.

But if the display -in the next anniversary for example- of a special type, like a special interview with Shaykh Usama or Shaykh Ayman, and with questions chosen by the channel, and with a good camera, we might find a channel that would accept its broadcasting. But they would accept this time, so as to get an exclusive press scoop: The first press interview of Shaykh Usama or Shaykh Ayman since 10 years ago! Particularly if the Shaykh is the one to be interviewed. This is because of the scarcity of his appearance during the last nine years. Because of the poor photographic quality of the last two releases -I do not know the photo quality this time- this led those believers in conspiracy theory to speculate if the person was the Shaykh, and you may have seen the program (Ben Ladin, alive or dead?) that was broadcast by Al Jazeera.

Accordingly, a high quality speech (HD) may receive some interest by some channels in the tenth anniversary. If the quality of the new Shaykh's speech is high, relative to the two previous speeches, you may think to compress it or take some measures to decrease the quality, to be similar to the previous ones, and I am talking seriously.

In general, and no matter what material we send, I suggest that we should distribute it to more than one channel, so that there will be healthy competition between the channels in broadcasting the material, so that no other channel takes the lead. It should be sent for example to ABC, CBS, NBC, and CNN and maybe PBS and VOA. As for Fox News, let her die in her anger. That is if there was no agreement with a specific channel to publish a specific material, or conduct an interview, or the like.

As for the second method, which I suggest, it is close to what the Shaykh mentioned of communicating with 'Abd-al-Bari Atwan and Robert Fisk. I suggest that we send the material-or materials-to a group of writers and professional or independent journalists, who have shown interest in al-Qa'ida issues, from different countries. In Britain, the two journalists Atwan and Fisk, and probably others, in America Brian Russ, Simon Hirsh and Jerry Van Dyke and others, in Canada Eric Margolis and Gwynne Dyer. In Europe, the Norwegian journalist who spent some time with the students in Kroner and released a film that was condemned in the West because he shows that the students are humans that have families and children and that they laugh and eat as the rest of the people. In Pakistan, Hamid Mir and Salim Safi, the owner of the program (Jerga) at Geo channel, also Rahimullah Yusuf Zia and Jamal Ismail, and at Al Jazeera …. (Put their names here if they exist). In Egypt, Dr. Muhammad 'Abbas and others, in Jordan Dr. Karam Hijazi, in Yemen 'Abd-al-Ilah Haydar Sha'i -if he is released by the government and is still concerned with al-Qa'ida issues, and so on. It would be good if we send it to 30-50 of those journalists and writers. We would inform each that he has been chosen to be amongst a group of international journalists and writers, and that they will receive special media material on the tenth anniversary of 9/11. It will be favorable if the message sent to them also includes what was mentioned by the Shaykh, of reasons that call them to be interested in this material and to cooperate in publishing its mission for the world, plus other convincing arguments. There would be a password and a site address to download the materials at the right time, let it be 5 days before the anniversary, for example. This is easy -as I think- on our brothers working in the networking.

Suppose that one-third of those corresponded with are interested, then we would have 10 international journalists that will display our mission in the newspapers and channels. If the experiment works, then I suggest to repeat it on every important occasion, and any instant we want to increase the number of those informed about some message or statement.

To rely only on Al Jazeera and the Jihadi forums on the internet is not useful. Al Jazeera channel, now seems to put requirements like other channels and agencies and papers to cover al-Qa'ida announcements. Namely to include a threat or to claim responsibility for an act. As for the messages of diplomatic tone, like the two Shaykh's messages about the flooding, is not suitable for publication in their media, as this face of al-Qa'ida should not be exposed to people.

As for the Jihadi forums, it is repulsive to most of the Muslims, or closed to them. It also distorts the face of al-Qa'ida, due to what you know of bigotry, the sharp tone that characterizes most of the participants in these forums. It is also biased towards (Salafists) and not any Salafist, but the Jihadi Salafist, which is just one trend of the Muslims trends. The Jihad Salafist is a small trend within a small trend.

By the way, Dr. Muhammad al-Misa'ri has excellent comments on
Jihadi forums, although his forum (al-Tajdid) is not any better,
actually worse as it seems to me. Al-Misa'ri was also correct in
his analysis about Iraq, in comparison with other Jihadi arenas.
To end the suspicion I would say: Whoever read my comments on
the Dr.'s book knows that I said something similar to what he
mentioned about the forums and the Islamic State of Iraq. All of
that before the al-Misa'ri announcement that he issued after the
killing of the State Emirs. My comments on the Dr.'s book were
two months earlier, so I did not stem my thoughts from al-
Misa'ri at all. But, there was some agreement on opinions -only
on these two issues. (As for the other issues, like his
definition of unification, some Fiqh theses, his exaggerated
stiffness with Shia, those adhering to the buried, rejuvenators
of myths and pagan appearances, not at all).

I would like to emphasize that I was at ease with declaring the
State for a long time. I was not at ease with al-Zarqawi's -may
God bless his soul- moves, which he took in the name of al-
Qa'ida. All of this is known to the Shaykhs Ayman, 'Atiyah and
Ubayd (Munir). My stand is not a new one, but I followed the
official stand of the organization, being afraid not to create a
seduction, and because I used to accuse my own opinion. This is
to note now, although I have accepted my own stand, I do not
discuss this topic except with the scholars like you and
sometimes with my brothers at al-Sahab. After all, it is but a
set of advice and opinions, I wish you give it some
consideration and discuss it, may God lead you and me to the
right opinions. I am not biased in my opinion, neither do I ally
with or differ from accordingly. If there was some sharpness in
introducing the matter, it is the style that I am used to in
conversation and in writing. I am, however, trying to make my
style more flexible and less sharp, and help is from God.

3- Showing the Fairness of our Case to the Whole World and the
European Peoples in Particular and the Obstacles placed in front
of that:

The virtuous Shaykh has talked about the importance of exposing
the justness of our case to the world and the Europeans in
particular, and that is when talking about the preparation for
the tenth anniversary to Manhattan battle. The Shaykh has
emphasized that context -as concerned the Europeans- in previous
messages and statements.

I was -in response to those directives, and after consulting brother Ubayd- starting to prepare a message to the Irish, and I started searching for the information and materials necessary for that to be collected. This was after I noticed the sympathy of the Irish people to the Palestinian issue, and the soft treatment by the Irish Judicial system of the Muslims accused of terrorism, and also not participating with its troops in Bush's Crusade wars (although it is participating within the European Union forces in training the Somali army). Also, what helped to prepare the message was the last economic crisis that affected Ireland a lot, thus forcing its youth to look for sources of living in the outside. The other matter is the increasing anger in Ireland towards the Catholic Church

after exposing a number of sex scandals and others. The people there are moving towards secularism, after it was the most religious of atheist Europe, and why do not we face them with Islam?

Also I was thinking of preparing an Arabic message to the Christians of the Arab region, calling them to Islam, and to caution them from cooperating with invader enemies of Islam who oppose the Islamic State. They should welcome the Islamic advance, as did their forefathers when the Muslims liberated Jerusalem during the time of 'Umar Ibn al-Khattab – May God be satisfied with him.

Then the attack on the Catholic Church in Baghdad took place, launched by the organization of the Islamic State of Iraq that we support, which is -if we like it or not- known to people as (al-Qa'ida in Iraq). This attack halted me, and I thought twice about my two project messages. As actions are more effective than words, their act and the contacts they carried during the attack, and the statement they issued later, do not help to gain people's sympathy. This attack came days after the declaration by the Catholics of the Middle East, of their disagreement with Israel in a way that made the Jews and their allies angry, the Catholics refusing to utilize the Bible to justify the occupation and seizing of Palestine.

Also the Catholics were historically the prominent enemies of the Jews, amongst the other Christians. They were also the original enemies to the Evangelist Protestant who were the vanguard of the Crusades. Their public in general, these days, is more sympathetic and understanding of the Muslims, than other

Protestant and Orthodox Christians. I do not eliminate the animosity, and do not say that if they had the chance they would not fight Muslims as did the Anglo-Saxon Protestants. I also do not deny the animosity of the Pope and other church heads to Islam and Muslims – why not, Islam is the biggest threat for the continuity of their power, particularly in Europe. I do not deny that they send missionaries here and there, asking Muslims to apostasy. But I am talking about the public and present situation, and the size of animosity, and the size of the missionary activities. We cannot compare their efforts against Islam to the efforts of the Evangelist Protestants or the efforts of the Coptic Church and other spiteful Orthodox.

Even in Bosnia, we saw the Catholic Croats standing next to the Muslims against the Orthodox Serb. I have seen lately, in a report about Venezuela, a picture of a wall, with (Islam is the heritage of all) written on it.

The conclusion is that, in general, the Catholics are a fertile ground for call of God and to persuade them about the just case of the Mujahidin, particularly after the rage expanding against the mother church (Vatican) as a result of its scandals and policies refused by many of its public.

But the attacks on the Christians in Iraq, like the Baghdad attack and what took place earlier in Mosul and others, does not help us to convey the message. Even if the ones we are talking to have some grudge against the mother church, they will not grasp in general the targeting of their public, women, children and men in their church during Mass.

From the strangest matters of this case, and what was reported by the media, was the threat of the attackers to kill the hostages and start an all out war against Christians in Iraq and the region unless the Coptic church (Orthodox) released Wafa Qastantin and Kamelia Shihata that are detained in one of its Monasteries. It is well known, to whoever has any knowledge of the Christians and their factions, that there are no ties between the Catholic Church and the Orthodox churches. There is historical animosity between the factions, as each side considers the other an innovator. Because we are living in the age of peaceful coexistence and dialogue exchange, they would be spilling each other's blood, as they used to do in the past.

To make the analogy: this operation -from the Christians point of view at least- as if an armed group belonging to a given sect have assaulted a Sunni mosque in al-Fallujah -not the Awakenings mosque- but a regular mosque-they captured the praying audience and threatened to kill them and rage an overall war on the Sunnah in Iraq, if the rejectionists Shia would release Sunni prisoners in the Husayniyahs (TN: Shia prayer rooms) of Sadr city in Baghdad or the visiting sites of (The Iranian city of Qum) Does this satisfy any sane person? Were we going to understand the motives that armed group or who is behind it, or who is allying with it?

Is it not, this policy of (Islamic State of Iraq) is exactly the Bush policy that rebuffed Europe and the wise men of the world. Bush said (either with us or with the terrorists) and did not leave a space for neutrality. Here this group in Iraq is telling the Christians (Either with us or with al-Maliki government and no space for neutrality. Either you pay the "Jizya" (TN: nonbeliever tax) to our fictitious state that cannot defend itself, and has no chance of defending you, or we will destroy your goods). Is this is the justice that we are talking about, and that the Shaykh talks about in his statements and messages?

Where is the proof that the Christians of Iraq have stood with the government or the Americans as a sect? In my opinion -and I could be mistaken- the issue has no relation to the cooperation between the weak and marginalized Christian groups with the government or the Americans. But it has a relation that the (state) group who believes the authenticity of their fictitious State and are biased to what was stated by 'Umar al-Baghdadi. He claims that the Iraqi Christians should sign another contract according to the rules of the Islamic State and pay the "Jizya"… Against what? Nothing.

It is irrelevant to rely on the statements of the scholars (the root in the blood of the infidels is the resolution unless a pledge or safety or Islam). This is out of place and outside the discussion. We are here talking about the interest and the priorities not about the roots of the issue.

How beautiful what Shaykh Usama mentioned lately -when talking about a media speech- that the strong statements that were mentioned by the ancestors were said during days of dignity and control, and therefore it is not fitting to the era of vulnerability. And I say: so are some of the rulings of the scholars concerning Jihad, as they were released when Islam was strong, mighty and defensible. So it cannot be implemented on the days of weakness like our present days. (I mean here what was mentioned by some -for example- favoring or stating the necessity of demolishing churches and burning the devious religious books and things like that that may not fit our today's Jihad. Because the nature of our fight differs from theirs, and we have different priorities, defending against the assailant for example, while the scholars were talking about the demanding Jihad, etc…)

Praise to God, where is the stand of the Islamic State of Iraq on Christians, from the stand of Shaykh Usama in his speech (The Solution) three years ago? Where is their stand from the message of Shaykh Ayman's address to the Copts in -as I think- the book of acquittal - ? (I reviewed the book and found it actually in chapter 14 under "notes on what is mentioned in the tenth series" and I recommend that it be read, as it shows the extent of violation of the stand of (Fictitious Iraqi Caliphate) to the stand of the two Shaykhs Ayman and Usama). Where does this stand go, from the flexible stand of Shaykh 'Abdallah Azzam, from the Christians in the Arab lands (look at the interpretation of "al-Tawba Surah" and the resistance he encountered from the attending youth)? Where does their stand go from the position of Shaykh Abu Muhammad al-Maqdisi, who refuses the idea of detonating the churches - caution: Just exploding a church, even if it was empty, how about if it is full of people?

Strange -I swear- the conflict between the statements of our leaders and scholars, and the acts of those allied with them -or you may say: those claiming to follow them!

In summary, a position must be taken on these behaviors and not well studied or well understood stands by groups of Muslims before the infidels. The position of the leaders and the organization must be clearly defined.

I do not see any obstacle or bad act if al-Qa'ida organization declares its discontent with this behavior and other behaviors being carried out by the so-called Islamic State of Iraq, without an order from al-Qa'ida and without consultation. I see that this is done immediately or lately, favorably sooner. I see that the organization should declare the cutoff of its organizational ties with that organization (TN: Islamic State of Iraq). The relations between al-Qa'ida organization and (the state) have been practically cut off for a number of years. The decision to declare the State was taken without consultation from al-Qa'ida leadership. Their improvised decision has caused a split in the Mujahidin ranks and their supporters inside and outside Iraq. What is left between al-Qa'ida organization and (the State), but the link of faith and Islam, which urges us to submit advise and apply the rule of propagating virtue and preventing vice, and the support of good deeds.

This is the only solution facing al-Qa'ida organization, otherwise its reputation will be damaged more and more as a result of the acts and statements of this group, which is labeled under our organization (the blessed with God's will). And among the repulsive issues -and certainly forbidden- the targeting of mosques with explosives and others- as what is happening in Afghanistan and Pakistan and sometimes in Iraq. We still need to clarify our justified issue to the Muslims before we clarify it to the Europeans (look at the next chapter for more on this topic)

I have read a new article by Robert Fisk expressing his reaction -and other people's reaction- to the attack on the church in Baghdad, and allow me to translate to you the most important parts and gist the rest:

The title of the article: The West makes it easier for al-Qa'ida to attack... November 6 2010

The speed with which the Baghdad church massacre by al-Qa'ida has frightened the peoples of the Middle East is a sign of just how fragile the earth is beneath their feet. Unlike our western television news, Al Jazeera and al-Arabiya show the whole horror of such carnage. Arms, legs, beheaded torsos, leave no doubt of what they mean. Every Christian in the region understood what this attack meant. Indeed, given the sectarian nature of the assaults on Shia Iraqis, I am beginning to wonder whether al-Qa'ida itself -far from being the center of world terror, as we imagine- must be one of the most sectarian organizations ever invented. I suspect that there is not just one al-Qa'ida but several, feeding off the injustices of the region, a blood transfusion which the West (and I am including the Israelis) here feeds into its body. (That is as if Fisk is comparing these strange injustices to blood transfusion, just as a blood transfusion revitalizes the sick or wounded, the same token these tyrannies did not rejuvenate al-Qa'ida).

In fact, I am wondering if our governments do not need this terror - to make us frightened, very frightened, to make us obey to bring more security to our little lives. And I am wondering whether those same governments will ever wake up to the fact that our actions in the Middle East are what is endangering our security. Lord Blair of Isfahan always denied this -(Fisk in that sense compares Blair to the representatives of the old empire, during the Iraqi invasion Fisk used to say "Lord Blair" the owner of "Kut al-Amara." Now as the winds of war are directed towards Iran, he is calling Blair as "Lord Blair Sahib Isfahan")- even when the 7/7 suicide bomber carefully explained in his posthumous video that Iraq was one of the reasons

he committed the slaughter in London -and Bush always denied it- and Sarkozy will deny it if al-Qa'ida fulfills its latest threat to attack France.

Now, as for al-Qa'ida, it is "All Christians" in the Middle East who are to be the targets as well, scattering these threats like cluster bombs around the region, up to two million of Egypt's Coptic community have to be protected at the two week Luxor religious festival. This is surrounded by hundreds of state security police, after the al-Qa'ida claim that that two Muslim women are being held against their will by the Coptic Church. That may have originated with a decision by the two women to divorce their husbands -by conversion to Islam- thus to end their marriage, since the church in Egypt does not allow divorce.

(Then Fisk talked on the problems evolving between the Sunnah and Shia in Lebanon, after the demand by Hizballah group to the government to reject the results of the international investigation concerning al-Hariri assassination. Then they discussed the acceleration of problems between Muslims and Christians in Lebanon, after the desecration of a Christian grave in Jiya, in southern Beirut. He also mentioned the statements of passionate Shia and Christians concerning the attack on the church in Baghdad).

The West does not have the necessary force to help the frightened Christians. The acts of faith-based politicians -the Christian faith- have brought about a new Christian tragedy in the Middle East.

(Then he mentioned a belief of the Americans that he met in the
state of California that Christianity was a Western religion,
rather than an eastern. Al-Qa'ida denied its responsibility for
grave desecration in Lebanon, because of its triviality. But al-
Qa'ida has a presence in Lebanon, as was stated by Bashar al-
Assad, the Shia Iranian and Hizballah ally, which makes him an
enemy to the organization of Bin Ladin. Then he mentioned a
statement to al-Hayat newspaper by Bashar, where he said):
"We are talking about al-Qa'ida as if it has a presence as a
strong and unified organization. This is not true, but it is
present as an intellectual trend calling itself al-Qa'ida. This
organization is the result of a situation and not a cause. It is
due to anarchy and weak development, it is the result of
political mistakes that represent some kind of political
heading. To say that this organization is present everywhere, in
Syria and all the Arab and Islamic states, that does not mean it
is widespread nor does it have popularity."

But al-Assad cannot acquit his regime nor the regimes of other
Arab states, whose security regulates all the political meetings
other those conducted by the state representatives. This forced
the Muslims, beginning a long time ago, to talk politics in the
only institution that they visit,

namely the mosque. The supreme irony this week has been to hear
our lords and masters praising the helpfulness of the Wahhabi
regime in Saudi Arabia for alerting the West to the aircraft
package bombs, when it was this same Saudi Arabia that nurtured
Usama Bin Ladin and his merry men over many years. (This is a
reference to the legend of Robin Hood, and its hero, who
disobeyed the British king during the Crusades and started to
block the roads. He was famous for stealing from the rich and
distributing it to the poor, and his gang was called "The Merry
Men".

Because the Middle Eastern dictators also like to scare their
populations (as if he wants to say that Saudi Arabia created al-
Qa'ida to frighten its people) Egypt's poor are disgusted by
their ruling elite. But that elite wants to ensure that there
are no Islamic revolutions in Cairo. And the West wants to
ensure that there are no Islamic revolutions in Cairo, or Libya,
or Algeria, or Syria, or Saudi Arabia, and you name the rest.
The immediate problem is that al-Qa'ida is trying to undermine
these regimes, as well as the West. (They mean al-Qa'ida). So
they lump Iraq itself -whether it is a democracy is a bit

irrelevant when it does not have a government, and is too busy executing its old Ba'athist enemies to protect its own people- along with the country's Christians and its Shia. And we are continuing to stage drone attacks on Pakistan and bomb the innocent in Afghanistan and tolerate the torture regimes of the Arab world. And to allow Israel to steal more land from the Palestinians. I am afraid that it is the same old story. Justice will bring peace, not intelligence wars against "world terror," but still our leaders will not admit this.

AH The Article

4- It has Become Unbearable and the Avalanche have arrived: The Tragedy of Tolerating the Spilling of Blood, Resources and Honor, and our Duty towards this Dangerous Phenomenon

The series of targeting the mosques and public places, by some who were referred to as the Mujahidin, is continuing and at its highest strength those days. So that the claims are not vacant, I will review some of the terrible events that I know, and what I did not know was graver.

- The detonation of a mosque near the village of Sharsada during the Eid prayers, in an unsuccessful attempt to kill Aftab Ahmad Khan Shirbow; instead, more than fifty of the village commoners were killed, and that attack was ordered by Baitullah Mahsud.

- Detonation of a mosque in Khyber area, in an attempt to kill (Haji Namdar) the head of the Organization for Propagation of Virtue and Prevention of Vice, and an individual from the students of (Wazir) tribe. He was not killed, but instead 15 of the people who were in the mosque were killed. It was ordered by Baitullah Mahsud. Haji Namdar was killed, after a number of months, by bullets targeted him while he was in a meeting.

- The detonation of another mosque during Friday prayers, in (Jamrud) area near Peshawar. More than fifty were killed in the explosion and scores were injured. The mosque was close to a barracks for government soldiers, and some of them were among the ones killed, but the mosque is open to all. It is attended by the regional people and the travelers, because of its proximity to the main road.

- Numerous explosions in all the areas, targeting the invaders soldiers or the soldiers of the agent's army or police officers,

27

or small government employees, or employees of private companies with government contracts, on places most crowded with pedestrians, residents and shoppers, without a reason to justify. It would have been possible to attack them in a more accurate manner, or attack them outside the markets and away from the residential areas and crowded streets.

- An explosion at the celebration of doctors graduating in the Somali capital, for the sake of killing 3 government ministers; they were killed with a huge number of the graduates. The Shabaab movement has denied their involvement in the operation, and God knows best.

- Explosion on a public playground in the city of (Liki Marwat) in Sarhad governorate -then- and 100 people were killed who were attending the ballgame. The reason for targeting the playground was the presence of a few individuals who belong to the (Lashkar) or what is known as a (Peace Committee) that was formed there. It was not proven that this committee has targeted the Mujahidin even once. And now after this sinful operation, no bearded person could enter the area without being investigated for being a member of the Taliban. It was said that the person responsible is a Taliban leader in Northern Waziristan, and his name could be (Badr Mansur).

- Explosions at the checkpoints and control points in a number of areas in an illegal way. These target the points at the peak hours with the presence of cars and pedestrians. They could have been targeted at other times, where the traffic is slow. There is another issue; the suicide bomber could be heading to carry an operation in another location, but he is intercepted at the point or trying to search his car or his body, then he would immediately explode himself not caring what could happen of killings and injuries to the people around him. He should have been supplied with a firearm to fight with until he died

or he may have used it to get the people away from him before exploding the bomb in a random way. I do not know who ordered that, or gave a fatwa about its legality?

-Explosion in a restaurant at the town of (Jandula) in southern Waziristan, in a failed attempt to kill (Turkistan Batani) and members of (Qara Zayn al-Din) allied with him. Only two were killed from the security guards of Turkistan and the rest (around 10 dead) were from the general public who were inside and outside the restaurant, from the tribes of Mahsud and Batani.

-Explosion in a market in the tribal Mohmand area, three months ago, targeting a tribal (Jirga). The targeters thought that it would take place inside the place, but it took place in another place as a precaution. The number of killed was more than 100, all or most of them shoppers that had nothing to do with the movement. The Taliban movement claimed the operation as stated by Ihsanallah Ihsan, who expressed sorrow for the fall of dead among the public, and we thank him for his frankness, at least.

-The operation of exploding the Islamic University in Islam Abad, where a number of female and male students were killed. It was claimed by (Qari Husayn Mahmud).

-The targeting of the main mosque in Talaqan town, in the Pakistani governorate Takhar. The cause of the explosion was to kill the mayor (Wali) of Kunduz governorate (Engineer Muhammad 'Umar) and he was actually killed with thirty others of the praying public.

-The explosion of the mosque of (Mawlawi Nur Muhammad) at Wana in southern Waziristan tribal area, at the middle of Ramadan. Al-Mawlawi was killed with about 30 of those studying the Qur'an at the mosque. The Uzbek group was blamed, and the group of (Hakimallah Mas'ud), for the responsibility of the attack.

-Lastly -but not least- the attack on the mosque in Dir Adam Khel during Friday prayers, which resulted in 70 dead and scores of injured. The one responsible -as it was said- is the so called (Tariq Afridi) and the target was either one of the tribal Shaykhs in opposition to (Emir al-Mu'minin Tariq Afridi) or Talabani group members opposed to (Tariq Afridi) group who were praying at the mosque. As there is a long record feud between them, in assassinations and kidnappings. The group of Tariq Afridi claimed that attack. The opposing faction is headed by (Mu'min Afridi) and they said he is in good relations with students of Wazir tribe and that he resides in Waziristan. All these details were taken from the newspapers and I am not 100% sure about the accuracy. But from what I know about the black reputation of Pakistani Taliban, I am confident of what was stated, particularly as these information verify each other. They were stated by journalists aware of the Taliban affairs, like (Rahimullah Yusuf Zia) and God know best. On the evening of the same day, attackers threw a bomb inside a mosque on the outskirts of Peshawar during the evening prayers. The target was one of the tribal Shaykhs who opposed the Taliban, or the family of one of the policemen. Five were killed, between them the imam of the Afghani mosque, and many were injured.

Note: Tariq 'Azam and Wali al-Rahman Mahsud contacted the newspapers one day after the attack on Dera 'Azam Khel, and insisted on denying any responsibility for Taliban Pakistan Movement from the act. They accused Blackwater Company to be behind the incident. They claimed that the telephone calls that were conducted with the journalists under the name of Tariq Afridi were forged. What is funny is that Tariq Afridi, the man accused of the operation, did not contact the journalists to defend himself. Maybe his telephone was not working or there was some problem with his number, or maybe he is more cautious than Wali al-Rahman in using the phone. It should be mentioned that, when calling the newspapers, 'Azam Tariq denied any relation between Taliban Pakistan Movement and Faisal Shahzad, who tried to blast Times Square in New York. Then there was a film broadcast by ('Umar Studio) the media branch of Tahrik Taliban Pakistan! So who would believe the statements of 'Azam Tariq after that?

I would like to point out that (Umma Studio), I think a media branch for the Uzbeks, have produced a film where they pledged with all rudeness to explode the mosques, as revenge for the attack on the Red Mosque, and to bombard other mosques at the tribal areas. In that film there were training and battles at Dir Adam Khel, Kohut, Ur Kazay and Mohmand and others. They also threatened to kill journalists, and showed a photo of a correspondent for Al Jazeera English, where the reporter was denying the responsibility of Taliban movement for the market explosions, while others were blaming the Taliban. But this stand of his did not help him much with those sinners.

I conclude these statements, with two stories that show the dangers of the situation and the ignorance that prevails amongst the ranks:

First story: A year ago or more, a discussion took place between me and one of the youth, from the sons of the Arab immigrants, about these explosions that are taking place in the mosques of Pakistan. I mentioned to him that this is not acceptable and that the leaders of the organization and the students of science do not see the mosques explosions and ask the people to stop it. Even if the mosque is in a military or government compound, and that they have issued statements about that. Even Shaykh 'Isa - may God release him- I have heard him saying that he does not agree on detonating Shia mosques in Pakistan, although he considers them infidels, according to Pakistani scholars.

(Of course there are exceptions, as Shaykh 'Isa was planning to attack the highest leaders of the military and government during the Eid prayers, and it was conveyed to me that al-Qa'ida brothers have attacked the military mosque in Rawalpindi. That mosque requires -different from other government mosques- a membership card to enter) The young man did not accept my story, and replied that most -or maybe- all mosques now are mosques of evil full of informers, spies and government employees and they have no mercy on them, in accordance to a statement by Sayyid Qutb in his interpretation of

"In the Shadow of the Qur'an" and that talk was stated to him by his father. I told him: fine, if you see that they are mosques of evil, tear them down, but do not explode them when the praying people are inside them. The discussion was ended and I did not know if he was convinced or not.

Imagine; a young man ready to detonate a mosque with what it includes, based on a generalization of what was stated by Sayyid Qutb, may God bless his soul.

The second story:
A group went to Kurum tribal area to fight the army, and they met with the local Taliban. They made an ambush for the enemy on one of the main streets. The army patrol was delayed. One of the people present asked (if the army did not come, what would we do), the leader of the Taliban group said (let us attack the Shia) the one asking replied (and if the Shia do not come), the leader replied (let us attack the hypocrites) meaning the general public and the passersby. The head of the outside group was angered and disputed him, the local leader was embarrassed and stated that he was joking. The head of the outside group replied (how would you joke like that in front of your soldiers and members?) This was conveyed to me by the brother who was heading the outside group.

-Thereafter: this is a drop from a flood, and a little from plenty, as I have tried to concentrate on events that I am sure are true, according to Mujahidin and who are allied to them, or whom I thought they were so. Otherwise the list is quite long; also, I did not talk about events related to robbery, kidnapping and other crimes committed by those corruptors.

It is known that taking over of mosques and spilling the innocent, was known through history to be associated with the worst groups and individuals, like al-Khawarij, al-Qaramitah, al-Hajjaj Bin Yusuf, the Crusaders, the Mongols and Tamerlane the national hero of Uzbekistan (although he is not from Uzbekistan, but it seems that they liked his toughness and brutality) then the Jews and the rejectionists. Then in this period, the Americans, the Arab and foreign tyrants, like the kings of Hejaz and Najd, Syria's rulers, and the Pakistani ruler Pervez Musharraf. Now who are famous for such acts that are counted on the side of the Mujahidin, like Hamas Movement and Taliban Movement in Pakistan and Afghanistan?

I have no doubt that what is happening to the Jihadi movement in these countries is not misfortune, but punishment by God on us because of our sins and injustices, or because the sins of some of us and the silence of the rest of us. I do not see that my statement is an exaggeration and intimidation, as the Qur'anic verses, the Hadith and the scholar's statements are plenty, and there is no need to state them. Some were stated by Shaykh Abu Yahya within his document (al-Rabiyun and the March of Victory), and I have mentioned some of it in a draft of a statement I have prepared on the subject, and will state it here afterwards, with God's will.

You may say: (but we have denied those who have committed these trespasses, and are still denying it and we guided them to the right path at every instance and in all occasions). I would say to them: yes, I know that, and you have done well, as some of the information that I have mentioned about the detonations at the mosques came to me originally from some scholars who conveyed to me some of their experiences in advice and counseling (which had faced failure, unfortunately, in most cases, because of the narrowness of the visions of those spoken to, their small minds, and the inclination of their hearts to brutality, ruthlessness, excess and intolerance to the statements of men and their banners).

I would say: You have done well, in what you have done in efforts in this matter, but allow me to state my humble opinion in the style that you are following in your denial. It seems to me that this style does not rise to the level of the repudiated acts and does not suit its type. You are sticking to secrecy in your denial and advice, and see in that a prevailing interest, and that pronouncing the denial is harmful,

as it causes a break in the ranks, or an exposure of our weak spots to the enemy to exploit it, and other arguments that may have some consideration chances.

As for the possibility of breaking ranks, it is that: just a possibility, and the fact that those conducting those acts, maybe it is better for them not to be in the ranks of the Mujahidin, as they are just like a polluted spot that should be removed and sanitized and cleared from the ranks.

As for exposing our weak spots in front of our enemies to exploit it, these attacks are -I swear- a greater shame and more horrible weak points, and it has been exploited by the enemies to a great extent. It has been exploited to distort the picture of the pious and loyal Mujahidin. Now many regular people are looking at the Mujahidin as a group that does not hesitate to take people's money by falsehood, detonating mosques, spilling the bloods of scores of people in the way to kill one or two who were labeled as enemies. While they shy away from listening to music or looking at a foreign woman – while those issues means very little to the common public, who see it as trivial issues. They are not, but no comparison to the sins that we are talking about. From that juncture, the Shaykhs and sermon speakers described the Mujahidin on their forums and life on the air that they are free people of the era-or the (Qaramitah of the time). They were able to persuade many Muslims of what they are claiming. The blame -or most of it- is laid on our shoulders. We contributed to that by not clarifying our stand on those forbidden acts in a sufficient way. We also contributed to the continuation of the perpetrators in their acts, by deferring the accusation from the contributors and blaming Blackwater Company instead.

I have learned that Shaykh Abu 'Abd-al-Rahman 'Atiyatallah -may God save him- has mentioned in his draft fatwa about the markets detonations last year, the possibility of having those acts committed by some Jihadi groups. He stressed those with aggressive rotten attitudes, however he deleted that paragraph before publishing the fatwa, upon the advice of some brothers – may God guide them.

Those who advised him to delete that part, they argued that we should not admit that such acts were committed from within our ranks: that means we have to impose a media silence! And this is a mistake from many aspects: The matter is religious and a fatwa and an order for virtue and a prevention of vice, and not a simple (organizational secret) of the type that we may impose a media silence on. Hiding the right, and delaying its details when in need, has strong religious implications, as is well known. Now that the matter is exposed known to all, near and far, our silence will lead to be despised by people and despising ourselves, as we look in front of all as "Mute Satans." We see the forbidden committed, and make no move, or look like compromisers, praising the killers while they are alive, and condole them when dead, and count them as good doers, irrespective of what we know about them of immorality. We look in the best of cases as inattentive who are not aware of what is happening around us.

Going back to the issue of our attitude in denial and adoption of secrecy, I would say: we are now facing a declared repudiated act, announced being committed on the people with no shyness or shame. It has engulfed the ranks like fire. The known repudiated act is judged differently from that of which no one is aware except the one committing it. The last type works on the secrecy, and not to announce it -with some exceptions- while the first type is where the denial is in the open. This benefits the others who would be willing or planning to do it or imitate the one doing it. And for other reasons, this disclosure of denial is what we ignored here. This made our denial incomplete and not qualifying to its basics, and God knows best.

At least, we should take our Prophet (PBUH) when he said: Oh my God, I disengage myself from what Khalid did, three times. He announced that until it reached us 14 centuries later, think about it.

Remark: What is basically required is not calling the actors one by one and to slander their personality that we might not know; what is required is to deny the act and to rather carry a renunciation, loving the actor for what it has in virtues and hating him for what he has of vices and deviating from the path of the Shari'ah. It would be required, in some instances, to caution the actors openly and caution people from then. It is as if this person or that organization became famous by committing atrocities, by the public and the private circles (and what he is famous for was true and proven) and if these acts were repeated by him and he did not confirm by advice or warning.

I may add here that what is required in announcing the denial - particularly at this stage- is the inability of the scholars for a secret and direct denial. This is because of the bad security situations, and what it requires in taking precaution from meeting people and staying in the abyss of the house and so on. This is in addition to what I have mentioned of our occasional ignorance of those responsible for those crimes.

Building on what was said, and as a first step in that direction, and for the sake of correcting the path and repenting what has happened, and to call for victory and relieve the affliction that is encountering us, I have prepared this paper.

I hope that God would help the scholars to study and review and correct, or record similar statements - copying here is desired for documentation and influencing the receiving side. They should remember the words dispersed here and there, as those embedded in the books and the speeches are not enough to explain the problem. What we need is direct speeches, defined and specialized on that subject.

This is the suggested text:

Acquittal and Warning

In the name of God the merciful the compassionate

God almighty has stated: "And fight those who are fighting you and do not be aggressive as God does not like the aggressors "

Qa'ida al-Jihad Organization has denounced, more than once, and on the tongue of its Emirs and scholars and symbols and those who speak in favor, any armed operation that targets the Muslims in the places of their gathering, and any operation that does not account for the sanctity of their blood, souls, bodies, belongings or money. This acquittal includes the explosive operations that takes place in the center of markets, streets, restaurants, hotels that are packed with Muslims. It also includes, as a first principal, the detonation of mosques on the heads of the innocent praying public, shattering their bodies. Associated with that is exposing the Qur'an and the religious books to indignation and destruction.

The acquittal of the organization was not just an empty media-driven step, but the organization was and still is giving advice after advice to those who commit those acts, directly and through its special channels. By denying them those horrible acts and guiding them to the right path, hoping to correct the path and stop the repetition of what happened. These efforts gave fruit in a few instances, and some people have returned to the straight path. But there are some who insist on following a wrong method and a distorted jurisprudence, for the sake of taking revenge from whoever wronged him or let him down or stood with his enemy, even if this revenge is carried out at the expense of innocent Muslims. This spirit of blind revenge and pre-Islamic (TN: religiously ignorant) intolerance is not from the manners of the Mujahidin, who are loyal and honest in their behavior.

Here we are, announcing it again in the open: We denounce any operation carried out by a Jihadi group that does not consider the sanctity of Muslims and their blood and money. We refuse to attribute these crimes to Qa'ida al-Jihad Organization. If it is to be proven that those responsible for it are connected with the organization, the organization will take the appropriate measures towards them. This position and the judgment is not to be changed if the act is carried out in the name of Jihad or under the banner of establishing Shari'ah and the legal measures, or under the name of promoting virtue and preventing vice. As long as it is forbidden in God's religion, we are disassociated with it. It is not acceptable to consider these personal crimes as a pretext to deny the duty of the compulsory Jihad duty, as a mistake does not justify a bigger mistake. We warn those responsible for those crimes, of disgrace in this lifetime and painful torture in the other. The consequences of injustice are grave, and injustice is the darkness of the Day of Judgment.

Injustice is one of the reasons behind defeat and disappointment, and the befallen miseries and sedition by the general public Muslims and the Mujahidin, as God has stated: (And fear tumult or oppression, which affected noting particular (only) those of you who do wrong and know that God is strict in punishment.) For those who insist on this criminal and pre-Islamic behavior should know that he is doomed to the same destiny that faced leaderships and groups and other trends in various arenas, after they shed the blood of Muslims, in bias to their group, doctrines and banners, by arguments that were weaker than the spider's web.

The Prophet (PBUH) has said (who left the obedience, and left the group and died, his death is a pre-Islamic death. Who fought under a blind banner, biased to a group or supports a group, and then dies, his death is pre-Islamic. Who diverted from my nation striking the good and the evil, and does not avoid the faithful, and does not honor a pledge, he is not from me and I am not from him) as narrated by Muslim.

I am surprised from that one allows himself or others to detonate a mosque full of praying individuals, or any other place where Muslims gather, just for the sake of killing one of the individuals present in that location. My surprise increases when this takes place in areas famous in manufacturing various firearms, where it is sold cheaply and could be easily purchased. If that targeted person really deserves to be killed, why not employ another method rather than the random attacks, which is not tolerated by any mind or religion. Which does not differentiate between and enemy and a friend, the child and the old man, the man and the woman and the Muslim and the infidel? Have you not remembered that you are fighting in the Muslim towns and not in the infidel's fortresses?

And if you say that this barbaric style is known in your tribal traditions, or your people's traditions, or tolerated by your Shaykh or Emir, we would say: It is not allowed in our Islam, and down with these traditions and opinions. A fight that is not guided by the Shari'ah rules is not honored. If the fight adheres to the tribal traditions and human opinions that violate the Shari'ah, whose ruling is no different from the constitutions and manmade laws, we should repudiate from and those rules should not be followed.

My Mujahid brother: He who is satisfied with those acts, or who orders them, or conducts them, is either an ignorant that needs education, or an agent planted amongst the ranks for the benefit of the enemies of the Mujahidin.

It is our hope that those in charge of those criminal acts that distort the Jihad and the Mujahidin only represents a gang of a few marginalized individuals. But we remind all about their duty in propagating virtue and preventing vice, and punishing the tyrant. As the Messenger of God (PBUH) said: (I swear by the one whose soul is in his hands, you would order the virtue and deny the vice, or God would send you a punishment from him, then you would pray and he would not respond to you) narrated by al-Tirmithi and streamlined by al-Albani.

Or as he said, peace and prayers be upon (If the people saw the tyrant and they did not stop him, God would impose on them his punishment).

As stated by him, peace and prayers be upon him (Support your brother if he is a tyrant or if he is under a tyrant. They said: Messenger of God we would support who is under tyranny, but how about the tyrant? He replied: by preventing him from being a tyrant).

And therefore, every Muslim or Mujahid, if he knows about an individual or leader from the leaders -even if he was his Emir-with the intent of such banned and tyrant acts, which are totally forbidden, he should advise him. If the person did not yield to his or other people's advice, he should report him. But not to the police of the idolater or his army or his security forces, as these are a bigger injustice and a horrible mistake and a criminal act. But to one whose knowledge and faith from the Emirs of Mujahidin and their scholars he trusts to take the suitable action against the perpetrators. This is in implementation of the statement of God almighty: (O ye who believe! stand out firmly for justice, as witnesses to God, even as against yourselves, or your parents, or your kin).

It is also banned on the Mujahid to obey his Emir in disobeying God, as stated by prayers by God be upon him (No obedience in a God's disobedience, obedience is only in doing favors). If the Muslim is ordered in a matter that violates the Shari'ah, he should not obey his Emir, even if his Emir was the drawn sword of God Khalid Ibn al-Walid -may God be satisfied with- (TN: a prominent army general in the early Islamic days). So how about when the one issuing the order is in a lower status? If he is mixed up about the order, and if it amongst the allowed or forbidden acts, and he was unable to consult a scholar, he should consult his heart, and to take care of his religion and his other life. He should remember that the original judgment on the Muslims souls, money and honor, the extreme forbidders. And that their blood is never allowed to be spilled, nor money taken or dishonor, or hurt him or branding him as an infidel, except upon a legal proof clearer than the sun in the middle of the day.

God stated: (If a man kills a believer intentionally, his recompense is Hell, to abide therein (Forever): And the wrath and the curse of God are upon him, and a dreadful penalty is prepared for him. O ye who believe! When ye go abroad in the cause of God, investigate carefully, and say not to anyone who offers you a salutation: "Thou art none of a believer!" Coveting the perishable goods of this life: with God are profits and spoils abundant. Even thus were ye yourselves before, till God conferred on you His favors: Therefore carefully investigate. For God is well aware of all that ye do(.The Women Surah 93-94. The Prophet (PBUH) stated: (The believer is within the realm of his religion as long as he did not target forbidden blood) narrated by al-Bukhari.

The Prophet (PBUH) stated: (The Muslim is who the Muslims are safe from his tongue and hand, and al-Muhajir is he who left whatever God has forbidden).

Finally, I remind my Mujahidin brothers that conducting the duty of Jihad and battle, and even dying for the sake of God, does not make us safe from the anger of God, if we spoil our Jihad by big sins and we did not seek repentance before it was too late. As a good example of that, the story of the group of people who were branded by the Qur'an for ridiculing God's verses, as they went out with Muslims in Tabuk battle. Another example is the story of the man who was killed in one of the Prophet's battles (PBUH). People said (he is a martyr), the Prophet (PBUH) denied him as a martyr saying: No, I have seen him in a robe in hell. Then the Prophet (PBUH) said: To 'Umar Ibn al-Khattab: 'Umar go and call on the people: Heaven is only entered by the believers. 'Umar said: I went out and called: That heaven is only entered by believers. Narrated by Muslim.

So, not every martyr in this world is a martyr in the Day of Judgment. Also, not all guilt is forgiven for the martyr of the second life. From the guilt that is not forgiven is the debt of money. As the Prophet (PBUH) said in the Hadith that was narrated by Muslim in his Correct book: (The martyr is forgiven of every guilt except the debt). Imam al-Nawawi —may God bless his soul-have said: (In his statement of May God pray and greet him (except the debt) is a notice on all the human rights. The Jihad and martyrdom and other good deeds do not eliminate the rights of the humans, but the rights of God violations are forgiven). If the individual is martyred and there were a few dinars of loan, he will be denied heaven until the debt is paid —as stated in some reporting. Now how about he who has killed scores or even hundreds of Muslim souls that he killed in absolute injustice? He is more eligible to be denied the heaven.

So let us take the initiative for repentance of our sins, the smallest to the biggest, with increased pleading for pardon and prayers, calling for God's victory and deferring his anger and punishment, almighty. We should avoid any wrongdoings of all types, and give justice to whom deserve it, before a coming day, where money and sons do not help except those who face God with a sound heart.

Our last request is to thank God, the Lord of Heavens, and may God pray on Muhammad and his kindred and his followers.

AH The Declaration.

If you are satisfied with this declaration, I suggest that it be reviewed by the wise men of Taliban Movements in both Pakistan and Afghanistan and the groups in other arenas. This declaration could be the beginning of a wider campaign in this context. Brother 'Ubayd had a good idea, and I add my voice to his, and that is to place at the end of every tape – which is sent presently from "Saladin Grandsons" and whatever – that it should contain in the future, programmed and Fiqh directives, cautioning from the common errors in Jihad. We would incorporate in it –for example– some Qur'anic Surah and Hadith that I have quoted in the suggested declaration like: (You the believers if you strike for the sake of God, make sure and do not say to those greeting you that you are not believers) or (The believer is within the realm of his religion as long as he did not target a forbidden blood) or (The Muslim is who the Muslims are safe from his tongue and hand, and al-Muhajir is he who left whatever God has forbidden) or similar Hadith. Ahead of it we place (The Mujahid Brother: remember the statement of God almighty…) or (To the Mujahid: remember the statement of the Messenger of God (PBUH)). We may place, instead of the Surah and Hadith, advice from us, like: No to detonating mosques and markets) or (spilling the denied blood and confiscating the stolen money is a tyranny, and aggression causes God's anger and delays victory) and so on.

There are other mistakes that may be confronted as much as possible, that I may discuss in another paper.

Finally, let us thank God the Lord of the heavens, you God we thank you and give witness that there is no God but God but you and we ask for your forgiveness.

In the Name of God…

Henceforth…

To Most Generous Brother Mukhtar Abu al-Zubayr (var. al-Zoubair)

I hope that you receive this letter from me while you are fine and well with all the brothers and followers…

Hereinafter…

We received your generous letter and I was happy reading what this letter contained about most jihad groups having united to join you; also about certain issues which occurred, of which you debated two important issues: 1) the issue of declaring the "country" (meaning the Islamic emirate); and 2) the issue of unity with the brothers within the declaration of the "country."

I see that there should be a practical working emirate on the ground but without declaring it in the media or confirming it in any paperwork, in order to avoid these documents leaking out to the enemies – should it happen for any reason.

This is my opinion, but you are there on the ground and you see all realities; whatever you see and witness live, the absent does not see. Therefore, you would balance out between the pros and cons on the issue of declaring or not declaring the establishment of the emirate; or you may balance things out on your side – as I see it – to make the declaration under the name of the Islamic Emirate of Somalia, with its named emir to be the Emir of the Islamic Emirate of Somalia.

Now, in relation to the issue of unity, I see that this obligation should be carried out legitimately and through unannounced secret messaging, by spreading this matter among the people of Somalia, without any official declaration by any officers on our

side or your side, that the unity has taken place. But there remains the situation of the brothers on your side and their talking about their relationship with al-Qa'ida, if asked. It would be better for them to say that there is a relationship with al-Qa'ida which is simply a brotherly Islamic connection and nothing more, which would neither deny nor prove.

And for the above matter, there are two reasons:

The first: If the matter becomes declared and out in the open, it would have the enemies escalate their anger and mobilize against you; this is what happened to the brothers in Iraq or Algeria. It is true that the enemies will find out inevitably; this matter cannot be hidden, especially when people go around and spread this news. However, an official declaration remains to be the master for all proof. Also, there will be fields open to those who would like to provide rescue assistance to Muslims in Somalia, to deny this reality which is not based on definitive evidences. Therefore, such would minimize the restraints on Muslims in the region of the emirate and likewise on the emirate proper.

The second: The matter is that some Muslims in Somalia are suffering from immense poverty and malnutrition, because of the continuity of wars in their country; I have a determined plan of action, using one of my sermons to press the merchants in the countries of the Arabian Peninsula to support pro-active and important developmental projects which are not expensive; we happened to have tried these in Sudan. Therefore, by not having the mujahidin openly allied with al-Qa'ida, it would strengthen those merchants who are willing to help the brothers in Somalia, and would keep people with the mujahidin.

The above are some of my viewpoints about what you proposed in your loving letter, including the other issues which you had, which Shaykh Mahmud ('Atiyah) will answer you about.

And before closing: we pursue your news and victories through the media; May God reward you blessings for all your efforts and your jihad.

Regarding your strike against the African Forces, you must review it enough to minimize the (damages) on Muslims from their onerous attacks against Bakarah Market.

Maybe your operations against them (TN: African Forces) could be during their arrival to or departure from the airport and without conducting your operational attacks against their headquarters unless those operations were large or through underground tunnels helping you reach the heart of the camp; and with time, an external attack. Anyway, we hope that you review this matter and may God empower and bless you with accuracy against your target.

In closing: I press upon you as much as I press upon myself to remain devout, patient, and persistent in upholding the high moral values which were upheld by an "Emir of reconciliation" toward his community, which is, with God's help, the dream of the Emir in his pardon, his justice, his patience, his good treatment of them, and his refusal to burden them with what they cannot not handle.

I would like you to pass on my greetings to all those respectable mujahidin brothers on your side for whom we pray to God the Almighty to render them victorious against their enemies and to protect them from the wickedness of traitors.

Our last supplications go to God, the Lord of the Universe, with prayers and peace unto our Prophet Muhammad, all his lineage and companions.

Peace to you and the mercy and blessings of God

Your Brother Zamaray

Friday August 7 2010

Attached is a book (titled) "Niqat al-'Irtikaz" (Fundamental Points)

(TN: End of Letter)

SOCOM-2012-0000006-HT

In the name of God, Most Gracious, Most Merciful

Praise God, He who promised and fulfilled, promised and forgave, and peace and prayer be upon the gentleman of the honorable, his perfect honored family and companions……

Honorable brother/ Azmarai, may God preserve you

Peace, mercy of God and His blessing be upon you. I hope that you and those with you are in the best of condition. And may God gather us on what is pleasing and satisfying to Him ,from glory of the world and winning of the hereafter…

Furthermore, these are some thoughts that I am adding to the letter which I previously had sent to you, last 12 of Dhul Al-Hijja (TN: No year given, most recent would be 19 November 2010):

Concerning our friend's letter (NFI) addressed to you; here is what I think. It is that those brothers might have sent the letter out of fear, too concerned about inflating the size and the growth of Al-Qa'ida, with God's blessing and strength. In addition, they think that bearing the burden of this huge body is overburdening, confining their energy, and exposing them to problems with many other parties. Especially, they desire and wish to walk toward development and construction. Therefore, they are satisfied with keeping those who resort to them and not exceeding that. I am afraid that this kind of perception, if that is reality, will lead them to exercising pressure on us to not to say so-and-so, or disassociate from so-and-so, denounce your connections with so-and-so, or deny your ties with so-and-so….etc. Thus, I see it to be very essential for Al-Qa'ida to confirm and declare its linkage with its branches, in order to become a reported fact, there is no use in denying it. Therefore, please reconsider your opinion not to declare the accession of the brothers of Somalia so as not to be pressured later on to announce our disassociation with them or with others…..And God is the conciliator to all the best…..

There is another issue, which I would like you to look into carefully; it is concerning controlling the affairs in general, membership and the affiliation in particular. There is no secret to you that, in the past, there were a lot of advantages and faults. However, what I would like to emphasize in this letter is the issue of individuals, those who pledge allegiance, and the affiliates. Therefore, from the last experience it showed that there were considerable variation between people and those individuals who pledged the allegiance. The problem is that Al-Qa'ida has become a broad field; each can enter, (TN: unclear possibly, sufficient) to declare his allegiance, does not wait to see whether he was accepted or not, even though the pledge is a contract between contractors.

In the last period, great figures with high quality have emerged, and also some figures have emerged did not benefit any groups by their affiliation, yet some kind of bragging and boasting appeared by joining Al-Qa'ida. And, the formulation of specific titles have been published by their owners in the network of information. This is a member of so-and-so, and that one is in charge of so-and-so, and this is straying from Al-Qa'ida familiarity. Moreover, if it comes from godly individuals, then it will have some positive impact deep inside. So what do you think if it comes from those individuals who are not on the appropriate levels?

In addition, in the last period, some figures have emerged collecting money in the name of Al-Qa'ida, and play at that… and I think you might have heard about the brothers of "Al-Zayat" (NFI) in general, some of them have abused the money to varying degrees. Anyways, the important thing, honorable sir, is that the issue needs to be controlled, to know who is member of Al-Qa'ida, what his function is, what side he follows, what is the way to impeach him, so as not to increase the friends of desire and greed and seclude those friends of religion and morals. And if the shortfall had sneaked upon the first generation, despite being near to the vow during the prophecy period, don't you think it will sneak upon us?

Things were stable until our master 'Uthman (TN: Third Caliph) – may God be pleased with him – started bringing his close relatives to power, and the sedition that followed his death may God be pleased with him, lasted what God wanted for it to last. Then, when Muslims had recovered and things started settling down during the year of the "Group"; our master "Mu'awiyah" marched them in a satisfactory way, until he started seeking to extract the succession of the nation in order to attribute it to his son. Then the sedition of Husayn, may God be pleased with him, followed by the sedition of Zubayr's son, may God be pleased with them both. Then sedition became widespread, the effect of which still exists to this day.

Anyway honorable sir, the intention is that it is predictable, with God's permission and blessing, achieving victory is near, and it follows the overflow of individuals, groups and their haste to pledge the allegiance. Therefore, starting from now please think about controlling the matter with a system that deals with people, each according to his religion, piety and contribution. And, governing the people with Shari'ah, which brings those who are moral and righteous closer to each other. Those who have groups established, nations, and whom victory descends upon, they fend off people of ambition and prejudice. God help us for all the best.

A final personal request, which is, I am asking you to pray for me, and my family for health in my religion, the world, and good offspring.

In conclusion, I am asking God to assume you in His care, preserve you, us, and all Muslims from all harm…

And I entrust you in God, Whose deposits do not go to waste.

Please destroy the letter after reading it, and may God reward you with the best.

Peace

Your beloved brother

Muharram 06 (TN: No year given, most recent would be 13 December 2010)

To the good brother Hakimullah ((Mahsud)), the Emir of Tahrik-e
Taliban in Pakistan (TN: TTP - Taliban Movement in Pakistan)

Greetings,

There are certain important issues that we like to bring to your
attention:

1: We have several important comments that cover the concept,
approach, and behavior of the TTP in Pakistan, which we believe
are passive behavior and clear legal and religious mistakes
which might result in a negative deviation from the set path of
the Jihadists Movement in Pakistan, which also are contrary to
the objectives of Jihad and to the efforts exerted by us. Here
are some facts to consider:

2: Considering Hakimullah as the sole Emir for everyone to swear
allegiance to, whoever oppose him and isn't a member of the
movement is an adulterer, the none differentiation between the
Jihad Emirate and the Great Imam post, and neglecting the daily
conditions of the Muslims; all of which according to the Shari'a
(Muslim laws) are a misconception of the real situation, and may
cause an inter-Mujahidin fighting.

3: (Of the passive behavior is) killing more people, taking them
as shields without basing their action on the Shari'a, killing
the normal Muslims as a result of martyrdom operations that
takes place in the marketplaces, mosques, roads, assembly
places, and calling the Muslims apostates.

4: The draft that was written by Hakimullah Mahsud is
unacceptable and we don't approve it because it contains
political and Shari'a mistakes. We already sent our comments on
this draft.

5: We are sending the attached short list on what is acceptable
and unacceptable on the subject of kidnapping and receiving
money, and we hope that you and the Mujahidin in Pakistan will
approve it.

6: We want to make it clear to you that we, the al-Qa'ida is an
Islamist Jihadist organization that is not restricted to a
country or race, and that we in Afghanistan swore allegiance to
the Emir Mullah Muhammad (('Umar)) who allowed us to carry
Jihad. Those that call us as guests do that for political

reasons and don't base this attribute on the Shari'a, and we ask you and all the Mujahidin not to use this attribute.

7: We make it clear to you that the brother Badr ((Mansur)) is one of the soldiers of the Qa'idat al-Jihad Organization who swore allegiance to Shaykh Usamah ((Bin Laden)), is with us, under our command, the Emir of a of a company of ours. Badr Mansur and other members of our group are not to be approached to join another organization or to deploy to other locations. Good manners and group work mandate that such a request be presented to his Tanzim (TN: al-Qa'ida) Emir and superiors.

8: We stress on the fact that real reform is the duty of all, and to succeed we should look for and correct our mistakes and take the advice of others.

We hope that you will take the necessary action to correct your actions and avoid these grave mistakes; otherwise we have to take decisive actions from our end.

We pray to God to grant us success,

Regards,

Mahmud al-Hasan (('Atiyatullah)) and ((Abu Yahya)) al-Libi

27 Dhu al-Hijjah 1431 (3 December 2010)

Brother ((ʻAbd-al-Hamid)), may God grant you success, these are questions from the Jaysh al-Islam brothers (in Gaza) along with responses to same from Shaykh Mahmud. For your reading, it may be of benefit.

In the name of God, the merciful, the compassionate

Peace be upon you, and God's mercy and blessings.

Praise be to God, and blessings and peace upon God's prophet, his family, companions, and those loyal to him…to wit:

These are questions which we ask you, our brothers, to show to the people of knowledge (TN: i.e. scholars), the crowns atop our heads, so that they can furnish us with their opinions, God willing…

First question: Is it permitted for funds to be taken from other organizations as support for us in jihad, as in the following examples:

Al-Jihad al-Islami (TN: Islamic Jihad) movement: Receives vast sums from abroad (Iran, in particular), and some of their people have adopted Shi'ite thought, God forbid. However, they have offered funding to us, in exchange for which we are to work with them and participate jointly in qualitative operations, as a sort of propaganda; the catch being that we would conduct the operation with funding through them, and afterwards it would be announced that we cooperated with them (TN: in the operation).

- The Fatah organization has also offered us funds purportedly to (TN: support) jihad, but there is another reason, namely their fear of becoming the target of our swords.

These funds would go directly towards the purchase and manufacture of weapons, and to support operations which we will conduct, God willing. When taking into consideration the suffocating siege against us, whether by the Jews, God's curses upon them, or by other organizations such as Hamas, who fear the growth of our influence and dominion…

Second Question: Is it permitted to invest funds in the stock market, buying and selling shares, for the goal of supporting jihad, or investing some donation-derived funds in stock markets and shares?

Third Question: Is it permitted to strike drug traffickers, eliminate them, and kill them, or (TN: not)? The technicality of the issue: Is it permitted to take the funds which they have gained from drug trafficking, and is it permitted to make use of the drugs which we obtain from them in:

1. Luring fallen addicts to serve as double agents against the Jews.

2. Selling them to Jews in order to harm them and take their money.

3. Bringing down Jewish soldiers, particularly border guards, by means of drugs.

This, by God, the Lord of success

Your brothers in Jaysh al-Islam

In the name of God, the merciful, the compassionate. Praise be to God, the Lord of all worlds. There is no power or strength save in God almighty. He is our Lord almighty and in Him we seek aid. We pray and wish peace upon the servant and messenger of God, our prophet Muhammad and all his family and companions and those who followed them in benevolence until Judgment Day.

First question: Is it permitted for funds to be taken from other organizations, on the premise of supporting us in jihad, as in the following example:

- Al-Jihad al-Islami (TN: Islamic Jihad) movement: Receives vast sums from abroad (Iran, in particular), and some of their people have adopted Shi'ite thought, God forbid. However, they have offered funding to us, in exchange for which we are to work with them and participate jointly in qualitative operations, as a sort of propaganda; the catch being that we would conduct the operation with funding through them, and afterwards it would be announced that we cooperated with them (TN: in the operation).

- The Fatah organization has also offered us funds purportedly to (TN: support) jihad, but there is another reason, namely their fear of becoming the target of our swords.

These funds would go directly towards the purchase and manufacture of weapons, and towards supporting operations that we will conduct, God willing. When taking into consideration the suffocating siege against us, whether by the Jews, God's curses upon them, or by other organizations such as Hamas, who fear the growth of our influence and dominion…

Response:

What I understood from the question is that the brothers are asking about the legitimacy of accepting funds from other organizations, if such is offered and given.

Doubtless there are technicalities in this… based upon, first of all, the intrinsic nature of these funds, permissible or forbidden, and then what interest, legitimate or corrupt, comes as a consequence to taking these funds.

So let us divide up the question on this basis, upon which I say the following, (TN: in knowledge that) success is (TN: only through) God:

If the money is intrinsically permissible, meaning it is not forbidden money. In principle, accepting it is permitted, as long as there are no other factors that prohibit this, as will come (TN: later in this discussion).

Permissible money is (TN: money) that which we have no knowledge of being forbidden; there are two types of impermissible money:

One of the two being: Intrinsically forbidden, such as wine, pork, the meat of improperly slaughtered animals, and the like, all of which can only be considered permissible to one in exigent circumstances.

The second one being: Forbidden by virtue of the means by which it was gained; there is much exposition and difference amongst scholars (TN: on this topic).

If it is attested (meaning that it is something witnessed) that the one who earned it did so illicitly, then the proper thing is that it not be permitted to be taken, such as (TN: gains from) theft or robbery, just as gaining it through an imperfect transaction, such as profits from interest, and funds gotten from trafficking in wine, drugs, and the like. It can neither be eaten of, nor accepted… with exception of the "thuman" (TN: 1/8th sales tax) on wine and pork can be…

…taken from the people of the dhimma (TN: non-Muslim subjects of an Islamic state), as our lord 'Umar said: "Let them sell it, and take the 'thuman' from it." This is a proper "athar" (TN: one of the utterances of Muhammad or his companions), and is the basis used by Islamic jurisprudents in this regard.

If it is not attested, and it is a matter of the mixing of permissible and forbidden (TN: monies), then this is an issue in which there are many differences and expositions, and we will most probably mention these later.

If it is (TN: money taken) from an infidel, does it differ from (TN: money taken) from a Muslim? Because the Prophet, God's blessing upon him, and his companions ate of the food and gifts of Jews and other infidels, and they did not ask them (TN: for the nature by which they were obtained). Likewise, in the story of our lord Ibrahim Khalil, which follows. This is also a source for dispute amongst scholars, and it requires exposition.

This applied jurisprudence is within the realm of that which needs exposition, by which I mean knowledge of (TN: the nature of) the monies, what is permissible to take and accept and eat of it, what is not permissible, from Muslim or from infidel, in the event of attestation (TN: of its impermissible nature) or in the event of mixture (TN: of permitted and non-permitted funds).

Jurisprudents speak of these issues in various chapters of books on jurisprudence and in fatwas. Among the passages which I point out to you to serve as a reference in this regard are as follows:

- "Kitab al-Halal wal-Haram" (TN: "Book of the Permissible and the Forbidden"); this is the fourth book in the "al-'Adat" (TN: "Customs") quarto within his "Kitab Ihya' 'Alum al-Din" (TN: "The Book of Reviving the Sciences of Religion") by imam Abi-Hamid al-Ghazali, God's mercy upon him. It is the basis for this issue, and has no precedent of which I am aware. If (TN: he made some) comments and researches on his choices within areas of applied jurisprudence in this regard, he (TN: wrote at great length) on issues of piety and the consideration of suspicions...!

- A collection of Shaykh al-Islam Ibn-Taymiyah's fatwas, particularly the 29th volume, which contains a number of fatwas on this issue. It includes writing and gems found nowhere else.

- "Jami' al-'Alum wal-Hukm" (TN: "Mosque of Sciences and Wisdom") by Ibn-Rajab al-Hanbali, God's mercy upon him, in his explanation of the hadith "That which is permissible is clear, and that which is forbidden is clear."

- Applied jurisprudence texts of Ibn-Miflah al-Hanbali.

- Al-Nawawi's collection regarding Sahib al-Mahdhab's statement "It is not permitted to swear allegiance to one whom it is known that all of his money is forbidden…"

In short, if we know, (TN: based upon) what has been decided in this matter (the matter of monies), that the money being given is not permitted to be taken and eaten of, then the matter is clear… and if we do not know that it is forbidden, then either there is suspicion, and caution is advised, or if it seems most probable to us that it is permissible or if its permissibility is certain, then it too is clear.

- If the money in and of itself is permitted to be taken, then it remains to us to consider what comes as a consequence to accepting and taking it, in which there are many scenarios which (TN: can be) envisioned, including: if doing so brings shame and degradation to a Muslim.

And: If doing so causes a Muslim to become obligated to an infidel or a libertine, which draws him into affection and adulation for them, and the like.

And: If dominion of the profligate or the infidel follows as a consequence (interference in affairs, dictation (TN: of orders), (TN: interference in) circumstances and the like).

And: If, as a consequence, an infidel or a libertine becomes stronger, greater, and increases in influence, i.e. strengthening the infidel or the libertine and aiding them.

It might not be something as this: The infidel or libertine may have some sort of benefit in giving it, which does not affect us much nor does it harm Muslims. The infidel may offer a Muslim money for the sake of kinship or the nation (for nationalist motivations and the like) and none of the corrupt consequences considered above will result. These are some of the things which affect the issue.

If it is taking (TN: money) from a just and proper Muslim, then this is clear. We will not discuss it and it is not a matter of question.

If the question is taking (TN: money) from organizations accused by our religion of being either infidel or libertine clothed in "innovation" or iniquity, and has committed grave offenses or perhaps even blasphemy through corrupt interpretations (TN: of Islam), and our judgment upon that in Islam still remains (TN: the same)!

Doubtless that some of these are damages in which the infidel and the libertine Muslim had some part in, and inevitably it is known that the libertine Muslim is not equivalent to the infidel in all aspects. For example: The internal ignominy brought upon us by a libertine Muslim is not equivalent to the internal ignominy brought upon us by the infidel. When a libertine Muslim obtains some form of dominion over us, it is not equivalent to dominion of the infidel over us, God forbid. All of these things are considered in their measure, based upon which there occurs a balance between the good and the bad.

As for exigency: As you know, exigency bears its own rules, and those in exigency deem it necessary in order to strengthen God almighty, and confines it to that situation (exigency is evaluated by its own measure).

Likewise, dire need, i.e., that which is close to but has not quite reached the threshold of exigency. In this event, the makruh (TN: acts/things discouraged but not forbidden) and the mushtabah (TN: acts/things of suspect permissibility) are allowed. The difference between exigency and dire need being that exigency justifies the prohibited (i.e. the forbidden), but need lifts away the "discouraged but not forbidden" status and the judgment of "suspect" (TN: from the thing) and brings leniency of judgment and so, we lift the sin/crisis from the individual in question whether or not a thing is "discouraged but not forbidden" or cause for suspicion, as we can bear the introduction of some ignominy in the interest of a greater good. As long as we are in need of taking money, then it is considered a "dire need"! God is all-knowing (TN: i.e. God knows better than I).

This response is my analysis, in brief, and the brothers know the circumstances, to which they (TN: can) apply what we have mentioned above…

On to something of an exposition on what came about in the question:

It is clear that you are in dire need and financial straits...!

As the al-Jihad movement's funding comes primarily from support (TN: provided by) the Rafidite (TN: "refuser"; common euphemism for Shi'ite) nation (Iran), which is not in and of itself harmful, by which I mean that it is permitted to eat of what is given of it and to accept it, God willing. It (TN: Iran) is to us an infidel state, and accepting monies from infidel states and kings is permitted, in and of itself, unless another prohibiting factor arises.

The evidence for this being the hadith (TN: utterance) of Ibrahim Khalil, God's peace upon him, and his acceptance of a gift from an infidel king. In this story of Sarah, when the king attempted to interfere with her, he was forbidden by God's will. He then gave her money and made a gift to her of a female servant (this being Hagar, peace be upon her). Ibrahim accepted this, and benefited from it. This hadith is in the two "sahih" (TN: the two texts containing properly attested hadith) and in others.

Al-Bukhari pronounced upon this:

It was Abi-Hurayrah, may God be pleased with him, who said:

"The prophet, God's peace upon him, said, 'Ibrahim, God's peace upon him, was traveling with Sarah. The two of them entered a village, wherein was a king or a tyrant. It was said that Ibrahim entered with a woman of the finest sort. (TN: An emissary) was sent to him, who asked, "Who is this with you?" To which he replied, "My sister." He returned to her and said, "Do not put the lie to my words, as I have told them that you are my sister. By God, there are no faithful on earth save for me and thee." He sent her to him (TN: the king), and he came to her, and she began to perform ablution and pray. She said, "Oh God, as I have believed in you and in your Prophet, and kept my womb chaste to all save my husband, do not give the infidel dominion over me." (TN: Upon which) he started and ran. Al-'Araj stated that Abu-Salmah bin-'Abd-al-Rahman stated: "Abi-Hurayrah stated that she said, 'Oh God, if he dies, it will be said that she killed him.' He sent (TN: for her again), and then came to her, and she began to perform ablution and pray. She said, "O God, as I have believed in you and in your Prophet, and kept my womb chaste to all save my husband, do not give the infidel dominion over me." He started and ran. 'Abd-al-Rahman said that Abu-Salmah said that Abu-Hurayrah said that she said "O God, if he dies, it will be said 'she killed him.' And he sent (TN: for her) a second or a third time, and he said, "By God, what you have sent me is naught but a devil. Send her back to Ibrahim and give her recompense. She returned to Ibrahim and she said, "I felt that God stayed the infidel and granted (TN: us) a servant girl."

Al-Hafiz Ibn-Hajar, God's mercy upon him, said:

The (TN: morals contained in) this hadith are the legitimacy of the brothers of Islam, the authorization of (TN: acceptance of) offers, license to submit to the tyrant and the rapacious, and to accept the gift of an oppressive king, and to accept the gift of the polytheist, and response to a prayer of sincere intent, and the Lord's satisfaction with he who is sincere in prayer and proper in deed. The counterpoint to this can be seen in the story of Ashab al-Ghar (TN: "owners of the cave") in which (TN: can be seen) the tribulation of the righteous in order to raise their qualities (TN: "degrees").

It is said that God revealed to Ibrahim, so that he could see the king with Sarah, and that he obtained naught from her, he mentioned this in "al-Tijan" (TN: "The Crowns") and pronounced: "He ordered that Ibrahim and Sarah be brought in to him; he then bade Ibrahim outside the palace, and came to Sarah. God made the palace as clear as a flask to Ibrahim, and he saw them and heard their speech." (TN: The moral of this being) that if one is beset by grief, he must take refuge in prayer. (TN: Another moral of this being) that ablution was practiced by peoples prior to our own, and is not limited to just our people, nor only to the prophets, so proved by Sarah, as the majority (TN: states that) she was not a prophet. So ends his words; I mention them in full for (TN: your) benefit.

Such is also found in al-'Ayni's exposition.

And this is the basis for this issue. There is more proof than this.

Including the prophet's companions', with the prophet's knowledge, acceptance in exigency of the gift of the infidel. And the Prophet accepted the gifts of infidels when no ignominy would result, and so accepted some of the gifts of infidels, as is found in many hadith, and he refused some of them, rejected them, and did not accept them, and said "I refused the dross of the polytheists," as was relayed by Ahmad Abu-Dawud and al-Tarmadhi. The meaning of "dross" being "their gift, present, and the like."

If you are not today capable of financing yourselves through legitimate means devoid of that which is objectionable, then accepting monies from other organizations, such as from some Islamic movements including Hamas or al-Jihad al-Islami movement, or even from nationalist movements who participate with you in striking the Jewish enemy, then (TN: accepting these monies) for the sake of using it to conduct jihad and to strike the Jews is better than abandoning the jihad due to paucity of funds.

So take it, if there is no other way, and strike the Jews…

Consider this further, and you best know your situation...!

And aim well (TN: "aim and be close")!

Because those movements (Jihad or Hamas, or even Fatah) are exploiting these acts and adopting them as their own, it is less damaging than would be the damage of abandoning the fight against the Jews, and God is all-knowing.

And if God opens the path for you, and you are able to fund yourselves and have no need for them, then abandon them, and work independently on your own path, granted to you by God.

We ask God the almighty to open the path for you, guide you, and strengthen you (TN: and purge you) of weakness, and make you rightly guided guides…Amen.

The second question:

Is it permitted to invest funds in the stock market, buying and selling shares, for the goal of supporting jihad, or investing some donation-derived funds in stock markets and shares?

The response:

The judgment upon this also depends upon the circumstances and regulations of these stock markets. I know nothing of the circumstance and regulations of these stock markets which would qualify me to speak about them. The methods of selling in (TN: the stock markets) have many complications, and are full of tricks, and I have no ability in this. May God strengthen us and you.

It is advised to ask some scholars who are specialized in this area, after editing your question well, and explaining the circumstances and regulations of the stock markets at which you are able to trade. May God make you successful and aid you.

Third question:

Is it permitted to strike drug traffickers, eliminate them, and kill them, or (TN: not)? The technicality of the issue: Is it permitted to take the funds which they have gained from drug trafficking and is it permitted to make use of the drugs which we obtain from them in:

1. Luring fallen addicts to serve as double agents against the Jews.

2. Selling them to Jews in order to harm them and take their money.

3. Bringing down Jewish soldiers, particularly border guards, by means of drugs

The response:

Praise God

As far as striking drug traffickers, eliminating them, and killing them: Yes, there is a technicality (TN: to the issue), which is according to the capability and authority of the mujahidin. The guiding principle for this, which you must learn and adhere to in this issue, is as follows: This is an issue within the realm of "propagating virtue and preventing vice," the guiding principle for its legitimacy being that it not lead to a greater vice.

This is the guiding principle; keep it, and may God bless you.

And so: If the mujahidin in some area or region are capable of carrying out hudud (TN: prescribed punishments for specific offenses in Shari'a law) and establishing Shari'a law or more, meaning that if they apply it, then the resulting outcome is in accordance with Shari'a law, and no greater harm or corruption is consequent, then this is up to them.

But we may say that at such time, it is their duty, the basis for which is this: It is (TN: their) duty to set up hudud, and to propagate virtue and prevent vice, and to do so by deed.

This is as the mujahidin today are doing in some sub-districts of Iraq, Afghanistan, Waziristan, and other places. For one in such as your case, it is obvious that you are not in this position, may God strengthen you and open the path for you.

What I believe (TN: is best) for you is not to do this, as I fear that great corruptions may result, and you will open yourselves up to things which are not within your power (TN: to control), and you will be beset with problems while you are yet weak. These sinful ones (if they be Muslims): There are technicalities pertaining to the permissibility, or lack thereof, of killing them. They are basically protected within Islam, and it is not permitted to kill them, although it is permissible in specific circumstances. Doubtless there is another exposition on this aspect.

However, if you are capable of taking their monies, in some cases, without there following any greater corruption, as we mentioned, then this is to you, and you may spend the monies for jihad in God's name.

And, in my conjecture, these cases are quite limited, if they exist at all. Such as: You stumble upon their monies, or one of their (drug merchants') convoys fall into your hands, and you then take their monies (not the drugs themselves), and spend them for jihad in God's name.

However, remember that the stipulation in this is always that it not lead to a greater corruption. God is all-knowing.

The second portion of the question, by which you also mean: The question regarding acceptance of gifts, presents, or alms from drug traffickers who are Muslims. This is what I understood from your question.

If this was the intended meaning, then: A man takes for himself, and accepts from them for himself, as in accepting their gifts, and eating of their food, then there is an exposition on this, and there is a difference amongst scholars regarding (TN: this point of) jurisprudence, as previously noted.

If their monies are solely derived from forbidden (TN: acts/items) i.e. all of it is from that which is forbidden (TN: acts/items) (such as drug traffickers), then most scholars (the mass of them) state that it is not permissible to take from them, or to eat of their monies (TN: sic)… some scholars choose (TN: the position that) it is permissible, saying: their sins are upon them, and nothing is upon he who takes of it. However, the former is most likely, God is all-knowing.

If their monies are mixed, then it is permissible to eat of the monies, and to accept what they give. However, it must be restricted, so as not to exceed the portion of their monies which are of the permissible sort.

Discourse on this issue is long, and (TN: you can) refer to some of the sources which we have indicated above.

If these traffickers, however, who traffic in forbidden (TN: items), such as drugs, give their monies as alms for jihad in God's name, then it appears to me, and God is all-knowing, that it is permissible to spend these monies for jihad in God's name

Because these monies were derived from forbidden (TN: items), then it is incumbent upon its owner to repent, and through repentance, relinquishment of these monies so that they are no longer in his possession. The way to do this being to place them in a "bayt al-mal" (TN: treasury), where they are used for the benefit of Muslims, including jihad and conquest in God's name, or to be given as alms.

Some scholars state: They would destroy these funds, as they are derived from forbidden (TN: items/acts).

This is quite weak, as God almighty has never ordered the destruction of monies, but proscribed the wasting of it. And in this case, destroying them would be a waste of the monies which contains no benefit, as there is no obligation to destroy it (nothing exists to indicate that this would be an obligation), and the clear good stipulates that it be spent in the interests of Islam and Muslims, and so should enter a "bayt al-mal" and become part of the resources of the "bayt al-mal" such as monies taken (seizure) from the corrupt, a punishment we have condoned, and the like.

This is what Shaykh al-Islam Ibn-Taymiyah, God's mercy upon him, chose, and expounded upon in sections of his fatwas (he expounded upon this issue in more than one fatwa in the 29th volume, and in others as well).

If the (TN: original) owner of the funds has not repented, but rather continues to commit sin, in this case the trafficking of drugs, then it is the duty of Muslims to take him to task, and it is the duty of the "wali al-amr" (TN: chief, or senior member) of Muslims to take this in hand, in which case the seizure of his money is permitted, to according to the most proper statements of scholars, by the "wali al-amr".

In brief: If the trafficker in wine or drugs donates some of his monies for jihad in the name of God the almighty, it is permitted to accept this and spend it on jihad in God's name, along with the duty of continuing to preach to him and to all men to submit to God, and to repent by abandoning vices and turning away from the forbidden. This is (TN: in order to) be cautious of assisting his trafficking in the forbidden. God is all-knowing.

If the mujahidin have no need of those (TN: funds), then perhaps it is best to leave them alone.

As for your question:

1. Luring fallen addicts to serve as double agents against the Jews.

2. Selling them to Jews in order to harm them and take their money.

3. Bringing down Jewish soldiers, particularly border guards, by means of drugs

All of this is not permitted...

The first is clear, as it is a proscribed means, the proscription against which is clear: Giving drugs or wine to people and contributing to and promoting this behavior to them...

all of this God has proscribed and forbidden, so by what evidence shall we permit it?! Just because those in question are "fallen addicts," it is of no matter to the (TN: applicability of) the verdict, and God is all-knowing. If they are Muslim youths who have committed this grave offense (taking drugs), then this is quite clear… if they are infidels…

…then it is also not permitted to use this means with infidels, according to all scholars… although some scholars have given license in other issues in this same vein which differ from the issue at hand, namely:

Such as Abu-Hanifah, God's mercy upon him, and his sanctioning of transactions with ahl al-Harb (TN: "people of war") (warring infidels) in dar al-Harb (TN: "house of war", i.e. lands not under Islamic rule) with interest, as his companions mentioned in "Bada'i' al-Sana'i'" and others, and the mass of scholars opposed him in this, and the statement of this mass is correct, which is that this is forbidden from being done with ahl al-Harb, just as it is forbidden with a Muslim or with one not of ahl al-Harb, whether in Dar al-Harb or Dar al-Islam.

Like Sahnun, of the Malikite imams, who sanctioned paying ransoms of wine or pork for Muslim prisoners of war, should the infidels so request: Ibn-Jizzi in "al-Qawanin al-Fiqhiyah" (TN: "Jurisprudence Laws" stated: "Should the enemy request a ransom of a horse or a weapon, it is paid to him, unlike the case with wine or pork." Sahnun sanctioned using these two (TN: forbidden) items to pay the ransom for prisoners of war, while Ibn-al-Qasim forbade it for being injurious to Muslims, and he who was ransomed with payment of wine or the like (TN: remains as one) who never returned.

Like the statement of Shaykh al-Islam Taymiyah in his fatwas "Leaving the Tatars or others to drink wine and to become intoxicated is better than forbidding it to them, because wine does not prevent them from remembrance of God, nor from performing prayer, rather it prevents them from (TN: committing) depravity and sin, and should they become sober, they would become more corrupt," as he mentioned in his "Kitab al-Istiqamah". This is a matter which pertains to the promotion of vice and prevention of virtue, meaning to refrain from discouraging them from this, if it is preferable (TN: to do so). God is all-knowing.

As for the second (number two): This is an issue of selling wine, drugs, and that which is forbidden in our Shari'a to the infidels for the purpose of harming them... the proper answer is that it is not permitted.

All of this is forbidden, encompassed in forbidding the sale of things there is no difference between selling to a Muslim or to an infidel, neither in war nor in peace. This is proper, as previously indicated.

As for the third (number three): The verdict for this is clear from the preceding; it is also forbidden and not permitted, and this is the basis: The forbidding of selling wine and the like to infidels of the ahl al-Harb, and forbidding using them as gifts to ahl al-Harb for the purposes of espionage and plying them. All of these are forbidden means, and are not permitted. As evidence of this:

The totality of evidence of forbidding the sale of wine and the like, and forbidding giving or presenting them, or giving them for the consumption to one who drinks it, or carrying it, etc... There is much well-known evidence for this, which includes both selling to an infidel and selling to a Muslim.

- Because this is contribution to sin and wrongdoing...

- Because it is a denigration to the image of Islam and its pure and noble message, and is an impediment to God's will.

O God, unless there is exigency, and we have no other means by which to free a Muslim from their hands; if they ask for ransom of wine or drugs, for example, and Sahnun authorized it, as seen in the precedent of paying ransom of wine and pork for prisoners, then this may bear the semblance of exigency, as the (TN: of the image of Islam) is safe from the damage of denigration in this case, if the enemy requests this. God is all-knowing.

Whereas if you have decided that there is exigent need for this, then you must weigh it, and limit it to exigent circumstances alone, and is not (TN: to be treated as) a permitted thing...!

Care must be taken to (TN: treat the matter) with secrecy and discretion, for fear of the spread of corruption to those who were faithful and for fear of denigrating the image of Muslims, and alienation (TN: of the congregation); we place our trust in God.

God is all-knowing and all-wise.

Praise be to God, first and last, and God's blessings upon our Prophet Muhammad, his family, and companions.

Written by (('Atiyatallah))

Shawwal 1427 (TN: corresponding to the period of time from 24 October 2006 until 22 November 2006)

And before closing: I make mention to you (plural) of a very important matter that came to me, which is changing the name of (Qa'ida al-Jihad), because there are several necessary and attention-worthy reasons to change it, of them:

1. This name (Qa'ida al-Jihad) was abridged by the people and only a few people remember this name; it has come to be known as (al-Qa'ida) and this name reduces the feeling of Muslims that we belong to them, and allows the enemies to claim deceptively that they are not at war with Islam and Muslims, but they are at war with the organization of al-Qa'ida, which is an outside entity from the teachings of Islam and this is what was raised repeatedly in the past as indicated by Obama, that our war is not on Islam or on the Muslim people but rather our war is on the al-Qa'ida organization, so if the word al-Qa'ida was derived from or had strong ties to the word Islam or Muslims; or if it had the name Islamic party, it would be difficult for Obama to say that. It is clear from the past also that they (the enemies) have largely stopped using the phrase "the war on terror" in the context of not wanting to provoke Muslims, because they felt that saying the war on terror could appear to most people to be a war on Islam, especially after they unjustly spilled the blood of innocent Muslims in Iraq and Afghanistan. We ask God the Almighty to have mercy on our Islamic brothers.

   For example, the name of our brothers in the Shabaab organization, Al-Arabiya (TN: news network) often identifies them with the Shabaab movement, only it avoids the name al-jihad or al-mujahidin.

2. The name of an entity carries its message and represents it. Al-Qa'ida describes a military base with fighters without a reference to our broader mission to unify the nation.

   Building on what is presented, it would be nice if you could discuss and come up with appropriate names that would not be easily shortened to a word that does not represent us. It would help if the name is a method of delivery of

our message to reach the sons of the Umma/nation. These
are some suggestions:

Taifat al-tawhid wal-jihad (TN: Monotheism and Jihad Group)
Taifat al-tawhid wal-difa' 'an al-Islam (TN: Monotheism and
Defending Islam Group)
Jama'at i'adat al-khilafat al-rashida (TN: Restoration of
the Caliphate Group)
Jama'at nasr al-Islam wal-aksa (TN: Support of Islam and
Al-Aqsa Group)
Jama'at wihda al-Muslimin (TN: Muslim Unity Group)
Tanthim al-Jihadi li-tawhid al-Umma wa-inkathiha (TN: Jihad
Organization for Unification and Rescue of the Nation)
Tanthim al-Jihadi litahrir al-aksa wa-tawhid al-Umma (TN:
Jihad Organization to Liberate Al-Aqsa and Unify the
Nation)
Hizb tawhid al-Umma al-Islamiya (TN: Islamic Nation
Unification Party)
Jama'at tahrir al-aksa (TN: Al-Aqsa Liberation Group)
Jama'at inkath wanahdat al-Umma (TN: Rescue and
Revitalization of the Nation Group)

SOCOM-2012-0000010-HT

(TN: this document is dated 26 April 2011)

In the name of Allah the most gracious the most merciful.

Praise Allah and pray on his prophet,

To the esteemed brother, Sheikh Mahmud, Allah protect him

Islamic greetings,

I hope this message will reach you, the family, the offspring, and all the brothers in good condition.

I received your first and then your second messages, Allah reward you for the totality of what it contained. To start, I want to talk about the most important point in our modern history, the point of launching the nation's revolution against the tyrants, and for which I ask Allah to make a start for reviving the dignity of the religion and its glory.

What we are witnessing these days of consecutive revolutions is a great and glorious event, and it is most probable, according to reality and history, that it will encompass the majority of the Islamic world with the will of Allah, and thanks to Allah things are strongly heading towards the exit of Muslims from being under the control of America, and the Americans worry about that, which is great; the Secretary of State indicated in her visit to Yemen that, "We worry that the region will fall into the hands of the armed Islamists" and that warning was directed to 'Ali 'Abdullah Salih and the remainder of the rulers during the revolution in Tunisia, before the revolution in Egypt that toppled Mubarak erupted. The fall of the remaining tyrants in the region became a must with the will of Allah, and it was the beginning of a new era for the whole nation.

These events are the most important events that the nation has witnessed for centuries, as since the nation has entered its current stage it has not witnessed any movements to save it that are as large as the all-encompassing movements that were launched with the grace of Allah these days, and it is known that comprehensive popular movements inevitably change the conditions, so if we double the efforts to direct and educate the Muslim peoples and warn them from the half solutions, while taking care in providing good advice to them, the oncoming stage will be for Islam, Allah willing.

Knowing that the movements calling for half solutions like the Brotherhood have witnessed a spread of the proper ideology among their membership in recent years, especially in the growing generations, and one of the Brotherhood members discussed that phenomenon in a lengthy question among the questions addressed to Sheikh Abu Muhammad; also it was mentioned in many of the media vehicles that there is a sizable direction within the Brotherhood that holds the Salafi doctrine, so the return of the Brotherhood and those like them to the true Islam is a matter of time, with the will of Allah. The more attention paid to explaining Islamic understanding, the sooner their return is, so preserving the Muslim movements today and adjusting their direction requires effort and attention, keeping in mind the necessity of being kindly to the sons of the nation who fell under misguidance for long decades.

That great duty, which is the duty of guidance and advice, which is connected to the fate of the nation, does not find he who fulfils it aware of the guidance that is disciplined with jurisprudence. I have asked in the past that the faithful in the nation select from among themselves a number of scholars and wise men, who then form a Shura council that follows up on the issues of the nation and provides guidance, opinion, and advice; but after they delayed in conducting that duty, and the nation entered that pivotal stage, it became incumbent upon us, the mujahidin, to fulfill that duty and to plug that gap as much as we can, which became one of the utmost duties after faith, so that the nation is liberated with the will of Allah and the religion regains its glory.

There is no doubt that the duties on the mujahidin are numerous, except that this great duty should take the main share of our efforts so that we do not shortchange it and expose the nation shake-up today, to what the revolutions against the Western occupation got exposed to in the past.

And we have to remember another important issue, which is that Jihad in Afghanistan is a duty to establish the rule of Allah (Shari'a) in it, and it is the path toward conducting the larger duty, which is liberating the one-and-half billion-person nation and regain its holies. So while we are conducting jihad in Afghanistan and bleeding down the head of the international apostasy, until it reaches such weakness that the Muslim people have regained some self confidence and daring, and removed some of the oppressive pressure that was exhausting and failing anyone who thought of crossing Americas agents, the pressure of the supreme power that threatened to keep whom it desires and remove whom it desires, and with the gradual deterioration of that pressure, the comprehensive revolutions launched at the hands of the people whose extreme majority are Islam loving.

So we have to get into expanding the programmed and directed media, and our efforts in directing the nation's research and deciding on a specific plan that we all discuss, as the oncoming stage is important and very dangerous and does not tolerate the apparent differences in our directives. Initially I would see that one of the most important steps of the oncoming stage is inciting the people who have not revolted yet, and encouraging them to get against the rulers and the methods, indicating that it is a religious duty and a logical necessity, so the arrows are concentrated on toppling the rulers without discussing the differences on issues, while paying maximum attention to spreading awareness and correcting the understanding, and we send to the brothers in all the regions to pay attention to spreading the book (understandings that must be corrected) by Sheikh Muhammad Qutb).

And due to our efforts in plugging that gap and preparing a plan to guide the nation, we must mobilize all the resources that have expressive abilities in speech, poetry, visual, or audio and devote them completely toward directing and guiding the nation's youth; and we leave running the work in Afghanistan and Waziristan to the resources that have field and administrative abilities, and do not have expressive abilities.

Please inform Sheikh Yahiya and the other brothers who have expressive abilities on the previous parts of the message, and inform me of their opinions without missing any of them, as every voice that can contribute in this stage should not be excluded.

General points after the second message:

- Enclosed is a statement to the nation in regard to the revolutions. Please review it and if there are remarks on parts of it by the brothers then there is no problem in revising it. Then send it to al-Jazeera Network, noting that I have enclosed a copy of it in a new card (TN: thumb drive or memory card) with nothing else on it, so please expedite its release and broadcast due to the importance and developments of the events.

- Regarding the paper you sent that is titled, "Elements for Research Regarding the Arab Revolutions," it is very important, so please start researching it and I might comment on it and on all your media activities after the revolutions in the next message, due to lack of time.

Enclosed is a file titled, "Suggestions toward Resolving Crises in Yemen," if you could rearrange the ideas in it and reshape them and publish it under your name, or if you do not see that as appropriate, put my son's Khalid name on it and direct the article to the scholars and dignitaries of Yemen. The situation requires expediency in that as much as possible.

- It would be nice to remind our brothers in the regions to be patient and deliberate, and warn them of entering into confrontations with the parties belonging to Islam, and it is probable that most of the areas will have governments established on the remnants of the previous governments, and most probable these governments will belong to the Islamic parties and groups, like the Brotherhood and the like, and our duty at this stage is to pay attention to the call among Muslims and win over supporters and spread the correct understanding, as the current conditions have brought on unprecedented opportunities and the coming of Islamic governments that follow the Salafi doctrine is a benefit to Islam. The more time that passes and the call increases, the more the supporters will be of the people, and the more widespread will be the correct understanding among the coming generations of Islamic groups.

- Regarding the operations that the brothers in Yemen are intending to conduct using poison, please be careful of doing it without enough study of all aspects, including political and media reaction against the mujahidin and their image in the eyes of the public, so please pay attention to the matter.

- Regarding the communications with the brothers in Iraq, please inform us on its progress and the reason for its scarcity.

- Regarding the brothers coming from Iran, you are the more knowledgeable of the security situation on your side and in Baluchistan, so arrange for them the most secure places, and Allah is the protector.

- Regarding what you mentioned about the British intelligence saying that England is going to leave Afghanistan if Al-Qa'ida promised not to target their interests, I think their stance is similar to the people of Damascus when Khalid Ibn Al-Walid entered it, and they became sure of being defeated, so they hurried to hold a peace treaty with Abu 'Ubaidah Allah be pleased with him, so I say that we do not enable them on that, but without slamming the door completely closed.

- As far as the French hostages with our brothers in the Islamic Maghreb, I want to warn that the atmosphere after the French standing towards the Libyan people does not condone killing the French, due to what will follow of negative reflections, after it became evident that most of the common people are supporting Sarkozy, so if we need to kill them then that should be after the end of Libyan events and their developments, and the better benefit as far as I see is to exchange the woman with the best that would benefit you and the brothers there, as far as the men, if the brothers can wait, then they should keep them until the elections, and if that is difficult then they should exchange half of them and keep the other half which should be the higher ranking and the more important ones, and if that also is difficult then they should at a minimum keep the most important man of them till the French elections, and it is better that the negotiations not be public and that they place a time limit on it so that the French do not postpone the exchange till the elections (TN: possibly after the elections) so that it's a winning card in their hands, even though the remaining period to the election is not that short.

- Regarding the British officer captured by our brothers in Somalia, I say that we attempt to exchange him for our prisoners with them, or with their allies, so if this happens then it is what we want, and if they reach a road block and they cannot keep him as a pressure card on France to leave Afghanistan before Sarkozy elections, then he is to be ransomed with money, and they be made aware of what I said about the ramifications of killing the French in this stage, even though the reaction to killing would be less if the killing was from their side vs. if it is from Al-Qa'ida in Islamic Maghreb side.

- It would be nice to ask the brothers in Somalia to inform us of the economical situations in the states they control, as it is obvious that enabling people's livelihood is an important part of the religion, and it is the most important duty of the Emir, so there must be an effort to establish an economical power, and I had in a previous message to you written some economical suggestions to be sent to the brothers in Somalia, then I did not receive from you an indication that they were sent, so if they were sent it is important to follow up on them, and they were not send because of an obstacle, I have enclosed them in the message to resend them to them.

- It would be good to send advice to the brothers in Somalia about the benefit of doubt when it comes to dealing with crimes and applying Shari'a, similar to what the prophet (PBUH) said, to use doubts to fend off the punishments.

- As far as what you mentioned of the desire of some of the
  brothers to go to the revolution fields in their countries,
  I have written in my message to you before I knew their
  desire the necessity of sending some qualified brothers to
  the field of the revolutions in their countries, to attempt
  to run things in a wise and jurisprudent manner in
  coordination with the Islamic powers there, while studying
  both sides of the benefits and which way is better before
  any of the brothers go. First of all, there must be
  confirmation of the safety of the route, that is for the
  brothers whom we would ask to go, or the brothers who did
  not insist on going, and for those whom you notice are
  highly excited and cannot withstand staying, so those whose
  conditions you accommodate and allow to go while doing the
  best to secure the best safe routes for them.

- As far as Sheikh Bashir Al-Madani (Yunis), if the place in
  which he is currently located is safe, then he should
  postpone his travel until the regime in Syria or Yemen
  falls, and as far as the brothers with him, they should be
  dealt with as I have explained in the previous item.

- I read the message of Sahib Al-Tayib, and your response to
  it, and it seemed to me that the message indicates that
  some information has been leaked to Sahib Al-Tayib through
  some of the scholars who are connected directly or
  indirectly to the government, or though some of the
  scholars who may have a personal opinion that follows the
  public opinion of the importance of stability in the Gulf,
  so they wanted to hint to Sahib Al-Tayib about the
  seriousness of instigating the situation in the kingdom so
  that he asks us about that, so he in turn only hinted at
  it, that is one way of reading that message, so I ask that
  you read it again in an analytical way and tell me about
  what you come up with by reading it, and also enclose a
  copy of it to Sheikh Abu Muhammad.

- Regarding brother Tufan and what you asked of reviewing his
  writings, due to the many duties and shortage of time, I
  will ask that Sheikh Abu Muhammad does that, so please
  enclose the writings of the brother to him, but in general
  I say that the stage now is to spread awareness in the

nation after all the flood of good, praise Allah, so it
should be given attention and good direction.

- Regarding Hamzah, Allah reward you for your effort in
getting him out, and as far as the options you presented, I
say the third option, which is that he should get out ASAP
to Baluchistan, where it is only a way to reach Sindh, so
he should not wait there except long enough to continue
travel, and should not meet with any of the brothers there,
and after he arrives in Sindh, he will contact a person in
Peshawar, whose number we enclosed in a message to Hamzah,
to agree on a specific location to meet in Peshawar.

Then Hamzah will inform the person who will accompany him
of the place that he agreed to meet with his friend in
Peshawar to take him to it, and he is a trusted person, and
we informed him that Hamzah will contact him in the near
future, and his name will be Ahmad Khan. The method of
getting out will reach Hamzah in detail when he receives
his message, which is enclosed.

As far as him getting training until you arrange for him to
get out, I say that he stays low in this stage and
postpones the training to another opportunity, and that he
does not get out unless for important necessity, and if he
has to go out, then he should not take his son with him,
which is what I pointed out to Sheikh Sa'id in the past
about distancing the non-concerned with the work as long as
there is danger, so children would be primarily included in
that caution, and I had asked for that after there was a
publication for Al-Sahab that showed a child standing next
to one of the brothers while the brother was preparing
explosives, so please draw the attention of all of the
brothers to that.

Note: This thumb drive (TN: the word used is the same
word used for telephone SIM card, so it is possible that
telephone memory cards, which are very small, are being
used for that purpose) contains a phone number of one of
our brothers contained in the message for Hamzah, so please
do not copy the message for Hamzah, and after Hamzah copies

the phone number on paper, destroy the card for fear of compromise.

- We were told that Hamzah sent you numbers of his brother Muhammad, and enclosed with it specific messages, so that one of the brothers would call him and relay the message to him. So, if there are still communications, it would be good that one of the brothers calls him from one of the places that are safe to call from, and informs Muhammad that Hamzah is telling him that his father wants him to go with his mother and siblings to Qatar ASAP, and to live there until the situation is resolved soon, Allah willing, and that they put the effort in obeying Allah and seeking knowledge, and that if it would be difficult to go to Qatar then they should go to Hejaz (TN: Hejaz is another name of Saudi Arabia), noting that Hamzah may have other points to relay to them and also the words that are between him and his brother Muhammad, so that Muhammad is assured that the call was from his side.

- Regarding the card (TN: possible ID card) and the license that are prepared for Khalid, please hand them over to Hamzah.

- Regarding the numbers that brother 'Abdullah Al-Sindi promised, please send them to us.

- Enclosed is a message from my son Khalid to brother 'Abdullah Al-Sindi, and a message from his mother to the family (TN: means wife of) of Sheikh Abu 'Abd-al-Rahman Al-B.M. so please expedite.

- Regarding the message that you enclosed to Muhammad Aslam, we transferred it to him, and regarding the sum of money that you said you sent to him, he told us about it, and we might keep half of the amount deposited with us and the other half with him.

- It would be good if you inform me about the funds arriving for the mujahidin from inside and outside Pakistan, and to mention the sums coming from each country individually, and of the sums that you mentioned in your message with the brothers in Somalia.

General points after the message before the first message

- Regarding what you mentioned in your previous message, that the main idea with the brothers on your side was that death is better than imprisonment, and accordingly, that a person should not get out from the circle of espionage (TN: the operating area of the drones), I say that the correctness of the heading does not guarantee the correctness of what comes under it, so when the heading is that death is better than imprisonment was followed with the assumption that leaving the area means imprisonment or capture; while in reality it is proven the American technology and its modern systems cannot arrest a Mujahid if he does not commit a security error that leads them to him so adherence to security precautions makes their technological advance a loss and a disappointment to them. In addition to that, adhering to security precautions is not an issue that a person will commit a human error in, if he really understands the importance of his mission and is capable of staying in hiding until the situation opens up, noting that there is a percentage of people who cannot do that, and those need to be handled in a different manner than the others, and it may be better to provide them with an opportunity in the field.

- As for those whom you have observed as being disciplined and capable, you arrange homes for them on the outskirts of the city, to distance them from the people, which reduces the security dangers, and they will be with trusted companions, and the companions will have some work as cover, as if they lived from it, especially for those who live close by and have observing neighbors.

- And one of the most important security issues in the cities is controlling children, by not getting out of the house except for extreme necessity like medical care, and teaching them the local language; and that they do not get to the yard of the house without an adult who will control the volume of their voices, and we with the grace of Allah have been adhering to these precautions for nine years and we haven't heard that any of the brothers were arrested after the events (TN: possibly referring to 11 September) while adhering to the precautions, and based on that, you can inform the brothers that I say that anyone who can adhere to the previous precautions should get out.

To sum it up, we are tasked with what is better and more beneficial for Islam and Muslims, and acceptance of what Allah decides, and there is no doubt that there are different views of what is better and more beneficial, especially with the differences in the fields of work for the brothers.

Note: what I mentioned above of arrangements to get the brothers out of the area is based on the picture you relayed to me in your previous messages, except that you mentioned in you last message that there is improvement in the security situation, so if that continues, which is what we hope for, then what I mentioned above will change according to circumstances.

- Regarding the companion, I wish that you expedite arranging the matter, as there is a written agreement dated 15 January 2011, that after nine months from that date we have secured a replacement for them to be in our company; and you know that arranging for a safe location after picking the suitable person takes time, so it would be good if you inform me of the developments about the companion in every message, and there is no problem if you mention that there are no developments.

- Regarding your meeting with the brother to arrange the affairs about the companion, you should never meet with him, but things in general should be arranged through correspondence. You mentioned in your last message the incident in which brother Riyadh was martyred; maybe it is an anomaly that happened, as the incident was contradictory to the security precautions that I asked you to implement, so please give importance to applying the precautions of not meeting any more than two persons and to reduce movements as much as possible.

- Regarding what you mentioned about Inspiration magazine, please send to the brothers in Yemen with the pointers to remember in that matter and explain to them the danger of its effects, in order to avoid repeating it.

- Regarding what you mentioned about the file that you sent in the past from brother Abu Al-Nur, you were right in what you mentioned, and because of that I did not confirm all that he said, but in general I wanted to encourage anyone that would provide advice, and be keen on handling any issue that is disagreed upon by the brothers in a quiet and kind manner.

- Regarding the operation that Taliban conducted, targeting one of the tribes, and what you mentioned of them saying that the tribe was hostile to the Taliban; even if that is true, the operation is not justified, as there were casualties of noncombatants, and due to its contradiction to jurisprudence, so please continue you advising of Al-Tahrik (TN: another name for Taliban).

- Regarding the message of my (late) son, Sa'd , Allah have mercy on his soul, I say that you delete the copies that you have and I will attach in my next message a copy that I will cut from it what deserves to be cut, then it will go to Al-Sahab archives due to the important information it contains, which exposes the truth of the Iranian regime.

- About what you mentioned regarding the picture of Sa'd, Allah have mercy on his soul, I say that you put his picture while he was working in the shop in Al-Sahab archives, but you do not publish any parts of it without coordinating with us, as for the pictures of him killed, they are not to be put in Al-Sahab archive.

- Regarding the serious warning that you included under the file "serious warning," Allah reward you, and it would be better that you attach such important items inside the file of your message to ensure that I receive them and read them.

- Regarding the French statement, and what you mentioned about not being sure that al-Jazeera had broadcast it; they have broadcast it and they interviewed some personalities to analyze it.

- Regarding the poem, Allah reward you with all good; and I say that you do not send it to the brothers.

In closing, I pray to Allah to protect you and guide you to what he approves of.

(TN: Religious farewell)

Signed :

Your brother, Abu 'Abdullah.

Monday 22 Jamadi al-Awal 1432 (TN: Monday 26 April 2011)

Dear Brother 'Adnan (Hafiz ((Sultan))):

I also asked you in previous letters to quickly write to ((Karrumi)), ((Abu-'Umar)), and their people with decisive, purposeful, guidance, because I am worried about the brothers making political gaffes. You must have heard Abu-'Umar's bad [speech] recently, and in my view [he made some] obvious mistakes. There were some things that should not have been said in a speech by a commander. The fact that they were mentioned in his speech - especially in the context of principles and being rewarded (TN: by God, for good deeds) - indicates that they are extremists and implies they are deeply entrenched and in a hurry [to act]... such things are a turn-off and [show] lack of judgment.

I wrote to them myself and chastised them and came down on them fairly hard.

I am afraid that if they continue using techniques such as this, they will spoil [things and] alienate the people, who could be won over by enemy after enemy. That would give our enemies and rivals an opportunity to exploit [the people], and they would wage a ruthless campaign of lies and malicious slander to distort (TN: the image of Abu-'Umar and al-Karrumi) and alienate [the people against them]. This requires closing any doors we can on the enemy and cutting them off; however, our brothers are making things worse by opening themselves up to evil and hostility!

What I mean is: Do not let Mahmud ((('Atiyah))) alone. I want you to have open and private messages issued publicly and in secret by 'Abd-al-Shafi (Kalim) - and even al-Sadiq (((Zamrai))), if possible - to al-Karrumi, Abu-'Umar, and their brothers, with guidance and advice. Send them direct and semi-direct messages that clearly and specifically talk about issues of "grassroots" politics, how to deal with the public and other factions, avoid rushing things, and undertake matters of great significance only [after obtaining] advice. [They should also be advised to] make every effort to bring people on board, to not describe any of the other mujahidin as illegitimate, and so forth, as appropriate. Such talk is premature, as people have different ideas, interpretations, and views.

Please move quickly on this.

Dear brother, write [to them] yourself, since al-Karrumi knows you and always asks me about you, calling you "(maternal) Uncle so-and-so." Have 'Abd-al-Hafiz (TN: AKA ((Abu-Yahya)) al-Libi, senior LIFG religious scholar and member of al-Qa'ida's Shari'ah Committee) write to the brothers, and he should never tire of writing and pressuring them; also have Ahmad (('Abd-al-'Azim)) write, as he is very influential with them and they admire him a lot. Anyone else who is influential [should write to them as well].

Another very important issue is that you must write to our brothers in the Ansar al-Sunnah (AAS), who are waiting for your responses to their earlier correspondence and grievances. Ask for help from 'Abd-al-Hafiz and Ahmad (TN: AKA ((Abu-Layth)) al-Libi, senior LIFG official and al-Qa'ida regional commander), and also try to have a letter issued to them from 'Abd-al-Shafi. At the very least, write to them using normal, polite language that would not cost them anything. They could be very simple, positive words of promise and that things will work out; that you will follow up [with them], offer advice and guidance; that you have written to the brothers and will [continue to] write. You should also urge them, the AAS, to unite with their brothers, as 'Abd-al-Hafiz did on the tape [recording]. You should mention that you believe duty requires this, and despite the failings and problems that exist, disunion is worse than all of that. On the contrary, together with their brothers, God willing, they will be an agent of reform and redemption, etc.

Of course, dear Brother, I have written to the AAS several times, most recently two days ago. I am in touch with them, offering advice and guidance to have them think better [of us], and trying to patch things up and bring them and al-Karrum closer together. But I protest to God so much about my isolation and being alone - there is no power or strength save in God - that I worry people will tire of me and [what I say] will become old and worn out to them!!

But I protest only to God.

"For me God sufficeth, and He is the best disposer of affairs." (TN: quote from the Qur'an)

(TN: The following begins as though it might be a separate message from that on page 1:)

Dear Brother,

We need guidance from you on the issue of using chlorine gas technology. It was reported that the brothers in Iraq have used it, but this was implicitly denied in a statement issued by the Islamic State of Iraq.

Also, the brothers where Mahmud is (TN: possible reference to 'Atiyah (('Abd-al-Rahman)) being in Iran) have the potential to use [chlorine gas] on the forces of the apostates, Jalal ((Talibani)) and Mas'ud ((Barzani)), and have already considered using it. However, I informed them that matters as serious as this required centralized [coordination] and permission from the senior [al-Qa'ida] leadership, because the gas could be difficult to control and might harm some people, which could tarnish our image, alienate people from us, and so on. Like we say, "it's not our business," or, "we already have enough problems," God help us.

They have put it on hold for now, but the best thing would be for you, brother 'Adnan, to examine this issue with your experts there and give us a clear pronouncement on that to tell the brothers!

God bless you and help you.

-- I have not received any news from Karrumi since the last message I sent you. I am expecting messages from them but have not received any yet. On the whole, though, their reports on the field and regarding trade are very good, and there is progress, praise God. However, the fighting against them is fierce in every respect, and I am constantly worried about only a few mistakes. None of the enemies scare me, I swear. No matter who they are, or how intimidating they may be, they are even more despicable and trivial than that. But I do worry about—ours and our brothers' mistakes, bad behavior, and lack of wisdom at times. That is why I always strongly urge you, Brother, to work together, follow through, and offer lots of guidance and assurance; perhaps God will deliver us and open the way to our brothers.

At any rate, our brothers are fine and well, and their reports from the field are promising. Many of the accusations against them are pure lies and fiction, and the campaign against them is fierce; they need help. We ask God to give them strength, deliver them and make them victorious over the ungodly and the unjust. Amen.

-- Maybe I will attach a file to this message with a selected collection of articles, statements and other items from the Internet, for your benefit.

-- We will try to make arrangements with the brothers in Lebanon to have one of their representatives visit us in the near future. God grant us success.

-- The al-Nasayib are well and doing fine. At the bottom I will paste the latest message from them. They send many regards, and have also requested some things from you.

-- Finally, many regards to you, the beloved one, and to Mansur, ((Abu-Khalil)), and any other dear ones around you who know us. Unfortunately, right now we are in a situation where we can only say "hello" to those we know [personally], and just barely!!

May God preserve, watch over and bless you all.
Peace be with you, and God's mercy and blessings.
Your admirer

9/4/(1432 H) - corresponding to 28 March (2011)

This is the message from al-Nasayib: (the brothers in Algeria)

Dear Brother, peace be with you, and God's mercy and blessings.

As for us, by God, we are fine, praise to Him, as is the whole family. Things are steadily improving: morale is rising, support is growing, and military activity has been improving recently. Every week there is a bombing, an encounter or ambushes. Overall, based on what I have been seeing, there is a resurgence. We ask God to make things easier and [help us]

surmount the difficulties. Regarding the enemy, they were thrown off by the recent strikes and have responded with continuous random shelling of the mountains. This has been very good for the brothers, as much of the ammunition has not detonated and the brothers are using it. The brothers are also used to the scare-tactic combing operations, which have been unsuccessful, thank God, except for last week, when five brothers were martyred in an all-day encounter; we ask God to accept them. Overall, the brothers have been impacted [most] by ambushes in the north of the country using infrared sensors (which were provided to the Algerian tyrant by the Americans). As for the desert, the brothers are concerned about the Russian Cobra helicopters (MI-34) with laser-guided missiles; they are impacting on the four-wheel-drive vehicles, which are indispensible in the Sahara Desert. Underlying that is the problem of badly needed money for good-quality weapons to counter these menacing helicopters; the mujahidin don't have single one of them, nor a single missile. Brother, it would be very good if the brothers there could let us know their expertise in that regard, that is, ways to counter the 6-km infrared sensors and MI-34 helicopters.

I cannot forget the response from the Libyan brothers along the front lines. The commander in the east informed us that four new brothers joined them last week, following a group of about 30 brothers before that, and there are more who want to come join. We ask that God enable our brothers to bring them in and train them in Tabsa [Algeria].

Peace be with you, and God's mercy and blessings.

SOCOM-2012-0000012-HT

In the name of Allah the most merciful the most gracious

Our honorable Sheikh, may Allah's mercy and peace and blessings be upon you…

I ask our mighty God that you are in good health and I hope that God grants you success and victory and support.

Furthermore:

- With regards to the lists and suggested classification, and in relation to the scholars (associated with knowledge), we did send to you our opinion and the opinion of the brothers in the "legitimate council." In summary, we don't favor the idea of classifications and lists with regards to the ones "associated with knowledge," because we are afraid of limitations and mistrust and so on. And we do see the issue to be left as is. I, personally, and the brothers, share the same opinion with regards to increasing the criticism dose and revealing and exposing scholars and evildoers. I pray to God not to increase them (TN: scholars and evildoers), because with all thanks to Allah, we have (a group of brothers who speak in our minarets) the power and the credibility and trust and stability within the nation's masses, which qualifies them to say few of the harsh words which are accepted by them (TN: The nation's masses). Also, large numbers of the rotten ones who are associated with knowledge and Da'wa are visible to the point that we can talk with confidence about them and reveal their defects, etc.

The issue with regards to the ones associated with knowledge and Da'wa has more sensitivity than other issues.

But, with regards to the educated and writers and thinkers and infidel reports and the masters of pen and paper who fight against God and the prophet and the companions, those we agree on publishing their lists and classifications. At the beginning, it would include a group of the "rotten heads" with addition to a profile on each person and personal photo if possible, and then we will publish it with God's help.

I did request from our brothers in the Jihadi media net to begin preparing these lists and folders and information so that it can be useful to us, and God is the one who grants success.

And with regards to the discussion about "Al Rafidah" (TN: the rejecters, or Shiites) and their danger, and the danger of the Iranian al-Safawi al-Majusi (TN: Safavids), the discussion that you sent us is pleasant and we are in the process of forwarding it (we might alter few of the statements, or add suitable ones) to the people of knowledge as suggested by you. With regards to Hamid Al-(('Ali)), it is an easy matter, it is not complicated for us to send it to him (God willing), but we also plan on sending it to other brothers, and God is the one who grants success.

Of course, with regards to Hamid Al-'Ali and the individuals around him, we say, "Don't advise an orphan how to cry." They are concerned with the "Rafidah" (TN: Reference to Shiites) and their danger is of great interest; in fact, they are overstated. They used to write to us and blame us for being negligent with regards to the "Rafidi" (TN: Shi'a) issue, and blame us for not envisioning the Iranian Rafidi danger and others, and they used to say, "The "Rafidi" danger is greater than the American danger!!" And so on…

Either way, we will work hard to send your discussion to Sheikh Hamid.

- With regards to the Iranian relationship and the problem with our detained brothers, we bring to you good news that they released a group of brothers in the last month (one group at a time), and all thanks to God the mighty. And the following individuals arrived to us:

- 'Abd-al-Muhayman Al-((Masri) and his family.

- Salim Al-Masri (from Jihad group) and his family.

- Abu Suhayb Al-((Makki) (originally from Yemen; during the crusaders offensive he was accompanying Sheikh Aba Sulayman Al-Makki Al-((Harbi))), and his family.

- Abu Suhayb Al-((Iraqi)), and his family.

- Al Zubair Al-((Maghribi)) (A brother who worked with the Libyan fighting group), and his family.

- And on the way now (maybe he is in Quetta or close by, the important thing is that he crossed the Iranian borders, and asks God to keep him safe) Khalifah Al-Masri, and his family.

And all thanks to God, the lord of both worlds.

They did send a message with the coordinating brother (a brother from Baluchistan in Zahidan; he is the one who they hand over to the brother and then he sends them to us) that they are going to hand over the family of Azmarai soon or maybe within a week, that is what they told him, so that he may make preparations for their travel to us.

They told him (TN: the brother from Baluchistan in Zahidan) the family (women, children, no men), that's what they told him…we ask God to ease their matter and to bring them safely, and to rescue everyone from the ones who are gone astray.

From our side, we are ready to receive them and working on facilitating the matter, and God is the one who grants success.

And what I mean is that they speeded up releasing the brothers during this period. And those brothers are mid-level brothers.

And they leaked to a few of the brothers who were released that in the near future they are going to release more groups of brothers. God knows.

And it is possible to include the following in the next group: Aba Hafs Al-(('Arab)), Aba Ziyad Al-Iraqi, Aba 'Amru Al-Masri, and others…

And we ask God for the release of the others (old ones and young ones)…Amen.

And we think that our escalation efforts (which include political and media "verbal" and the threat which we sent to them, and the apprehension of their associate, the trade deputy in the consulate in Peshawar; and other things they saw from us, brought fear to them), could be one of the reasons for a speedy process on their behalf.

But, they (the criminals) did not send any messages to us, and they did not talk to any of the brothers about it. (TN: Could be reference to releasing the brothers)

Of course, this is nothing strange coming from them; in fact, this is their mentality and method. They don't want to show that they are negotiating with us or reacting to our pressure, they just do these acts to appear as if it is one-sided and as a matter of initiative on their behalf.

We ask God to repel their evil… Amen.

- I did send to Aba Muhammad your forthcoming project about the economic crisis, and he responded by sending a few remarks, and I did see in his remarks plenty of similarities, including removing a few statements which we saw unsuitable…etc.

Unfortunately, I think I misplaced his letter and I cannot find it right now.

This is all I could think of, and may God bless you.

- Also attached are a few text files from the net. And if we are able to, we will send you a hard disk which contains several useful subjects from the net. Can we send a hard disk to you?

We ask God to care after you and support you…Amen

And may peace and God's mercy and blessings be upon you...

Your loved one

'Atiyah

Thursday 11 June 2009

A Letter of Hope and Good News to Our People in Egypt

In the name of God. Praise be to God, and prayers and peace be upon the prophet, his family, and companions

Beloved Muslim brothers wherever you are, God's peace, mercy, and blessings be upon you.

This the fourth part of the Letter of Hope and Good News to Our People in Egypt and I will dedicate it to the popular eruption that is going on in the Arab world in general and in Egypt in particular. In the last part, I promised to talk about the issue of Southern Sudan, but I have decided to postpone this for another part, God willing.

First, I would like to repeat the greetings to the free and honorable people who erupted in Tunisia, Egypt, Jordan, and Yemen, and those who rose up and resisted the corrupt rulers, the corrupters, the Zionist Arabs, the fighters of Islam and the hijab, the spreaders of immorality, the collaborators with Israel against al-Mujahidin, the imposers of the siege on Gaza while supplying Nile water and gas to Israel, and the deniers of medical treatment and trade in Egypt for the people of Gaza, while allowing tens of thousands of Israelis to enter Sinai without a visa to commit immorality in order to fill the pockets of the greatest criminals with this illegitimate money.

Those are the corrupt and corrupting rulers who joined the United States in her war against Islam and the Muslims in the name of "terrorism," and from whose airports and seaports aircraft and warships deployed to bomb Muslims in Afghanistan and Iraq, and who turned their prisons to torture stations in the service of the crusade.

A greeting to every honest and free person who sacrificed his life and his comfort to resist the corrupt and corrupting in Tunisia, Algeria, Egypt, Yemen, Jordan, and all the other Muslim lands. Greetings to those brave and free, and I pray to God to have mercy on their martyrs, grant their families patience and comfort, heal their wounded, and end their imprisonment.

My free, honorable, and zealous brothers, your Mujahidin brothers are with you, facing your enemy, confronting the US and her Western allies who appointed Mubarak, Zayn-al-'Abidin Bin-

'Ali, 'Ali 'Abdallah Salih, 'Abdallah Bin-al-Husayn, and others as rulers above you.

The US's reversal of its policy to support the oppressors and the tyrants and its attempt to deal with the Muslim people through the policy of softness, deception, and soft power are the direct results of the blessed attacks on New York, Washington, and Pennsylvania. Since those attacks, the US and all Western countries have started to redraw their policies.

(I am afraid that this sentence might be inappropriate and might be perceived by many people as braggadocio and an attempt to monopolize the accomplishment. I think that our best and closest to the truth speech should include words. such as "participation" and "contribution." We should say that this change was caused by the unity of the efforts of the children of this nation ,including al-Mujahidin. God knows best.)

The US's concession and reversal is not sufficient and will not please any free and honest Muslim or anyone who wants justice among the non-Muslims. Therefore, your Mujahidin brothers promise you that they will continue to attack the US and her partners until they leave the lands of the Muslims and stop supporting the tyrants and the oppressors through the help of God. God is my witness.

My free and honest brothers in Egypt, this is a very sensitive phase, and you have to make sure that you are protective of your faith, honor, and dignity. You should insist upon your principles, beliefs, and faith ,and you should work on strengthening them.

There are many who are watching and would jump on the opportunity to derail your movement so as to achieve their aspirations and goals.

My free and honest brothers who are loyal to their faith and their nation, your blessed movement erupted to confront the oppression and the corruption of the ruling regime and to change it. So when we talk about change, let us present the issue in a medical approach by talking about the disease and then about its cure.

What is the disease that the corrupt regime most recently represented by Egypt?

Egypt suffered from the authority of a secular regime that fights Islam, corrupts, steals the country's treasure, is defeatist in front of Israel, and is loyal to the West, which is headed by the US.

In previous parts, I talked in detail about that regime.

Here, I want to point out that secularism in our Muslim world in general and in Egypt in particular, was not the choice of the Egyptian people. The Egyptian people have repeatedly demanded to make the Islamic Shari'a the source of law and legislation and to have an Islamic regime. Al-Sadat deceived the Egyptian people by adding the second article to the constitution which states that Islamic Shari'a is the main source of legislation in Egypt. With this deceitful text, the secularist approach in Egypt continued. Secularism was imposed by the occupier through his cannons and spears and was imposed once again by those who replaced the occupier through fake elections, oppression, and cruelty. I explained some of these details in previous parts. The demand of the Egyptian people for a Shari'a-based regime is considered one of the most obvious truths about Egypt.

The Shari'a-based rule was and continues to be the demand (TN Arabic grammar correction) of the overwhelming majority of Egyptians. Since the '40s, hundreds of lives were lost, tens of thousands were imprisoned, and twice that number were tortured for the sake of achieving it.

External powers (TN Arabic grammar correction) and their local agents in Egypt made sure to demote the Shari'ah-based rule through oppression and deceit. The demotion of Shari'a-based rule and the strengthening of secularists were among the most important instructions by the American administration, especially after the events of 9/11. Whoever wants evidence of this should read the RAND Center publications, especially the books "Civil and Democratic Islam," and "Building Moderate Muslim Networks." These books emphasize that the US's interests are with secularists and reformists because they are the true allies. They also talk about the importance of attacking and demoting Islamists in general and Jihadists in particular.

These Western powers that invaded our countries, stole our resources, and violated our independence, realized that their main enemy is an Islam that is capable of mobilizing Muslims to form a superpower that would challenge their control and confront their crimes.

The West encouraged and continues to encourage the robbers and corrupt tyrants and oppressors to seize power in our countries, because they are obedient and useful for accomplishing interests and because they are easy to bribe in exchange for dangerous concessions that affect our security and sovereignty. In return, the West will get whatever it desires from our independence and resources. They turned a blind eye to the crimes of the rulers and the corrupt elite that surround them and join them in corruption.

For 30 years, the US was silent toward the corruption and the embezzlement by Mubarak, his family, and his inner circle. It did not start talking about transition of power in Egypt until the security forces failed to suppress the uprising of the Egyptian people who are starving for dignity and freedom.

Anyone who monitors the statements of the US administration and its president and the statements of Western leaders would notice the gradual shift from talking about protecting stability in Egypt to asking Mubarak to resign. They were not only saying that they want Mubarak to resign; they were asking for an orderly and controlled transition that would allow change of faces, and perhaps regime, but would maintain the current policies. They want to continue with the policies that fight Islam and demote the Shari'a, even if the overwhelming majority of Egyptians demand it, and policies that do not oppose to the American and Western military presence in Afghanistan, Iraq, the Arabian Peninsula, the Gulf, and the Islamic Maghreb. They want to continue with a policy that helps that presence and supplies it with whatever it needs, including supplies, fuel, airports, seaports, bases, information, forces, and polices that ensure the survival of Israel, continues the pressure on the Palestinian people in Gaza and elsewhere in order to give in to the Israeli aspirations and accept a government headed by compromisers and defeatists, and ensures the continuation of the Zionist project for the destruction of al-Aqsa and the Judiazation of Palestine.

This is the democracy that the US wants for us; a democracy that is especially designed for the Third World in general and the Islamic world in particular. We witnessed this democracy in the election of the Rescue Front in Algeria, and we witnessed it when the US and the West boycotted the government that was formed by Hamas, and in the US's appointment of Karzai as president even after it admitted that he rigged the election.

At first glance, it might seem that the US and the West have contradiction and double standards in what they are allowed to do and what they forbid other from doing. This democracy that they claim and what they brag about is not appropriate and not allowed for others. However, a deeper look would reveal that this is true democracy, for democracy is in actuality a religion that worships an idol called "the mood of the majority" with total disregard to religion, morality, values, or principles. For them, everything is relative and can be changed depending on the number of votes (and depending on the wishes of financial powers, pressure groups, and large companies. The reality is that democracy is a game of lies because it lacks honesty). He who looks at Western history in general and American history in particular would find scandalous examples of this. The US and the West imposed Israel on us and brought an entire nation and settled it in Palestine and uprooted an entire nation from its land and refused to allow it to return to it with total disregard to the opinion of the majority and the right to self determination for the uprooted.

The majority in the US and the West wanted to expel the Palestinians from their land; therefore, they were expelled. "This is democracy and let these people go to hell."

Democracy is not a principle, morality, or values. Democracy is a religion based upon honoring the mood of the majority. The mood of the majority in the West, the US, and Israel does not want for our countries to have governments that represent their people; instead, they wish to have submissive governments that follow their orders.

More specifically, they want our countries to have a democracy that will allow the continuation of their occupation of Iraq and Afghanistan and will allow their armies and fleets to continue to control the sources of oil. They want a democracy that will accept the Israeli military supremacy with nuclear weapons, which al-Barad'i did not dare to demand that they be inspected or impose any sanction against Israel because of them. They want a democracy that bans Shar'ia-based governance even if the overwhelming majority of our people want it. They want a democracy that accepts the confiscation of most of Palestine and giving it to the Zionist entity. They want a democracy that will continue the siege on Gaza and the suffocation of the resistance against Israel. They want a democracy that will fight jihad in the name of fighting terrorism.

They want a democracy that will impose secularism on us and will prohibit us from committing to Islam, such as the democracy of Turkey that they try to market to us. They want a democracy that will change the foundations of our social behavior so that we will accept perversion and accept a family that is not based on a husband, wife, and children; instead, it would be based on a very ugly image of filth. They want a democracy that will change our educational curriculums to make us accept the occupier, the aggressor, the robber of our resources, and the fighter of our faith. They want a democracy that will promote an Islam that is without Jihad, Shari'a, promotion of virtue, prohibition of vice, loyalty and disavowal, and unification.

This deceit by the Western governments goes beyond democracy and applies to their complaints about freedom of press and the bad treatment of journalists in Egypt, while they are the ones who bombed Al Jazeera's offices in Baghdad and Kabul, and they are the ones who detained Taysir 'Alluni for conducting an interview with al-Shaykh 'Usama Bin-Ladin, may God protect him, after the invasion of Afghanistan (or for sympathizing with Taliban).

To strengthen a regime that is loyal to her, the US shamelessly and disgracefully intervenes in Egyptian affairs, issues instructions and orders day after day, sends it representatives for direct involvement, and contacts the government and some opposition factions as if it is dealing with a farm or a branch of a company that it owns. This humiliating style in the American treatment of Egypt became deeply rooted by Mubarak and by al-Sadat before him.

So, this is the disease that the corrupt Egyptian regime represents. As I said before, it is a secular regime that fights Islam, oppresses, corrupts, steals resources, is defeatist in front of Israel, and is loyal to the West that is headed by the US.

So, what is the cure?

The cure is to amputate this corrupt regime and replace it with a good, just, and Shari'a-based regime that spreads Shura and justice and will allow the nation to participate in selecting their rulers and holding them accountable and will allow their active participation in managing their affairs through their representatives, and will work on redistributing the nation's wealth and on stopping the theft, embezzlement, wickedness, and immorality, and will confront the Western hegemony over our countries, and will aid in ending the oppression of any oppressed person in our nation, in Palestine, Iraq, Afghanistan, and every corner of the Islamic world, and ending the oppression of every oppressed person in the world, because oppression is forbidden to Muslims and non-Muslims.

The Prophet said, "God said, 'My people, I banned oppression for myself and I banned it amongst you, so do not oppress.'"(Footnote 1)

The removal of the tyrant and the amputation of the corrupt regime is nothing but a step or steps on the path to a cure. It is like a surgeon who cuts open the abdomen of a cancer patient, who will not heal until this cancer is removed and the abdomen is stitched back together and the patient is cared for until he recovers.

(Footnote 1) I suggest that at the beginning you should include the poem that I attached to you in a file named "Good News."

The removal of the tyrant is like a doctor cutting open the abdomen of a cancer patient and leaving him (it is not a good analogy).

The honest, free, and the zealots for their faith, honor, and dignity should not be satisfied with the removal of the regime that deserves to be removed; instead, they should continue to with jihad and struggle until the Islamic regime that achieves justice, freedom, and independence is established.

The free and honest should not allow the US or others who are waiting to pounce and steal the fruit of their uprising and eruption.

At the beginning of the demonstrations, the US tried to preserve the tyrant and hoped that he would be able to suppress the popular uprising. Then, it moved to the second option, which is being implemented at this time, to remove the tyrant and to transfer power to other trusted members of his regime. The third option is for the US to work on getting rid of the regime and transfer power to a democratic or undemocratic regime, as long as it is loyal to her.

The US's and the West's greatest fear is a rise of Islamic regime in Egypt and other Muslim countries that will achieve justice and confront their supremacy.

The free and the honest should not accept the remnants of the regime or a secular regime that is loyal and submissive to our enemies. You should not be deceived by 'Umar Sulayman, for he is Mubarak's man and a loyalist, the trusted man of the American intelligence, and the one who was praised by Israel. Also, they should not be deceived with Husayn Tantawi, for he is Mubarak's man and a loyalist and is trusted by the Americans. Didn't Obama praise the Egyptian Army? Didn't the American politicians consider it the guarantor of the so-called "stability"?

The Egyptian Army has many free and honest people who are loyal to their faith and nation. Wasn't it the Egyptian Army who had within its ranks Khalid al-Islambuli, 'Ata Tayil, Husayn 'Abbas, 'Abd-al-Hamid 'Abd-al-Salam, 'Isam al-Qumari, and Sulayman Khatir (may God rest their souls)?

Unfortunately, Mubarak and the Americans appointed a leadership for that army that is loyal to them.

Wasn't it the Egyptian Army leadership that allowed the thugs to come in with their horses, camels, and weapons to attack demonstrators on the Bloody Wednesday?

Before that, wasn't it the Egyptian Army who supervised the military trials and who issued more than 100 death sentences under Mubarak and put many times that number in prisons and jails? It is aiding the American military and intelligence effort against our nation.

It also provides military bases for the Americans and facilitates supplies and storage for those forces.

Isn't it the entity that participates in the joint training with the American forces and NATO, including Bright Star, in which the joint forces train on occupying Egypt for when an anti-American regime gets established there?

Isn't it the leadership that receives American military aid of about 1.5 billion dollars each year so as to make sure that the Egyptian Army is at the service of the American interests?

Isn't it the leadership that ordered the siege on Gaza?

From the American perspective, the leadership of the Egyptian Army is the guarantor of the surrender treaties with Israel and cooperation treaties with the US, the guarantor that Sinai will continue to be demilitarized, and the guarantor of the safety of the southern Israeli border and the continuation of the siege on Gaza.

Speaking of the military courts, I should remind every free, honest, and zealous in Egypt to not forget his detained brothers in Mubarak's prisons, for they sacrificed their treasure, life with their families, and were tortured, humiliated, violated, and detained for a long time in their struggle against that corrupt and corrupting regime. Free and honest people, saving those detainees is a responsibility on your shoulders and you will be held accountable for it in this life and in the life to come.

I call on every free and honest person in Egypt to continue his struggle, Jihad, and resistance until the corrupt regime falls and an Islamic regime rises. I specifically call on the lions of al-Azhar, and I tell them, "O lions of al-Azhar and Islam, this is your day. Rise and lead the nation in her struggle for establishing the Islamic regime. You can lead the nation if you unite, insist upon and grab onto the truth, and you get rid of the dwarves that Mubarak imposed upon you. The roar of the lions of al-Azhar is starting to echo loud, so continue, be patient, and spread patience."

Lead a campaign by your nation to rise and topple the corrupt regime and build the Islamic regime upon its ruins. Prove to them that there is no safety without faith, no peace without Islam, and no freedom without unification.

Regain your freedom that was stolen from you, for it is your right to have the endowment of al-Azhar returned (TN Arabic grammar correction) and the right of the scholars of al-Azhar to choose their shaykh from among them, and not by a tyrant. Regain your right to have an independent union that represents your opinion and defends every persecuted amongst you. Why is it that every profession, even dancers, has a union and organizations representing them except for al-Azhar?

(TN: The following is a poem)

Get up and greet al-Azhar and let the world hear it,

For it deserves our praise.

They are more important than kings and have more authority.

There would be so much fear and uncertainty if it were not for them.

They know so much about Shari'a and the are great examples of morality.

Al-Azhar became the center of the Muslim world.

Awareness of Muslim issues started in al-Azhar.

You are doing God's work on Earth.

You are the defenders of the Muslim world.

Because of you, no ignorant will be allowed to roam the lands.

(TN: end of poem)

My free and honest brothers in Egypt, there are some who want to become the rulers of Egypt by making a deal with the Americans. A deal that would guarantee that her interests and crimes continue in exchange for fake political life and false freedoms that are convenient for the US and would take us back to the fake political life at the time of the monarchy.

There are some who would like to solve Egypt's problems by submitting to the US and seeking her help. These people are intentionally ignoring the fact that the US is the root of the problem.

The free and the honest in Egypt should understand the nature of the conflict and that the local enemies are agents (TN Arabic grammar correction) for the external enemies. Political freedom cannot be achieved away from liberating people from polytheism and submission to the foreign invaders. It cannot be accomplished except through expelling the occupation forces from

Egypt, Arabian Peninsula, Afghanistan, Iraq, Palestine, and other Muslim countries. It cannot be achieved except through a just redistribution of wealth so that the bite does not get stolen from the mouth of the poor in order to be deposited in the accounts of the thieves abroad.

They need to understand all of this to make sure that the fruit and the gains of their uprising do not get stolen.

Before I finish my words, I want to send three messages:

My first message is to the people of our beloved Tunisia, the Tunisia of Qayrawan (TN: Cyrene), the Tunisia of Jihad and steadfastness. I say to them: The tyrant ruler is gone, but the tyrant regime is still there. Continue your Jihad and struggle until you remove all the tyrants in your country and have the banner of Islam, freedom, pride, and justice fly over your country.

The second message is to our people in beloved Yemen, Yemen of faith and wisdom, the reinforcement of Islam, its servant and its supporter. I tell them: Remember your Mujahidin brothers who are confronting the tyrant, corrupt, and corrupting regime. I urge them to uproot this regime that turned Yemen into a base for spying and supplying for the crusade and which filled its pockets with the illegitimate crusaders' money in exchange for killing Yemenis. You started your uprising, so continue with it until Yemen is free from the crusaders and their agents.

My third message is to our Muslim nation everywhere. I tell her: the US's defeat can be seen on the horizon, and her servants are starting to fall. Join Jihad and aid those who wage jihad against them.

Finally, praise be to God, and prayers and peace be upon prophet Muhammad, his family and companions.

God's peace, mercy, and blessings be upon you (Footnote 2).

(Footnote 2) I suggest that at the end of the letter you should include the poem that I attached to you in a file named "Oppression, Go away and Vanish 2" with a picture of Mubarak and his son. It would be great if you cold also include pictures of the police beating up the people and an appeal to the Egyptian people to break the siege on Gaza. Also, there are pictures of the beating of demonstrators in Egypt on the first tape named "Gaza's Sacrifices and the Conspiracies." Also, there are pictures of Mubarak at the end of it. May God grant you success.

From Shaykh ((Mahmud))/(TN: Report on) Senior shaykhs and other issues pertaining to the Arabian Peninsula

(TN: In red lettering) This file contains messages from one of the trusted brothers who is a middleman for me in the Arabian Peninsula and is a religious student with ties to the senior shaykhs and clerics.

My Dear Shaykh ((Abu 'Abd-al-Rahman)),

Peace be upon you, and God's grace and his blessings. I met with a group of well-known senior shaykhs who signed on to the recent Statement of Victory of the Sunnis in Iraq over the Safawis (TN: derogatory reference to the Shi'a-majority government). I asked them their impressions of your latest statement and of the statement by the brothers in the Islamic State of Iraq (TN: ISI). I also showed your message to them to all but one person, and I have begun building bridges with them. I met other people, as well, and showed them the statement.

The senior shaykhs with whom I met included Shaykh 'Abd-al-Rahman al-((Barrak)) (who was very moved by your message to him); Shaykh ((Abu Zafr)); Shaykh Sa'id Al ((Zu'ayr)); Shaykh Muhammad al-((Habdan)); Shaykh 'Abd-al-'Aziz al-((Jalil)); Shaykh Yusuf al-((Ahmad)); and Shaykh Muhammad al-((Farraj)) (I went to his home twice and prayed at his mosque, but it was unable to meet with him).

They shared with me important information and their reflections on current events. The most important thing of value pertained to Shaykh Abu Zafr; we agreed to meet together over several sessions to determine the structure of several reports about certain matters that must be brought to your attention after I return from the pilgrimage, God willing.

There are many details that I will share with you regarding the statement about supporting the Sunnis in Iraq and the story behind it, as well as what precisely took place during the meeting, and who wrote it. I will also tell you about who wanted to have a statement issued about the attacks against the ISI saying it's not a legitimate organization, etc.

I have indeed begun writing the report and I've finished the main point in it and the beginning of it. All that remains is writing the bulk of the details and drawing the connection

between what was said by the various shaykhs. I will begin
wrapping up the report after my return from the pilgrimage,
because I'm traveling tomorrow, God willing.

There is an urgent piece of information that Shaykh Abu Zafr
asked me to relay to you: He wants you to ask your friend, whom
you will send to Abu Zafr, to stop demanding the report about
the senior shaykhs in the Arabian Peninsula. This is because
the shaykh says that the courier that you use is good, and we
consider him a good man, but he cannot be trusted with such
secret information because he is weak when he is in custody.
The shaykh asked around about him, and was told that when that
brother was in jail, he gave up all the brothers' secrets in no
time. He cannot keep secrets, and with the slightest bit of
pain, he gives up everything he has. There may be someone in
Medinah who could be called upon for a favor and the blessings
of whose worthy prayers would be sought, but the person who told
this story would not allow them to be spoken of. So the shaykh
doesn't mind if the brother comes, but he is not to be given any
secret information of any importance. Many casualties resulted
from this brother having been in jail in the past, and from his
many confessions and his having revealed the secret of our
activity. So ask him quit asking the shaykh for the report for
the time being, because the shaykh is busy and doesn't have the
time right now to write it, so he shouldn't keep insisting on
it.

In general, Shaykh Abu Zafr and I agreed that we will prepare
the complete report about the senior shaykhs and then they
shaykh will put the final touches on the main points. I will
then put it in its final wording. The shaykh mentioned to me
his position regarding your statement and the statement from the
brothers in the ISI. In general, the shaykh did not support
their recommendation because they will be turned against you,
particularly the statement from the brothers in the ISI, which
included the general vouching that was at odds with your
statement, in which you vouched for only two people who had no
issues.

Naturally, the shaykh knows my true name and my home address. I
agreed with him on a code word for communicating in the future.
None of those senior shaykhs knows my alias, the one by which
you know me. I am very careful to make sure neither side knows
the other name, be it my true name or my alias. It's enough
that each side knows one of the two, for reasons of security.
There is currently no benefit in their knowing both names. I
also met with someone close to Shaykh 'Abdallah al-

((Ghanayman)), who told me some new information about the shaykh.

At any rate, I will begin the report about the response from the senior shaykh to your message and the news they're hearing. These meetings lasted several hours, so I will try to summarize what was said as best I can.

(TN: new message)

My Dear Shaykh Abu 'Abd-al-Rahman,

Peace be upon you, and God's grace and his blessings. May God accept your best works along with ours.

(TN: in blue text) What is the brothers' assessment of Harith al-((Dari)) and the Association of Muslim Scholars?

Thank you for your explanation about ((Fadl-al-Rahman)), the Politician and Ultimate Holy Warrior. I met a good brother from Sarhad who is a close friend of Fadl-al-Rahman, and I was going to meet The Politician during the pilgrimage, but I ran out of time and wasn't able to meet him. I was deceived by what I'd heard, and your explanation helped. Praise be to God that I didn't meet him. During the pilgrimage, I met two Shaykhs: Muhammad al-Hasan Ould al-((Dadu)) and Safr al-((Huwali)). These were quick meetings, not much more than greetings asking how things were, because circumstances weren't conducive to more. The reason for meeting The Ultimate Holy Warrior was to ensure coordination so that some brothers I know could join the father's group, because I'd heard he had some ties to them. He promised he would do that, but after winter. I wanted to go through you to make them religious students, or just new brothers through him. If you know any trusted brothers who could help them get there, that would be great. There is a group of brothers that want to join with the brothers in Khorasan. The best of them is a religious student in a European country who has wanted to join the brothers ever since things got more difficult for him in his country. The last one, I know only from the network, because he is a deputy of the Amir (TN: senior leader) of the Worldwide Islamic Media Front. Do you have a way to help in this matter for brothers with no experience?

103

Is there a trusted brother from among the Mujahidin who can
record tapes of the brothers in the Arabian Peninsula in his own
voice? They need to provide commentary to videos, but everyone
is afraid to reveal his voice. So is there anyone suitable for
this on your end whose voice is suitable for commentary during
films and whose accent is that of the peninsula region?

I want to ask you a question about the veracity of what a very
close friend of Shaykh Yusuf al-(('Ayiri)) told me. He said
that Shaykh Yusuf was expelled from al-Qa'ida, or to be more
precise, that he was removed from al-Qa'ida leadership in the
Arabian Peninsula after rejecting the bombings. I was told he
sent a secret letter of counsel to ((Abu 'Abdallah)) about the
matter. The decision to remove him was made by ((Sayf al-
'Adl)), and news was handed down via the Doctor. Shaykh Yusuf's
friend told me that this news reached him from Shaykh Yusuf via
a middleman working between the two men. Do you have any
information about this? He vehemently denied it.

How true is what I hear from people aligned with religious
students, who may be biased, that Shaykh Ayman al-((Zawahiri))
is the most influential man in the organization, and that Abu
'Abdallah is like a puppet on his hand, and that Abu 'Abdallah
has given authority to Zawahiri to run everything, though the
former disagrees with some of Shaykh Ayman's behavior? (This is
what some of the enemies or hated families in the peninsula and
elsewhere are saying). This really has me agitated, and I don't
accept it. But I wanted to verify with you the role of Shaykh
Ayman. Has al-Qa'ida been tinged with his ideology and
opinions, and is Abu 'Abdallah not the most influential man in
the organization?

Thank you so much for the explanation about the senior shaykhs.
If you don't mind, I would like you to include among them Shaykh
'Abd-al-Qadir (('Abd-al-'Aziz)) and Shaykh Abu Muhammad al-
((Maqdisi)). I have been eager to ask you about this, because I
recognize in you a balanced judgment of character, and I trust
your opinion and think of you thus, though God is the ultimate
judge, and my recommendation of you does not come before His.

While I was on the pilgrimage, God deemed that I should meet two
people: Muhamamd al-Hasan Ould al-Dadu and Safr al-Huwali, but
they were quick meetings that consisted of little more than
greetings and small talk about goings on. I had wanted to meet
a group of senior shaykhs during the pilgrimage, but I didn't
get the chance.

What is the truth in what is being said about Harith al-Dari
having been targeted more than once by my brothers in the
Mujahidin Shura Council? Is this only between Harith al-Dari
and myself?

(TN: in red text) Very important explanation about the statement
in support of the Sunnis in Iraq against the Safawis, for which
I praised you:

The statement was adopted by the senior shaykhs of al-Qasim, led
by Shaykh 'Abdallah al-Ghanyman. It was written in
approximately ten pages that have been abridged to roughly four.
The part about denouncing differences and arguments and the
importance of closing ranks was written by Shaykh 'Abd-al-'Aziz
al-Jalil, as he himself told me (this portion was supposed to
appear in a separate statement, but because of the disagreement
about the wording, they decided to add it to this statement).
The statement was signed during the meeting that takes place
every four months that included the most well-known of the
peninsula's senior shaykhs. 70 senior shaykhs attended the
meeting, where they were presented with the statement. Only 38
agreed to the statement; the rest refused to sign it for various
reasons, including an objection to the wording or fears that it
would lead to greater pressure on them, along with other
reasons, despite the shared apprehensions regarding the State's
fears about Iran's intentions. The statement had included four
lines containing an attack against the ISI, saying it was an
illegitimate state, that sort of thing. A group of the senior
shaykhs, chief among them al-Barrak, were adamant that the lines
be removed, and the rest of the shaykhs were forced to oblige
their wishes because of the importance of the signatures from
the dissenting group, especially that of al-Barrak.

In truth, there was much talk from the shaykhs in these meetings
because they lasted for so many hours. I will give you a
heavily abridged presentation of the finer points:

The shaykhs with whom I met included:

1. Shaykh 'Abd-al-Rahman al-Barrak
2. Shaykh Sa'id Al Zu'ayr
3. Shaykh Bashr al-((Bashr))
4. Shaykh Muhammad al-Habdan
5. Shaykh Yusuf al-Ahmad
6. Shaykh 'Abd-al-'Aziz al-Jalil

7. Shaykh Muhammad al-Farraj (I wasn't able to meet with him; I prayed in his mosque and went to his home several times, but he wasn't there)

They all welcomed further contact and each read the message, with the exception of one to whom I did not show the message or bring up its subject because the situation wasn't appropriate for it. This is a positive indication, in addition to what al-Jalil and al-Habdan both said about how happy they were with your statement and the statement from the brothers in the ISI.

1. Al-Barrak: The shaykh was quite moved by the message and said, "May God keep you well, Brother 'Atiyah. Really, you have lifted me above my home, and I am but a lowly worshipper." He prayed for victory and ability for the ISI, which is being hounded by worshippers of the cross and their lackeys, and he said he will work on the matter of Shaykh (('Umar)) as much as he can.

2. Bashr al-Bashr: He was pleased with your message and appeared comfortable when he was dealing with me. He said, "I would recommend that Shaykh 'Atiyah and the ISI not post a statement praising those men. They will turn on you. They are generally against you, as is a majority of the Senior Shaykhs in the Arabian Peninsula. Shaykh (('Atiyatallah))'s statement is better because it praises al-Barrak and al-Ghanayman, unlike the other, more general one that praises those undeserving of praise." I have a lot of important, secret information that the Shaykh will record, and which I will send to you, God willing. He will give me the main points, and I will take care of the wording. He mentioned that there is a wicked campaign to have a statement issued against the ISI laying bare its practices, and saying that it is expanding its takfir and killings and that you issued a fatwa to the nation unilaterally announcing them to the State, etc. However, this campaign met failure, praise be to God, as both he and Shaykh Sa'id bin Zu'ayr informed me. Several senior shaykhs in Riyadh are taking over developing the campaign, along with representatives of the factions in Riyadh. I will send you a report explaining this matter further, with exactly what was said, etc.

Tell me everything you want me to relay to al-Bashr, because I'm going to go see him soon, God willing.

The two most watched people in Riyadh are al-Bashr and Abu Malik 'Abdallah al-((Rays)). The latter is the biggest supporter of the Jaysh al-Islami (TN: Islamic Army), and his opinion of al-Qa'ida is well-known: Shaykh al-Bashr was assigned full time to secret work roughly a year ago.

Shaykh al-Bashr told me that three senior shaykhs - 'Abdallah al-((Sa'd)), Yusuf al-Ahmad, and Muhammad al-Habdan - supported the Mujahidin, but he doesn't think they are able to be of much benefit to the Mujahidin at present in consultations, etc., because some of them are more concerned with accountability, denouncing vice in the marketplace and the media, and other such things.

He mentioned that he met the Amir of the Jaysh al-Islami in Iraq on two occasions, and that he also met with a delegation from the Islamic Courts, whom me advised to crush the transitional government in Baidoa before Ethiopian support could arrive.

Shaykh Bashr is with you, heart and soul, and he told me that he would inform me of any updates he had, which I will send to you.

The name of Shaykh 'Abd-al-Rahman al-((Mahmud)) was recommended to me by al-Jalil, and Shaykh Bashr agreed to go see him. He told me not to go to Abu Malik al-Rays because of his well-known position, which I had not known of.

Meeting with one of al-Ghanayman's students: I met with a student of Shaykh 'Abdallah al-Ghanayman, and he told me that the shaykh was in good health and was one of those who had tried to hasten the dissenting statement. The shaykh relies on the students close to him for help, as he is an elderly man and needs people to move him. The biggest problem facing al-Ghanayman is that his students aren't devoted to their shaykh. Otherwise, if this weren't the case, I would have seen something else, and the shaykh's signature would have been put on it. The shaykh had promised himself that his books wouldn't be printed until after his death, but his students recommended to him that the books be printed, and all the money be sent to the Mujahidin. The shaykh was really happy with this suggestion, and said that if the money was going to be sent to the Mujahidin, then he would recent his earlier position. It is said that he had refused to welcome Shaykh Salih al-((Fawzan)) into his home, but I think that's unlikely. But perhaps he didn't welcome him in the usual way, or not in a way suitable to man of al-Fawzan's notoriety, because Shaykh 'Abdallah thinks

that al-Fawzan has gotten more involved with the Sultans than is
necessary. On a sidenote, I asked one of Shaykh

Salih al-Fawzan's students about the shaykh's relationship with
the State, and he told me that the shaykh was terribly afraid of
the Salul family. I told him that was strange, and that the
shaykh was a man of conviction, particularly when it comes to
the Mujahidin and the Islamic groups, and to sticking to the
Salafist path. What he was saying about matters of jihad was
completely unacceptable, and he was supposed to be a man who
stood firm in confronting the Sultans. The student said I was
right, but the reality was that the shaykh was totally unable to
confront the State.

Perhaps I will have a private meeting with Shaykh 'Abdallah al-
Ghanayman, God willing, about matters, and maybe I'll also meet
with students of Shaykh 'Ali al-((Khudayr)). There is a famous
quote from Shaykh Nasir al-(('Aql)), who is well-known for his
knowledge of doctrine. He said he didn't know anyone under the
sun who knew more about Salafist doctrine than did Shaykh
'Abdallah al-Ghanayman.

3. Sa'id Al Zu'ayr: He prayed for Shaykh 'Umar, and he said to
me, "Tell Shaykh 'Atiyah that the reason the brothers have
stopped is the lack of a practical means on the horizon to
achieve victory for the shaykh, and statements do no good." The
shaykh was advising consulting the senior shaykhs of the Arabian
Peninsula because most of their hearts were not with the
Mujahidin, and because those who are sitting should be sending
their questions to the Mujahidin.

It was strange when he told me a bit of information that differs
from what I know. He told me that there is a need for Mujahidin
in Khorasan and Iraq, and that no one says there isn't a need
except for the failures. The shaykh told me there are
representatives from Khorasan and Iraq that he meets with
regularly.

He also said that there are many religious students on the front
lines in Iraq; Shaykh Bashr had mentioned this same point to me,
and had advised that I doggedly peruse the volumes of fatwas and
true believers.

He said there are three pieces of advice that he thinks are very
important for the brothers in the ISI: The first one is to be

very wary of newly-joined members. No matter their status or
capabilities, they must not be placed in leadership positions in
the shura council, as there are many dangers lurking. Victory
lies ahead, so one must remain on the lookout for penetrations
and be extremely wary of newcomers. Benefit from them, but just
don't put them on the shura council, for example.

The second piece of advice is to remain eager to draw in the
largest number possible of soldiers from other factions to the
Promised State. Honor their arrival and know that the base of
jihadist groups wants what God has, and wants martyrdom. These
groups have no particular ambitions or special opinions. So
honor their arrival and the arrival of any of their commanders
that come, so that we might not lose victory. Whoever of the
senior shaykhs of Riyadh tries plainly to ruin this will see
their efforts met with failure, praise be to God.

The third piece of advice is to not consult the senior shaykhs
of the Arabian Peninsula. There is no good in consulting them.
They rest on your victory, and they let you down. It is a
sinister person who lowers the necks of the Mujahidin for
someone sitting around to ride upon them. Put the affairs of
the Jaysh al-Islami in order now with Safr al-Huwali and Nasir
al-'Umar, who got in trouble when their necks were lowered.

4. 'Abd-al-'Aziz al-Jalil: He really responded when we started
communicating, and he asked me a bunch of questions to be sure
of me. He prayed for Shaykh 'Umar and for Muslim prisoners, and
he said that they had reached the stage in which they hope there
will be a brother with whom they can meet to confirm some
things, and so they can convey some things. I was supposed to
meet him in Muna, as well, but things didn't work out then,
either.

5. Muhammad al-Habdan: He responded when we started
communicating and told me that he has an open channel with al-
Barrak at a moment's notice to stay in touch with him, and he is
prepared to serve you as he is able.

6. Yusuf al-Ahmad: He is the one person I didn't show your
message to because circumstances didn't allow, and it wasn't a
suitable time. But I did ask him about the dissenting
statement, and he told me some of the information I mentioned
above, which I gathered from the senior shaykhs to better
explain the issue of writing the statement.

He said that there are representatives from some of the factions that attended the meeting, or more precisely some senior shaykhs who support well-known factions and have close contact with their representatives. They told them some stories against the ISI, saying they did this and that, and that Abu Hamzah al-((Muhajir)) is the problem and ((Zarqawi)) is heaven compared to him. They said Abu Hamzah is much more bloodthirsty and more enthusiastic about takfir, is tyrannical in his dealings with others, and has no patience for anyone who disagrees with him, etc. The stories say that they kill shaykhs and proselytizers who disagree with them, be they from different factions, brothers, or what have you. Unfortunately, the ISI messenger did not come to respond. On a separate note, Shaykh, the brothers have a representative and he went to several of the senior shaykhs like al-Barrak and al-Bashr. But to the pro-ISI shaykhs, any word they say can be counted against them. So the Jaysh al-Islami or the 1920's Revolutionary Brigades, etc., are not like the ISI. The accusation of supporting al-Qa'ida is there.

In order to better illustrate the position of some senior shaykhs who support jihad but oppose al-Qa'ida, I give you an article written by one such shaykh who follows this approach. May God help you as you read this; it will require effort and patience. The words will raise your blood pressure and arouse your anger; in fact, a draft of the article before the final copy even included an unconfirmed accusation that takfir book used by the Taliban and Bin Laden was written by Zarqawi, and to which ((Abu Qatadah)) responded. It was supposed to be published in Mufakkirat al-Islam, and they agreed to do so, but then they decided against publishing it before the Eid holiday, saying that the ISI would kill all the publication's correspondents if it published it (this is the essay that was called the Essay on the Family of Perversion).

Shaykh 'Abd-al-'Aziz (('Abd-al-Latif)) was recommended by one of the brothers as a good person to visit.

For your benefit, here are the links to the web pages of senior shaykhs mentioned in this secret report:

Al-Barrak:

<http://www.islamway.com/?iw_s=Scholar&iw_a=lessons&scholar_id=1
66>

Al-Bashr

<http://www.islamway.com/?iw_s=Scholar&iw_a=lessons&scholar_id=194>

Muhammad al-Habdan

<http://www.islamway.com/?iw_s=Scholar&iw_a=lessons&scholar_id=177>

Sa'id al-Zu'ayr

<http://www.islamway.com/?iw_s=Scholar&iw_a=lessons&scholar_id=106>

Yusuf al-Ahmad

<http://www.islamway.com/?iw_s=Scholar&iw_a=lessons&scholar_id=242>

Al-Farraj

<http://www.islamway.com/?iw_s=Scholar&iw_a=lessons&scholar_id=244>

Your student and admirer in God.

In the name of God most merciful

To Shaykh Mahmud, may God protect him,

I hope that this letter finds you while you and your family are in good health

I offer my condolences to you for the death of our beloved brothers. May God have mercy on their soul and consider them among the martyrs.

This is the path of Jihad. God said, "You will sacrifice you money and yourselves for the sake of God."

They struck us and we will strike them back. Anyone who looks at the enemies in NATO, especially America, will know that they are in big trouble. This year has been the worst year for them in Afghanistan since they invaded it. The number of their dead has never been this high according to their own reports. Their financial crisis continues. Britain has lowered is defense budget and America is reducing the budget of the Pentagon.

Anyone who knows the world and knows politics, knows that it is impossible for them to continue with the war. There is no difference between them and the Soviet Union before it withdrew from Afghanistan. As for the local enemies, as you know, they are in big trouble and the government is in danger of falling, especially after the floods and the increase in the number of those who are suffering from the financial crisis. Their difficult situation was the reason for the crisis between them and NATO.

You know of the size of the disagreement between the two sides after they closed the border. Through the generosity of God, the situation is moving in the direction of al-Mujahidin. You should be patient and strong and God will reward us.

-Regarding the brothers in Wasiristan in general, whoever can keep a low profile and take the necessary precautions, should stay in the area and those who cannot do so, their first option is to go to Nuristan in Kunar, Gazni or Zabil. I am leaning toward getting most of the brothers out of the area. We could leave the cars because they are targeting cars now, but if we leave them, they will start focusing on houses and that would increase casualties among women and children. It is possible that they have photographed targeted homes. The brothers who can keep a low profile and take the necessary precautions should stay, but move to new houses on a cloudy day.

A warning to the brothers: they should not meet on the road and move in their cars because many of them got targeted while they were meeting on the road. They also should not enter the market in their cars.

Note: there is no comparison between the fortification of Kunar and Zabil and Gazni. Kunar is more fortified due to its rougher terrain and the many mountains, rivers, and trees and it can accommodate hundreds of the brothers without being spotted by the enemy. This will defend the brothers from the aircrafts, but will not defend them from the traitors.

Also, the brothers should enter those areas to fight and attack the enemy.

-As for you, if you think that it is dangerous to move by car, then you can stay in the area, but you need to do your work through two brothers, and only one of them should carry your messages to the brothers. The key individuals for your work are your first deputy, second deputy, military commander, and four or five other brothers.

They can through their own ways deliver the messages to the other brothers. The brother should visit you no more than once or twice a week.

The other brother comes to you only for necessary issues only, even if this slows down the work. We pray to God for things to change. You should know the locations of the brothers, but they should not know your location, except for the carriers.

Note: tell the brothers that the ban is not only to those who come by car. The amir should not meet anyone except the two carriers. The Americans have great accumulative experience in photography of the area due to the fact that they have been doing it in the area for so many years. They can distinguish between houses frequented by men at a higher rate than usual. Also, the visiting person might be tracked without him knowing. This applies to locals too.

Inform the brothers that this is the arrangement for every amir at this time.

It is important to have the leadership in a faraway location to gain expertise in all areas. When this experienced leadership dies, this would lead to the rise of lower leaders who are not as experienced as the former leaders and this would lead to the repeat of mistakes. Remind your deputies that all communication with others should be done through letters.

-In a previous letter I asked you to get an oath from the brothers that would include:
1-Obediance and jihad for the sake of restoring the caliphate
2-Keep the secret of work
3-Safeguad the work that they are responsible for and provide advice to the leadership

Take the oath even from brothers who gave the oath in the past.

Regarding the first and second deputy, send me the text of the oath and let me know which brothers can take on this responsibility in the future.

-Regarding brother Muhammad Shawqi Abu-Ja'far, if he arrived at your location, please arrange for him a safe place and explain to him in details the danger in moving and all security precautions.

If he is on the road, then make the arrangements for him, he might be with the brothers in Kunar. Explain to him in details about the situation in Pakistan, Afghanistan, and Wasiristan. Then, he can give you his opinion about the location that he is in. He should be informed of the nature of work and he should be consulted on things that are being discussed.

-In your letter, you talked about your relationship with Abu-Salman al-Baluchi. I know that he is good Mujahid and got detained in the past, but some of the Baluchi people that he knows work for the Pakistani intelligence. Therefore, I advise you to be careful and not talk to him about your news and secrets. Also, for that reason, my son Hamzah should not be at his place or anywhere near him.

Regarding my son Hamzah and his mother, I wish you take all the security precautions that were mentioned before in order to disrupt surveillance on him. He should move only when the clouds are heavy. Then, 'Um-Hamzah goes to the middle-man on my side. I asked him to make all the remaining arrangements. I also asked him to make sure that they read the letter before they go in order to alert them to some security precautions including not taking with them any of the things that they had in Iran, such as their suitcases. As for Hamzah, if you find my companion that we talked about, please send him to Peshawar and the surrounding area and ask him to arrange a house that can hold two families in addition to his family. He should stay there with Hamzah. If you did not find him yet, then please have a trusted Pakistani brother accompany him. Make sure to tell Hamzah that I am of the opinion that he needs to get out of Wasiristan if he is there, and he should not go there if he is not there. What I said regarding Hamzah applies to 'Uthman and Muhammad if they come from Iran.

Regarding the deputy position, Shaykh Abu Yahya should be the one for a year from the date of the appointment of Shaykh Sa'id (may God rest his soul), but he should give his greatest attention to the issue of shari'a research that we talked about in the past especially for Somalia and the Islamic Maghreb. The brothers in the Islamic Maghreb might experience divisions. To avoid this, the research that you said that you are going to prepare on dealing with the apostates should be sent to them. It should be complete and comprehensive and it should include the opinions of the scholars. This is a very important issue. I have attached a letter from myself to Brother 'Abd-al-Rahman. You can look at and it contains my order to him to be your second deputy. Our situation cannot accept baseless excuses from anyone. Do the same thing with 'Abd-al-Jalil. Appoint him as a second deputy if you need to for a year from the date of the arrival of your letter to him with the possibility for renewal.

I have sent you also a file named Attachments for Shaykh Mahmud and it includes parts of the Yemen message. Since you lived there with the brothers for a while, please read it and make some adjustments in it to make it appropriate for your area. If possible, please add it to the files of brother 'Abd-al-Wadud or you can send it to them as part of your correspondence to them. Please let us know which sections you will send to them. Do not send the parts that I sent to them in the letter of the general policy.

-We did not receive the letter from shaykh Abu-Yahya which mentiones the Islamic Maghreb.

-In the last letter when I used the term "external work," I meant the work of shaykh Yunis and the work inside western countries.

-It seems that there is a misunderstanding regarding the issue of Jihadi media. It is a main piece of the war and I did not mean that it should be abandoned. I just wanted to point out that the level of interviews did not reach the desired level and I called on you to do better.

-Regarding the program Witness to History (TN: a program on al-Jazirah), I do not like it because the host of the program uses improper language sometimes.

-Regarding my letter to brother Basir, if you get any important comments from Shaykh Abu-Muhammad on the letter in general, please send them to me. Also, if you or shaykh Abu-Muhammad have comments on any of the paragraphs, you can delete these paragraphs and send the letter to brother Basir.

If you did not get anything form Abu-Muahammad due to the difficulty in communicating between you two, and if you do not have any important comments, then go ahead and send it to Basir because it contains a request to the brother to provide us information on the situation in their area and clarification on some of the events that took place in the Muslim world.

Regarding the negotiations for the release of the Afghani prisoner in your area, you should be careful in the way that you deal with the negotiators. Many mistakes can happen when you receive the money. This also applies to donation money. You should take all security precautions. My suggestion is to rent a house in Peshawar and the money should be delivered in it. After the mission, the brother leaves the house.

Make sure to get the money exchanged at money exchangers. You should also get rid of the bag that the money was in because it might have a chip. The brother should take the money, get in a taxi, and go to the center of the market and get to a roofed section of the market. Two brothers should be waiting for him there and he should give them the money to bring it to you. The money should be in euro or dollars. After that, he should evade surveillance and stay away from the brothers that he gave the money to.

Negotiators should not be met in Wasiristan (the area where the American aerial photography is active), unless there is a perfect plan that would prevent the enemy for tracking those negotiators or the brothers. You should know that the news of the negotiations might reach the Americans.

Note: the brother should not be one of the leaders.

-Perhaps you monitored the trial of brother Faysal Shahzad. In it he was asked about the oath that he took when he got American citizenship. And he responded by saying that he lied. You should know that it is not permissible in Islam to betray trust and break a covenant. Perhaps the brother was not aware of this. Please ask the brothers in Taliban Pakistan to explain this point to their members. In one of the pictures, brother Faysal Shahzad was with commander Mahsud; please find out if Mahsud knows that getting the American citizenship requires talking an oath to not harm America. This is a very important matter because we do not want al-Mujahidn to be accused of breaking a covenant.

-Due to the abundance of blessings, you need to establish a special section for planning military operations at the fronts. It is should have experienced brothers and you should provide them with the latest equipment. You should also task some brothers with summarizing books on warfare and publish these summaries and give them to the brothers and the leaders. As for the brothers who are in charge of planning, they should be kept in a safe location outside the battlefield. They should conduct studies and preparations before operations. They should also film and document operations in order to learn from mistakes and avoid them in future operations.

Also, attention should be paid to the medical aspect, especially during withdrawal after the operation.

-Please have brother 'Azzam translate the book the Most Important Things About al-Qa'ida by Robert Fisk and then send the translation to me.

-The tenth anniversary to the attack 9/11 is coming and due to the importance of this date, attention should be paid to start preparing for now. Please send me you suggestions on this.

We need to benefit from this event and get our messages to the Muslims and celebrate the victory that they achieved. We need to restore their confidence in their nation and motivate them. We should also present our just cause to the world, especially to the European people. We will have a lot to show, therefore we should not depend on one media outlet to cover that event. If al-Jazirah shows responsiveness, we should contact the correspondent of al-Jazirah Arabic and English and tell them that we are willing to cooperate with them in the area of covering the tenth anniversary by answering any questions that you think the public is interested in. You can point out to them that this way they will be showing the other opinion. Note: all correspondence, letters, and negotiations should be in the name of al-Sahab.

We should also look for an American channel that can be close to being unbiased, such as CBS, or other channel that has political motives that make it interested in broadcasting the point of view of al-Mujahidin. Then, we can send to the channel the material that we want the Americans to see. You can ask brother Azzam about the channel that you should send the tape to and let me know your opinion and his.

I also think that you should write to 'Abd-al-Bari 'Atwan and Robert Fisk and tell them that the tenth anniversary is coming and it is the harvest of a fierce war between al-Mujahidin and America. This is a chance to explain our motives for continuing the war. The wise people would tell you to give people their rights in order to be able to focus on other vital issues such as global warming. They have the option to stop the war, but we do not have any option, except to defend our nation. This is a conflict between the biggest cultures in the world at a time when the climate is changing rapidly.

Tell them that we suggest that they make a documentary on this anniversary and we will provide them with printed, audio, and video materials.

Please have them give us their video material and the names of specialists that they will use in order for us to establish a vision for the film and to be able to clarify the events. We should shed light on the fact that In some past documentaries on a-Jazirah, some specialists confirmed that the events of 9/11 are the main reasons for the financial crisis that America suffers from.

-Regarding what the brothers in al-Sahab-Urdu mentioned in the statement on the floods, I am in support of giving advice and constructive criticism even when it is directed at me, for this is the duty of Muslims. Thank you for letting me know what the brothers wrote.

I also need you to read the statement and read the comments that the brothers added, but pay attention to the following:

A- All talk about climate change and the catastrophes that were caused by it. After the Copenhagen conference, they stated that the main reason for these catastrophes is the sins.

B- The attack was not directed at the victims who lost their children and money.

C- We dealt with relief organization during the Afghani Jihad and we have never seen what the brother mentioned. I am not saying that it did not happen, but I think that the brother is exaggerating. I called on Muslims to establish an organization that would be guided by the principles of Islam. As Muslims, it is our duty to save those Muslims.

D- Reminding the people of Pakistan to repent and return to God. This is an issue that I wanted to talk about. During those events, I was thinking these floods were caused by sins, but I did not say it because I wanted to be sensitive to the fact that some parents were able to save two children and watched their third drown. For that reason I wanted to talk about helping those who are in need.

One of the main criticisms toward the brothers is that the brothers were saying that floods were caused by sins.

The Prophet never told anyone that they are in pain or crisis because of their sins, but he did call on them to join Islam. That was the case of the Jewish man with the sick child, who the prophet invited to Islam, but did not tell him that his son was sick because he was not a believer.

E- Regarding the talk about a network of pipelines and wells in the Gulf especially in the land of the two sanctuaries (TN: Saudi Arabia), the reality is that water is getting drained by agriculture and most countries are getting their water from a few water desalinization stations on the gulf. Whenever a war starts in the region and some oil tankers gets attacked, the oil will get in the water and pollute it. Also if the stations themselves get attacked, 20 million Muslims will be at risk of dying out of thirst. You know that rebuilding a damaged station would take a long time. For that reason, I highlighted this issue so that people can take some steps on their own. The presence of apostate regimes should not keep us from alerting Muslims because they could be harmed. For example, If we know that the high dam in Egypt is about to crumble, we should inform the millions of Muslims of this danger. It is our duty to support and save the Muslims whenever we can.

You know that prophet Yousuf warned the people of Egypt of the deadly famine that was coming at them and he saved them from it.

You also know, that a statement should not be taken out of context s and no statement is independent of what is before it and what is after it. In summary, talking to the Muslims about repenting and abandoning sin is a duty, but the statement was not directed toward the victims of the flooding. Please study the matter and let me know what you find.

-Enclosed are the letters to Shaykh Abu-Muhammad and to brother Abu-Mus'ab 'Abd-al-Wadud. Please give these letters to them.

-I want the brothers in Islamic Maghreb to know that Planting trees helps al-Mujahidin and gives them cover. Planting trees is not expensive and it should be done immediately after rain. They should ask people to keep animals and livestock away from them. Trees would give al-Mujahidin the freedom to move around especially if the enemy sends spying aircrafts to the area.

It is best if they can get the trees from a plantations or they can even create their own plantation.

-Please send me the America Statement by Shaykh Abu-Muhammad. Also, please send him a copy of the letter of Sahib al-Tayyib to me and a copy of my letter to him. Also, please send me a copy of my letter to brother 'Abd-al-Wadud in the exact format that you will send it to him in.

-Please send to the brothers in Algeria the file that was written by Shaykh Bashir al-Madani about the Islamic Maghreb and which I sent to you in my previous letter. Ask him for his comments on it and see if he has as any information on this issue.

-Please let me know regarding what you mentioned in the past about arranging a direct way to deliver information to the brothers in the media.

-Al-Jazirah mentioned that some newspapers reported that one of the methods that al-Qa'ida uses to kill Americans is to put razors (TN: plow) on a truck and the driver pushes it to between them. Please let me know if this accurate and let me know the source of it.

-Regarding the separation of Southern Sudan, I am thinking about what you said and perhaps we will know something about it in the coming days through the media.

-As for what you said about the chaos, I am not in favor of it and if we were together you would know that you and I are in agreement on this. I might write to you about this in details.

-Enclosed is a special chip for the media. It contains Statement to the American People. With it is also a letter from my son Khalid to the brothers at the media. It is important to have it and the statement delivered to them. Tell the brothers that this statement should be broadcasted before the American congressional election. Also, a copy of the statement should be given to the correspondent of al-Jazirah-English. Also, another copy of it should be given to an American news agency. Tell the three channels that we want to broadcast the statement on 29 October. If the channels do not broadcast the statements, the brothers should be ready to broadcast it on the internet on 30 October.

-Regarding what you mentioned about informing the middle-man that you received the money that he sent, it is OK to do that if you write on a very small piece of paper that can be folded very tightly so that it would not get noticed.

-In your letter, you mentioned that you did not receive the chip. This true, we did not send it because of a problem with it and due to the shortage on time, I was not able to change the letter. I apologize.

-Enclosed is the article attributed to our brother Sayf al-'Adl.

-Regarding the money, I like for them to be in Euros. I do not see a problem in sending them all at once.

Finally, let me know how the widows and the orphans are doing. Also, please let me know how the children of Al-Jufi (may God rest his soul) are doing. Please make sure to keep the children and all the families away from the areas that are being photographed and bombed.

I pray to God almighty to protect you and protect all the brothers around you. May he grant you success.

God's peace mercy and blessings be upon you.

Your brother, Zamray
21 October 2010

In the Name of God, Most Merciful, the Most Compassionate
Thanks to God, the God of all, God bless our prophet Muhammad,
His Family, and His friends.

To the Generous Brother Abu Basir, God bless you
Peace and Mercy upon you

I hope you will get this letter and all brothers and their
families are in good health and working your way to God
Almighty.

We received your letter and our brother's letter (Abu Hurirah
al-San'ani) through our brothers (NFI). We were very happy to
receive your letter that answered our questions. The letter
provided us with information about you and your situation, and
we were following your news very closely through the media.
In reference to your statement, "If you want Sana'a, today is
the day," we want Sana'a to establish an Islamic State, but
first, we want to make sure that we have the capability to gain
control of it. Even though we were able to militarily and
economically exhaust and weaken our greatest enemy before and
after the eleventh (TN: September 11), the enemy continues to
possess the ability to topple any state we establish.

Our greatest enemy is unable to provide stability in those
countries and the mujahidin, with the help of God, are fighting
it (TN: greatest enemy) with its allies. At the same time, we
have to remember that the enemy toppled the Taliban and Saddam's
regime. Additionally, you know the experiences in (Syria, Egypt,
and Libya) and the enemies' alert in Yemen can't be compared
with the enemies' state of alert in Afghanistan. The enemies
considered Yemen as one of its own because of its geographical
location, which is in the heart of the Gulf where the largest
store of oil is in the world. We do not want to trouble
ourselves and our families in Yemen concerning this matter at
this time. Things needed to be prepared and will organize for it
(NFI) to be successful because if we fail, people will not help
us the second time. I believe that Yemen should be peaceful and
kept as reserved military for the Ummah (TN: Islamic State). It
is well known that wars need reserve military and to keep the
enemy in the open fronts until the enemy becomes weak, where we
would be able to establish Islamic State. Therefore, the more we

can conduct operations against America, the closer we get to uniting our efforts to establish an Islamic State, God willing.

Based on this, our opinion is to appoint scholars and tribal shaykhs to accomplish a practical truce among them, which will help the stability of Yemen. Even though we learned that 'Ali 'Abdallah ((Salih)) will not be able to agree on the truce, proving that the government is escalating the situation to an internal fight and the government has no authority. Therefore, the people of Yemen will continue supporting the mujahidin. The government will be responsible for the war, not us, and it will show the people that we are careful in keeping the Islamic Ummah united and the Muslims safe on the basis of peace.

- We do not see escalation as necessary at this point because we are in the preparation stage; therefore, it is not in our interest to rush in bringing down the regime. In spite of this regime's mismanagement, it is less dangerous to us than the one America wants to exchange it with. 'Ali 'Abdallah Salih has been unable to suppress the Islamic activity and has been considered to be a non-Muslim man and supporter of the West during the past years. On the contrary, the salafists and the jihadist salafists were able to take advantage of his regime and target America from Yemen, as some of the mujahidin went to Somalia or traveled to us, which allowed us to assign our brothers to conduct international operations.

If the government does not agree on a truce, concentrate on the Yemeni emigrants who come back to visit Yemen and have American visas or citizenship and would be able to conduct operations inside America as long as they have not given their promises not to harm America. We need to extend and develop our operations in America and not keep it limited to blowing up airplanes.

- We would not be able to send you a brother to help you at this stage. We should keep our movement low for security reasons and not move unless under extreme, necessary circumstances, especially the leadership, who are in the media. They need to avoid meeting people. If they need to move, they have to stay away from gas stations and restaurants. The driver should have plenty of gas and food before leaving the city to avoid stopping on the road. The intelligence services place officers in the gas stations, rest areas, restaurants, coffee shops, etc.

- Avoid killing anyone from the tribes.

- It is crucial to have one of the organization's leaders in the south.

- Do not target military and police officers in their centers unless you receive an order from us. Our targets are Americans, who kill our families in Gaza and others Islamic countries. The soldiers (TN: Yemenis) need to be careful and not protect the Crusaders. We have to protect ourselves, especially if they try to stop us during an attack on the Crusaders. This is a very important point, which allows people to support the mujahidin and will reduce the soldiers' morale.

- It is important to attempt to take a vow and truce from supporters of al-Qaida without enforcing it and accept them as your coworkers. With time they might join you.

- The first commanders should be screened well (TN: background investigation).

- In reference to the issue of abandoning weapons, this would never happen because, with education and iron, our religion will be victorious. Weapons are part of our survivors and history. Men without weapons are incomplete, and any men who leave their weapons have no respect by others.

I need to remind you about the general politics of al-Qaida concerning the military sector and media. Al-Qaida concentrates on its external big enemy before its internal enemy. Even though the internal enemy is considered to be a greater nonbeliever, the external enemy is more clearly defined as a nonbeliever and is more dangerous in this stage of our life. America is the head of the nonbelievers. If God cut it off, the wings would be weakened as 'Umar, peace be upon him, asked al-Harmazan, as he knows more about the land of Faris (TN: Iran). He replied, "Yes, the Faris of today has one head and two wings." He asked him, "Where is the head?" He replied, "It is in Nahawand." Then he mentioned the location of the two wings. He suggested to the commander of the faithful, "If you cut the wings, the head will fall down." 'Umar replied to him, "You liar. You, the enemy of God, because I will go straight to the head, and I will cut it

off, as has been said, if God cuts the head off the wings will
be weakened."

Even though these politics are clear in the minds of our leader
brothers, it is very important to remind all of our brothers
about it with a note to the new generation, who joined the jihad
road and were not advised about this issue. Thus, they conduct
separate operations rather than concentrating on the main
objective as we heard in the news about operations in Ma'rib and
'Ataq against the government forces. I hope these operations
were important for the mujahidin's self-defense only.

I provide an example to clarify al-Qaida's general political
policy in concentrating on America, which means that the enemies
of the Ummah, for example, is a malicious tree with a huge trunk
of 50 cm around and has many different sizes of branches,
including the countries of NATO and other regimes in the
regions. We want to cut this tree at the root. The problem is
that our strength is limited, so our best way to cut the tree is
to concentrate on sawing the trunk of the tree. We need to
concentrate on cutting around 30 cm in the bottom of America's
leg (trunk). Even though we have the chance to attack the
British, we should not waste our effort to do so but concentrate
on defeating America, which will lead to defeating the others,
God willing.

Here is an example for you, the mujahidin were able to cut the
root of the Russian tree, and after that, all the branches fell
one after the other, …

…from the south of Yemen to Eastern Europe, without spending any
effort on these branches at that time. Therefore, any arrow and
mine we have should be directed against Americans, disregarding
all other enemies, including NATO, and concentrating on
Americans only.

For example, if we were on the road between Qandahar and Helmand
and army vehicles of Afghanis, NATO, and Americans drove by, we
should choose to ambush the American army vehicles, even though
the American army vehicles have the least amount of soldiers.
The only time you are allowed to attack the other army vehicles
is if those army vehicles are going to attack our brothers. In
other words, any work to directly defend the mujahidin group

will be excluded from al-Qaida's general politics policy because
the mujahidin group should be able to carry out its mission,
which is striking American interests.

Anyone following up with the latest events should know that our
work and messages concentrate on exhausting and straining the
American, especially after September 11. We will continue to
pressure the Americans until there is a balance in terror, where
the expense of war, occupation, and influence on our countries
becomes a disadvantage for them (TN: Americans) and they become
tired of it, and finally withdraw from our countries and stop
supporting the Jews.

It is very important to remember that timing is very important,
as the present history confirms. We should realize by now that
in order to establish an Islamic State, we should destroy the
international infidels because they are against an Islamic State
no matter how little it (TN: State) is, as happened in Morocco.
Shaykh al-Khatabi established an Islamic Emirate in Morocco, but
the Crusaders blockaded and terminated the Emirate. The reason
they do not want an Islamic State is because they know that
Muslims are special, and for a short period of time during
Prophet Muhammad and his successors, the whole world respected
the Muslims.

Today, the head of the infidels (TN: America) is controlling and
supporting the countries in the region. Additionally, it has the
ability to topple the Islamic State in Afghanistan and the Iraqi
regime. Even though it is exhausted, its strength to destroy an
Islamic State in the region remains high during this time. The
most important thing is that local and international
professional adversaries are planning to destroy the Islamic
movements; therefore, we need to be proactive and face all of
their plans and continue to deplete and exhaust it throughout
the open battlefield in Afghanistan and Iraq to get it to a
weaken point, which will stop it from destroying the country
that we want to establish. Also, we might have to wait for a
year or longer to establish this objective (TN: Islamic State)
through the Muslims' unity and their effort to join the jihad.

You know that many jihadist groups did not succeed in gaining
their objective because they concentrated on their internal
enemy. Therefore, the Syrian Muslim Brothers got themselves in
trouble, especially in Himah, when thirty years ago the event
(NFI) shocked the people. Additionally, other events took place
as of the Islamic group attempt in Egypt, including the
situation with our brothers in Libya, Algeria, and the Arab
Peninsula. Even though some of the work was targeting the
American centers, not the regime, and was useful in getting
America to leave its huge military bases in Saudi Arabia and in
educating young men about the jihad. Then the jihad started
facing problems for the abovementioned reasons.

Meanwhile, the resistance movements against the foreign
occupation enemy were able to accomplish huge successes during
the last ten years in the Islamic world, and the latest one was
in Afghanistan. The reason for this success is that…

…the Russian occupation of Afghanistan allowed us to gain the
people's heart. It was very important to us to gain the
Afghanis' support because the people's support to the mujahidin
is as important as the water for fish; therefore, any movement
has to have the people's support in order to survive, as
happened in Gaza when all the people supported the Islamic
Resistance Movement; even though, the people are unaware of the
wrongdoing by the mujahidin. The enemy entered Iraq without any
knowledge of the area or the Iraqi people, who have a strong
tribal background; therefore, the Iraqis supported the
mujahidin. Many Iraqis joined the mujahidin against the
Americans until some mistakes happened when some of al-Anbar
tribe's children were attacked without a reason of self-defense
(they were not a threat to the mujahidin), but they were
registering in the security force compound. This attack resulted
in the tribe working against the mujahidin. At this time, the
mujahidin learned their lesson, which is not to kill any of the
tribe members.

There is a very important point that needs to be addressed and
understood, which is that God's law needs to be obeyed by all
the mujahidin stating that there was no imminent threat from the
tribe's members, and they were going to join the security forces
for financial reasons. This lesson should be taken into
consideration because members of the tribe were planning to join

the security force and might be a threat in the future, but they would not kill themselves to protect Americans. Additionally, these people have no problem killing their own cousins; therefore, if they attack us and we kill one of them, we will have no problem with them. But we should avoid killing a group of them during their presence in the security force compound to avoid any desire for revenge against us. It is important to study all the mujahidin's attempts and efforts to learn from their mistakes.

It is clear that the Arabs are in the depths of intolerance and revenge. Some of the mujahidin brothers worked with us in the past and returned to Yemen and got involved in some of the tribes' fights.

They were unable to separate themselves from this culture (revenge). America pressured the Yemeni government to attack the tribal areas as happened in al-Mahfad and Shabwah, which led some of the tribes to be against the government. On the other hand, the mujahidin were able to work with the tribes and establish a good relationship with them because the mujahidin have a good understanding of the meaning of revenge among the tribes. As Prophet Muhammad ordered Abu Hudhifah not to kill al-'Abas Bin 'Abd-al-Mutalab, but Hudhifah refused to abide by the order.

A friend of Prophet Muhammad, 'Abdallah Bin 'Abdallah Bin Abu Bin Salul, asked the prophet if he was going to kill 'Abdallah Bin Abi and requested to kill him.

He stated that he would not be able to see his killer because he would kill his killer and go to hell. The prophet told him that we will be his friend as long he is with us. When 'Umar became the leader of a tribe (Ibn Abi Majazatah), Prophet Muhammad asked him "How things with you 'Umar? If I had killed him when you told me to kill him, you would have honor, and if you order me now to kill him, I would kill him." This hadith proves that anyone fighting under the American flag against the Muslims should be killed, but the argument here is the timing as Prophet Muhammad stated, "If I had killed him when you told me to kill him."

The time to establish an Islamic State is near, and the jihadist ideology is spreading abroad, especially among the youth and the new generation in comparison to other Islamic movements that did not fulfill the redundancy among the Ummah except the jihadist Salafi ideology that works well with Ummah issues. We should develop the speech of al-Qaida to be convincing, easy and clear. Additionally, it has to be sensitive to the people's issues and suffering and to the general public.

Some of our brothers might have provided harsh statements to some of the Salafists, God bless them, concerning the establishment of an Islamic State. We need to understand our present circumstance, which is different from theirs, and we need to understand the difference between our strength and our weakness. We have to concentrate our statements on the most important, which is the meaning of only one God, and steer people away from praying to more than one God. Also, we need to pay attention to the words and meaning of our statements in order to avoid words that could be used for different meanings within the Islamic law without giving up any of our principles by using words that will relate the intended message, for example, using the word "clients" rather than the word "agents." During this stage, we need to relay the truth to the people in the easiest and nicest words. Some people do not like the word agents and consider it insulting. Therefore, if we use the word "clients" instead of the word "agents," and say that they (clients) betrayed their religion and their Prophet instead of using the traitor rulers, it would help more Muslims listen to us. That way we would be able to alert the Muslims about their loyalty to oppressor rulers, which is our goal.

...We need to stay away from words that will affect the people's support to the mujahidin. Additionally, the mujahidin should feel that they are in the international Crusaders' propaganda against them, which is concentrating on giving the wrong impression about the mujahidin to Muslims. Therefore, it is important to carefully write our statements in order to avoid all accusation against us from the enemy, who accuse us of being animals and killers. The Muslim people should feel that they are part of the battle, and they are in need of speeches that fit their conditions without forgetting that the Ummah (Muslims) are the main supporters of the mujahidin. Thus, we should be careful and provide statements that would be welcomed by the people and stay away from flagrant attacks, criticism, or disrespect of the opponents.

In reference to Hamas, we should understand that Hamas has many supporters who are supporters of Islam even though they forgot the meaning of some of the important Shari'ah law. We do not want to help the devil against them. As time passes, we will explain their leaders' mistakes, which will help them to pay attention to their mistakes and avoid them (NFI).

We need to understand that a huge part of the battle is the media, and the cable channels today play a stronger role than the Hja'in poets during the ignorant era. If the cable channels concentrate on promoting a specific person, they will have success, and the opposite is correct. If those channels do not want that person to be successful, they will destroy him. This shows that we are at odds with most of the channels and al-Jazeera has a different agenda than ours. It would be better for us to stay neutral, even though this channel sometimes commits mistakes against us. These mistakes are limited, and if we confront it, al-Jazeera will raise propaganda against us and could hurt our image within the Muslim world. Therefore, it is important not to have an enemy in the moderate poets if there is no reason to do so.

Conclusion: Even though the government is weak and might fall, the opportunity to let it fall and establish a different government is open to others but not to us. The reason for this is very simple: It is not possible to compromise on any part of our religion or bargain on our religion in order to satisfy America to support the new government. Many people will say anything and leave their religion under the pretext of being in the best interest of al-Da'wah. Please discuss the matter of conducting a truce with government with the others.

…If you decide on the truce, you should announce it with its justification and its conditions, which includes the closing of the American counterintelligence offices, expelling all American security and military forces in Yemen, and preventing the Americans from violating the sovereignty of Yemen through the Yemeni scholars and the tribal shaykhs, so people will understand your position and their position.

Finally, I would like to remind you that America will have to withdraw during the next few years because of many reasons, the most important of which is America's high deficit.

In closing, I send my greetings to all of our brothers in your area, and I ask God to help us all for what He wants and likes us to do, make you follow the correct directions, make you stay in your area, keep us on the road of jihad, and give us victory against the infidels. I hope to meet with you in the near future, God willing. God bless our prophet Muhammad, his Family, and his friends, and the last of our prayer is thanks to God.

...Except that I would like to point out how important it is for us to keep in mind the views of the Muslim Ummah (TN: Muslim population) on getting involved in a comprehensive war against the enemy. The Ummah is fighting an internal enemy, which are the leaders of the Arab World. The Ummah is also fighting an external enemy, which is America. Although the former is far more blasphemous, the latter is clearly the unbeliever.

At this stage of our war with our enemies, America poses a greater threat to the Ummah than any other enemy.

America is the head of the infidels. If God wills it, America's head can be cut off. Once the head has been removed, then it would be easier to cut off America's wings. This is exactly what Omar, may God be pleased with him, said about the Persians.

When the Muslims were at war with the Persians, Omar consulted with Hurmazan, who was supposedly the expert on Persian affairs. Omar asked Hurmazan about the best way to attack Persia. Hurmazan replied, "Persia's power today can be described as a power with a body, head, and wings." Omar asked, "Where was the head?" Hurmazan replied, "Nahavund." Hurmazan also told Omar about the two powers which represented the wings. Hurmazan then told Omar, "Oh, Emir of all believers, I have the answer to your question on how to defeat Persia: Cut off the wings, then the head becomes easier to remove." Omar immediately replied, "You tell a lie! You are the enemy of God. I must cut off the head, first, then the wings will be easier to remove."

I have come up with my own scenario on the situation. I have probably mentioned this before. The enemy can also be described as a wicked tree. The trunk of that tree is 50cm wide. The tree has many branches, which vary in length and size.

The trunk of the tree represents America. The branches of the tree represent countries, like NATO members, and countries in the Arab World. We, on the other hand, represent a person who wants to cut down that tree. Our abilities and resources, however, are limited, thus we cannot do the job quickly enough. The only option we are left with is to slowly cut that tree down by using a saw. Our intention is to saw the trunk of that tree, and never to stop until that tree falls down.

Assume that we have cut up 30cm of the trunk of that tree. We, then, see an opportunity to use our saw to cut into one of the branches. Say a branch that represents the United Kingdom. We should ignore that opportunity, and to go back to sawing the trunk of the tree.

If we are to allow ourselves to be distracted by sawing this or that branch, we could never finish the job at hand. We will also lose momentum and, most importantly, waste our jihad efforts.

We want to saw the trunk until the wicked tree is down. God willing, once the tree is down, its branches will die thereof.

You saw what happened to the Russians in Afghanistan, when the Mujahidin focused on sawing the trunk of their wicked tree. Their tree fell down, then its branches died out, from South Yemen to Eastern Europe. Mind you, the Mujahidin had done very little to help kill those branches.

We must then aim every bow and arrow and every landmine at the Americans. Only the Americans, but no one else, be it NATO members, or other countries.

Assume that we are on an ambush mission between Qandahar and Helmand, and we have just spotted enemy forces. The enemy forces consisted of three separate convoys. One convoy belonged to the Americans. One convoy belonged to the Afghan army. One convoy belonged to a NATO-member. Also, assume that the Afghan and the NATO-member convoys carried far more troops than the American convoy.

What should we do? The rule is that we must only attack the American convoy, but no one else.

Of course, there are exceptions to this rule. Not to state the obvious, if the Mujahidin knows that a non-American force was on its way to attack their positions, and that force was not on a regular patrol mission, the Mujahidin must intercept it.

Accordingly, the Mujahidin in every country will use force against the local authorities only if they come under direct attack. The Mujahidin need to preserve their strength, so they could use it in their fundamental mission. That is to attack Americans and their interests.

One must leave room for the possibility that Americans, or their interests, may not be present in some countries or regions. Also, when Americans exist in fewer numbers in a given country, they tend to be under heavy protection. So each country or region has its own variables as far as targeting Americans and/or their interests.

When Americans or their interests are not found in a given country, the Mujahidin group in that country must look for American targets in neighboring countries or regions. The Mujahidin group in that country should not opt to attack NATO members and/or NATO interests, because they happen to be vulnerable targets in their country.

Also, to avoid targeting conflicts between the al-Qaida branches, each Mujahidin group must be certain that it is the only al-Qaida group operating in a country where it intends to target Americans.

You may find it suitable to target Americans in South Africa, because it is located outside the Islamic Maghreb. Also, South Africa is not covered by the brothers who are located outside that region. The same can be said about other African countries.

The Muslim land has been spoiled by America's hegemony, and the leaders who rule that land. The leaders of that Muslim land had totally given in to America's hegemony, in exchange for favors which only serve their interests. Those are the same leaders who also abandoned the Law of Islam.

The road is open for us to resurrect the religion, and to restore dignity to the Muslim people. To restore dignity to the Muslim people, the Muslim land must break away from that American hegemony.

It is that same hegemony which had forbidden any government in its sphere to rule with God's law.

To break away from America's hegemony, we need to involve America in a war of attrition. The war must be enduring, however. The goal is to weaken America until it can no longer interfere in Muslims affairs.

Once the American enemy has been defeated, our next step would be targeting the region's leaders who had been the pillars of support for that American hegemony. These are the same leaders who not only abandoned the Islamic Law, but also helped America extend its hegemony all over the Muslim land.

Once those leaders have been defeated, God willing our next step will be building our Muslim state.

Going back to the earlier question about fighting the apostates.
I say: You know that throughout history, many resistance
movements in the Muslim world had fought and won against many
foreign enemies. The last of those fights was in Afghanistan.
The reason the resistance movement in Afghanistan had won was
because it had the support from the Afghan public. The Afghan
public was highly charged, and it supported the mujahidin with
every possible means, to expel the Russian infidels who had
occupied Afghanistan.

The public support to any resistance movement is extremely
vital. A resistance movement cannot last without the support of
the public, just like a fish cannot live without water. Also,
when the movement's public support is diminished, the standing
of that movement is diminished, too.

Most people in Gaza rallied behind the Islamic resistance
banner, because they had a common foreign enemy. Although at the
time, the Gazans had known little about the shortcomings of
their leaders.

In Iraq, the enemy entered the country and then occupied it. The
enemy, however, made a very big mistake when it ignored the
Iraqi tribes. The enemy was also ignorant about the region and
its people.

The enemy, in one way or another, had stirred up the Iraqi
tribes, which led them to declare unification. As a result of
that unification, the Iraqi public became united against a
common enemy. Then, the Iraqi public became supportive of the
Mujahidin, who were also fighting that same enemy. The Iraqi
public had sacrificed tens of thousands of men who fought side
by side with the Mujahidin. (Translator note: Here, the author
is making reference to the Sunni tribes and Sunni public.)

The Mujahidin made a few mistakes in Iraq. The mistakes were
committed because of hasty and poor decisions by some of the
brothers. Those mistakes involved a number of military
operations. If the Mujahidin had closely examined those military
operations beforehand, the situation would have been better.
Those who were in charge of those military operations had
totally ignored anticipating the benefits or drawbacks those
operations might generate.

The biggest mistake was made when the Mujahidin targeted and then killed members of the Anbar tribes near a police recruitment station. The Mujahidin could have easily chosen not to carry out that operation. The Mujahidin were not under direct attack by those members of the Anbar tribes. Also, the members of the Anbar tribes were not on their way to attack the Mujahidin in their hideouts. That attack had caused the tribes to withdraw their support for the Mujahidin. The attack also stirred up very bad feelings.

As you know, a killing of a tribesman is taken very seriously by any tribe and it often becomes a leading cause for all sorts of vengeful wars.

Imagine the general Iraqi political climate at the time. Also, imagine what was the tribes' reaction when they first heard about the Mujahidin killing hundreds of their tribesmen.

It is extremely important to pay close attention to timing. Timing is everything. This saying has been proven to be true now and then.

We must fully understand that now is the time to begin the work toward building our Muslim state. To do that, we first need to tackle the guardian of the universal hypocrisy, America. We need to deplete America of its power.

The body of the international hypocrisy has always been highly unreceptive to the creation of any Muslim state, and no matter how small or big that sate was. There are many examples which can attest to that.

When Shaykh Khitabi created a Muslim state in Morocco, the crusaders quickly reacted, then reorganized their forces and besieged that state. The Khitabi state was defeated soon after that siege. That took place well before the crusaders had a foothold in the Muslim world.

Despite our deep disagreement with the Algerian Salvation Front (FIS), to make a point, the Front was also harmed by that body of universal hypocrisy. When the Front overwhelmingly won the first round of elections in Algeria, which meant that it was going to win the general elections, the top French officials drafted a plan to move in against the Front, if the Algerian government wished it to. The United Kingdom and all of Europe were standing by to help the Algerian government defeat the Front and, if necessary, by force.

The West greatly worries about a resurfacing of a Muslim state.
The West understands what sorts of potential the Muslims have;
potential that has been implanted by Islam in its followers.
Such potential is not present among followers of other faiths.

Because of this Islamic potential, the Muslims were able, in a
very short period of time, to spread Islam throughout the world.
That short period of time was between the time of the Prophet,
Mohamed, may peace be upon him, and the time of the first four
Wise Caliphates.

The maps which had been drawn by the Sykes-Picot Agreement and
other more recent maps have been acknowledged by all world
leaders. However, if a new Islamic state is to emerge, these
maps will become something of the past. The Islamic state will
be seen as a threat, and the West will deal with that state as
if it had taken over some of its own territories. So, the West
and other continental and regional countries will likely band
together to defeat any new Islamic state.

Today, America, the guardian of the West, is by far the most
influential country in the region. America is the lifeblood of
that region. America is also the biggest supporter of that
region's status quo. America is strong enough to have toppled
the Iraqi regime, and the Islamic government in Afghanistan.
Since then, America may have been weakened, perhaps,
tremendously, but it is still powerful enough to topple any
state and anywhere, particularly any newly founded Muslim state.
Our work, hence, must go on until we exhaust and weaken America
to the point where it could not threaten or defeat any state
which we create.

So, it is rather urgent to work hard at organizing the Muslim
people, to unify their efforts and resources. Some of the Muslim
people may have not experienced a call to Jihad because of one
excuse or another. Nonetheless, the Muslim people must be united
first before the preparation for building a Muslim state begins,
God willing; even if we have to put off the creation of that
state for a few years.

There is another important issue which must be fully understood.
That is the intent for applying Islamic Law is to create an
environment in which God's codes are supreme to any other codes
in a given land. Our duty is to ensure that such a condition
exists. We also have to evaluate, and very carefully, our

decisions, which had taken into consideration the common good perspective within the domain of the Islamic Law.

It is common among ordinary people to enlist in the armed forces for monetary incentives. Once enlisted, if these people are ordered to step forward to a battlefield and fight, they would likely do so. These people, however, would not fight on behalf of America, even if they had been ordered to do so. These people would not have the motivation to kill their own cousins whom America wishes to destroy!

Assume that some of those enlisted people, who often would belong to this or that tribe, would be willing to fight us. Also, assume that during one of their offensives, we kill one of them. The reaction of the tribe, to which the deceased belonged to, would likely be insignificant in this case, because the incident only involved one person and, after all, it happened during an offensive operation. Imagine, however, that same tribe's reaction if we were to initiate an attack against a group of tribesmen, then kill many of them as they were trying to enlist with some unit of the armed forces. That tribe's reaction would be undoubtedly severe. That tribe would press hard against us.

The killing of a greater number of tribesmen often boosts tribes' vengeful attitudes. The Mujahidin, hence, must be extremely careful about initiating operations to which they know little about the consequences. The Mujahidin should also study past mistakes so they may learn from them.

Tribal wars have often undermined the stability of many communities. Tribal vengeful attitudes at times could be intense and uncontrollable. Many tribal wars throughout history can attest to that. Even some of our Mujahidin brothers had been sucked into tribal wars. When some of the Mujahidin left us to go back to their homeland, they found their tribes at war, and so, they joined in. They put their faith to the side, then joined an ignorant bunch. Those Mujahidin had always been true to their faith, to say the least, but they could not abandon the tribesmen's ignorant and vengeful attitudes.

Many governments in the region also made big mistakes when they ignored tribal attitudes. Those governments, and because of outside demands, would often kill their own countrymen without given enough thought to the consequences of their actions. As outside pressure increased on those governments, those governments, in return, intensified their actions against their own tribes. That led many tribes in those countries to turn against the governments.

If the Mujahidin treat the tribes well, the tribes will likely be on the Mujahidin's side. The tribal communities take the spilling of blood within its community very seriously. You know the story about Abu Huthaifa, may God have mercy on his soul. Remember what Abu Huthaifa said during the Badir battle. When Abu Huthaifa learned the Prophet's instructions about not to kill al-Abbas Bin Abid al-Mutalib, Abu Huthaifa said, "We are to kill our fathers, our sons, our brothers, and members of our tribes, but ignore Abbas! By God, if I am to face Abbas, I would kill him!" Abu Huthaifa then regretted having said that.

You also know the story about Abidallah Ibn Abidallah Ibn Abi Salul. Abi Salul, who was a companion, may God have mercy on his soul, had this dialogue with the Prophet, peace be upon him. Abi Salul: "I heard that you were planning to kill my father, Abidallah Ibn Abi Salul. If you are still determined to do it, then let me do it. I would bring his head to you. Oh, by God! The Khazraj had never known a man to be more loving to his father than me. I am afraid that if you let another Muslim kill him, I would avenge my father's killing, because I would not be able to stand seeing a killer of my father walking freely among the people. So, if I decide to kill the killer of my father, that puts me in line with the sinners, because I killed a Muslim man, because he had killed an infidel."

The Prophet said to Abi Salul, "Instead of all of that, we need to treat your father well and we can also have a good relationship with him, but as long as he stays with us."

The Prophet then instructed the tribe of Ibn Abi, the tribe of Abi Salul, to be in charge of Abi Salul senior, and to punish him if he did wrong. The Prophet, peace be upon him, then turned to Omar, may God be pleased with him, and asked, "what do you think, Omar? If I had killed Abi Salul senior, as you had suggested, I would have started a vengeful tribal war. Look at the situation now! If I ask the Abi Salul's own tribe to kill him, they would do it."

You know that any Muslim who fights against other Muslims on behalf of America, NATO counties, or the apostate states, must be fought back. This, however, should be done at the right time.

The timing issue can be understood if we look at an incident during the battle of the Trenches. That incident involved Huthaifa Bin al-Yaman, may God be please with him, and Abu Sufian. The Prophet, peace be upon him, said to Huthaifa, "Go to those people, then live amongst them. Learn as much as you can about those people, and what they are doing. Do not talk to anyone about this, however, until you come back to us." Huthaifa said, "May God be pleased with him." While there, Abu Sufian said, "Oh, Qurish people! Your prestige is at stake, and you are living in a land where your livestock has disappeared. Banu Quridhah tribe has held back, and today we have just learned about their unpleasant stance. We are confronted with a storm (the Muslim people forces), as you see, which appears unwilling to die down. We cannot start our fires or protect our homes from the strong wind. So, get ready to move, because I am." Abu Sufian then jumped on his camel while it was still at rest. He struck the camel hard, then the camel stressfully stood up. Whenever Abu Sufian's camel stopped, Abu Sufian would not wait for his camel to sit, instead, he would jump off, and quickly. Abu Sufian was always in a rattled mood. If it was not for the Prophet's instructions `not to talk to anyone about this until you come back to us.' I could have easily killed Abu Sufian with an arrow."

Abu Sufian was the head of the infidels. Also, it appears that there is no doubt that killing the head of the infidels at the time would be in the interest of Islam. However, killing Abu Sufian had proven to be not in the interest of Islam, especially during that period of history. There were so many reasons not to kill Abu Sufian. One of reasons was that killing Abu Sufian would have given his tribe, Qurish, an incentive to avenge him, then launch a war on the Prophet, and his followers. That was mainly why the Prophet instructed his followers not to target Abu Sufian, to spare the Muslims any additional burdens.

The same can be said about fighting the infidels, or holding peace agreements with them. When the Muslims are strong, they fight the infidels until they either become Muslims or pay a penalty (the jizyah). When the Muslims are weak, our Prophet, peace be upon him, taught us to do what is in the best interest of the Muslim people.

The Prophet, who never uttered nonsense, taught us the following. During the battle of the Clans (Ahzab), the Prophet, peace be up on him, offered the Ghatfan clan one third of the city of Medina's harvest, in exchange for the clan not to fight the Muslims, and to go back to their territories.

Instead of the Muslims taking the wealth of the Ghatfanis, the Muslims gave them one third of their economy's output! The city of Medina where the Muslims were living at the time enjoyed a strong economy, and its harvest was counted among the best. So, a Muslim leader must do what the Prophet did, to compromise in difficult time. The duty of the Muslim leader is to ensure implementation of God's commands, and to defend God's religion.

Also, we need to learn about what the Prophet, may peace and blessings be upon him, did during the Hudaybyah peace agreement with Qurish. Qurish at the time was the head of the infidels in the Arabian Peninsula. The Hudaybyah peace agreement produced great and positive results for the Muslims.

As we are on the Jihad path, we need to do what the Prophet had done and to put God's religion above everything else. Our desire is to do just that -- to create a Muslim state, which would rule by the Almighty God's commands. This is feasible, God's willing.

Creating a Muslim state, however, cannot happen overnight. We need to be realistic about so many factors. Some of the factors include having to build the proper foundations for the state.

God did not send the entire holy Quran to the Prophet at once, although the Quran had been complete in Heaven. The Sword verse, for example, had existed in Heaven, as the Muslims were instructed by another verse "to hold back their hands (from fighting)." There is no doubt that God indented that "hold back" verse to serve certain goals which were to be for the benefits of the Muslim people.

I believe that another of God's goals was that the Muslims at the time did not possess the proper resources to create and be able to defend a Muslim state in Medina. Then, when God willed it, the Muslim state was created in Medina with the help of the Ansar supporters. Despite the fact that the state was considered too vulnerable and perhaps subject to what could be devastating wars. It was the Ansar supporters, may God be pleased with them all, who stood firm with the Prophet, and his state in Medina. This shows how important it is to ensure having the necessary support and loyalty of the people before building a state, be it ordinary, or influential tribesmen.

Note that when the Ansar, may God be pleased with them, decided to support the Call to Islam (Da'wa), they were told that all other non-Muslim Arabs would unify against them. Note that the

Ansar had not been told that "the whole world would unify against them!"

We must gain the support of the tribes who enjoy strength and influence before building our Muslim state. When God sent his prophets, may peace and blessings be upon them all, it was their tribes who were the first to reject them. Those were the prophets who enjoyed the support of God and His miracles!

This is part of God's worldly reality in which His own prophets had to experience. If God wishes to change that reality, He would have done it for His prophets! We, on the other hand, must understand this reality and plan our work accordingly.

If it is unfeasible to gain the trust of an influential tribe in a certain area, we should create a new Mujahidin group within that tribe. The basis for the tribal Mujahidin group is faith and not financial compensation. The tribal group must be based on similar foundations which had been used to create the Mujahidin groups. We think it is the best option. God knows best!

The group should consist of as many members as possible. We must urge members of this group to unify, and to trust one another. Members of the tribal group should agree to pledge allegiance to jihad, to assist in the creation of a Caliphate-based Muslim state. If some members of the group do not wish to pledge, however, this should not be an issue.

You must have an open mind with members of the tribes. You must also accept the members as part of your work. With time, and as long as the members find you inspirational and forgiving, they will come to your side.

You must give special consideration to members who have special status among their tribesmen. Also, you should make use of the members' skills and qualifications.

Creating a new tribal group, based on faith and brotherhood, God willing, will help us establish better relationships with the tribes. This will eventually help us build strong ties with the tribes, similar to what tribesmen have which are, for the most part, based on natural instinct.

It is important to study every issue that is involved in our work. Also, every aspect of a foundation which we want to use to build our state must be thoroughly examined. The work we want to undertake is a just cause, but we must be realistic every step of the way.

God has ordered us to be clever about planning for our future, as we depend on Him for assistance. I would like to support this point with an example.

Assume that the Mujahidin are on a Da'wa mission to spread the word of God but they had to stop because of a river in their path. The Mujahidin must build a bridge if they are to cross the river. The engineers decided that, to build the bridge, they needed the following material and labor: Two tons of iron ore, one thousand ton of cement, one thousand square meters of wood, two thousand tons of crude iron, two thousand tons of sand, and two hundred workers.

The Mujahidin, however, did not have all the materials ready, but they decided to build the bridge anyway. The bridge then collapsed as they were building it, due to the insufficient and missing building materials.

What the Mujahidin has done was a double failure, because they wasted material, as little as they were, and time. If the Mujahidin, however, waited until they had all of the material ready, then built their bridge, they would have succeeded.

Also, having a great number of Mujahidin laborers who are very eager to build the bridge is not enough to do the job. Having a good cause and the willingness to endure hardship for the sake of God's religion is not enough to do the job either. God is the Almighty, most powerful!

I have to point out that one of the things the local and foreign enemies are good at is the ability to destroy Muslim movements. They are experts in this area. The enemies know how to weaken a Muslim movement by provoking it to step into a fight which is beyond its strength. The enemies understand when to lure a Muslim movement into a fight, especially during the time when a movement is in the process of building itself up.

When a movement gives in to enemies' provocation, while knowing it does not have the resources to fight, the enemies will quickly have the upper hand in deciding the time and place for that movement's destruction.

Having a highly motivated force is an important factor in wars, but it is not the only factor. The leadership should not, thus, be driven by its force's high motivation while ignoring other equally important factors.

(Translator note: a poem)

"Making a decision must be made before heroes' enthusiasm,

Making a decision is a priority, and it is

Second!"

(Translator note: The word "second" in the poem was possibly in reference to the decision being second to God's, and to the Prophet's guidance.)

We must find Islamic alternatives that will help us avoid falling into enemies' provocations, and so not to waste our efforts and resources. The alternatives should include plans to help us build the future Muslim state. Also, the alternatives should include plans to help us topple the apostate leaders and stop them from returning to power.

That was one issue. The other issue, far more important, is to accumulate enough resources to help defend the future Muslim state.

A future Muslim state can defend itself only if it has the public support and has been meeting the demands and needs of its people. That is an important factor in sustaining and defending any future Islamic state.

The enemies will fight any future Muslim state that we create. In addition, the enemies, to say the least, will impose all sorts of sanctions against our state.

You know that most Arab populations have been living under so-called modern states. Such states have long abandoned the Muslim traditions of early history. Some of the Muslim state's functions in early history included applying the Islamic Law as the law of the land, providing internal security, and defending the state from foreign powers. The society, on the other hand, provided for itself.

In a modern state, the public expects the state to provide it with jobs and financial assistance. Indeed, this has become a tradition in many modern state societies. Modern states intentionally make their populations dependent on them, so as to control them. But when the state is unable, or refuses, to provide what is expected of it, the people in that society revolt, and the sate becomes unstable. Also, note that many of the things that were considered complimentary in the early days are now part of the essentials.

A revolutionary movement today needs more than just the military might to topple a government or control a country.

While putting aside the external enemy, a movement needs to have the resources in place to meet the needs and demands of the society, as it makes its way to controlling a city or a country.

A movement cannot expect, however, a society to live without for a long time. Even if that society happens to be a great supporter of that movement. People often change when they see persistence in a shortage of food and medicine, and the last thing they want to see is having their children die for lack of food or medicine.

Also, a Mujahidin movement must remember that it needs to provide the basics for its mujahidin fighters or so-called logistics support.

Economic factors are very important. The Mujahidin may win a war against the enemies, but they may lose what they gained in that war due to economic sanctions. Imposing economic sanctions are one of the enemy's favorite nonconventional weapons.

As for Afghanistan and Somalia, they are the exception to the rule. Somalis, for two decades, have been providing for themselves. Somalis have not asked any government to step in to provide basic necessities. Somalis live their daily lives the same way their ancestors did, and before the creation of the modern state. They farm, raise livestock, and trade. In Afghanistan, 20% of its population raises livestock, which is among the highest percentages in the world. The total expenditure for the Muslim Emirate in Afghanistan was little compared to what other modern and poor countries had.

The Afghan population is considered to be outside the modern-state system, and unlike Arab populations.

When the Islamic group in Egypt (the Muslim Brotherhood) killed Sadat, they had a plan to topple the government and then establish a Muslim state. Their plan was to have their members throughout the country, control government buildings, the mass media, and so on and so forth.

If God had willed for the Islamic state to be born in Egypt, it would have not probably lasted more than a few weeks. The Egyptians, who were about sixty million at the time, needed about 150 million loaves of bread, per day. That was just bread alone! Assume that the Muslim state in Egypt had come under international sanctions. So, what would happen when Egypt could no longer import wheat from its major supplier, the United States? Egypt has been dependent on American wheat for many decades, especially after it had abandoned helping the Egyptian farmers plant more wheat, or coming up with alternatives. Egypt has made its citizens so vulnerable to world's wheat producers, mainly the United States. Egypt's wheat reserve was good for two weeks during that time. So, how could a newly Muslim state meet the wheat demands of the Egyptian population while it was under international sanctions? How long would the public tolerate having to go without? That has nothing to do with whether the Egyptian public liked or disliked the Islamic state. A dangerous shortage of food causes death and people do not want to see their children die of hunger.

Before building a Muslim state, the Brotherhood could have thought about food security for the Egyptian people. Sudan, for example, would have been an ideal supplier of wheat, considering that Sudan was controlled by a Muslim government. The Brotherhood could have worked with the Sudanese to help it grow more wheat well before it thought about toppling the government. The Brotherhood could have also maintained a two-week reserve system for wheat.

The same can be said about the rest of the Arab countries. Most Arab countries are totally dependent on world's wheat suppliers.

I would like to point out that it is rather important not to expect people, and tribes in particular, to endure more what they can handle. For example, we cannot expect the public to endure constant enemy's air bombardments. We are not talking about a war in which men can show off their prowess, but a war in which air bombardments do not differentiate between a man, a woman, or a child.

Our Waziristani brothers, for example, said that they were
frankly exhausted from the enemy's air bombardments. The enemy
has been given almost a worldwide approval to violate the air
space of other countries and to attack anyone whom it views as
its enemy. The enemy does all of that under the pretense of
chasing al-Qa'ida. The time will come, and soon, when the enemy
will not be allowed to violate other countries' airspace.

It is known that they teach in military and war science that if
a war breaks out between two countries, the two countries do not
send all of their forces to the front line. Instead, they hold
back some forces, especially forces with special training.

Today, the Muslim Ummah as a whole can be viewed as an army with
several regiments. The Ummah uses these regiments in a wise
manner. So, if an opponent attacks the Ummah with tanks, the
Ummah then advances its artillery regiment, to counter the
opponent's tanks. If an opponent begins an air strike campaign,
the Ummah then advances its anti-aircraft regiment. The anti-
aircraft regiment must also deceive the enemy about the location
of the other regiments since they would be most vulnerable to
the air strikes.

Praise be to God, the jihad war is ongoing, and on several
fronts. The Mujahidin work, and may God give them the strength
to endure on the jihad path, will continue to target the
guardian of universal apostates, America, until it becomes weak.
Once America is weak, we can build our Muslim state.

The more operations are carried out against America, God
willing, the closer the time will be to organize the resources,
and unify the efforts to establish the state of Islam. Only
then, the Ummah will be able to change its status quo of
weakness, degradation, and disgrace.

The Ummah should put forward some, but enough, forces to fight
America. The Ummah must keep some of its forces on reserve. This
will be in the Ummah's best interests. The Ummah will use the
reserve in the future, but during the appropriate time.

In the meanwhile, we do not want to send the reserves to the
front line, especially in areas where the enemy only uses air
strikes to attack our forces. So, the reserves will not, for the
most part, be effective in such conflicts. Basically, we could
lose the reserves to enemy's air strikes. We cannot fight air
strikes with explosives!

We have plenty of time to view and examine the appropriate time to begin our jihad work against the apostate regimes in the region. God says, "Against them make ready your strength to the utmost of your power, including steeds of war, to strike terror into the hearts of the enemies, of God and your enemies, and others besides, whom ye may not know, but whom God doth know. Whatever ye shall spend in the cause of God, shall be repaid unto you, and ye shall not be treated unjustly." (60).

We still have a powerful force which we can organize and prepare for deployment. The organization process and the preparation for deployment will need time.

Let us assume that the ideal time to build a Muslim state in the region will be three years from now. So, it would unwise to begin fighting the apostate regimes in the region now when the pre-requisites and conditions for the Muslim state have not been met.

Our main goal, and yours, is to resurrect the religion of Islam, and to build a Caliphate-based state in every Muslim country. So, for now, we do not need to be diverted from our goal by going to war with the apostate regimes in the region. This is not the time for it.

Our goal is to build our state, then spread God's Call to the rest of the world. We can, God willing, accomplish this goal, as long as we stay put on the path of jihad.

We need to concentrate our jihad efforts in areas where the conditions are ideal for us to fight. Iraq and Afghanistan are two good examples. We do not have to rush to other areas of conflict, especially in areas which appear to have unfavorable jihad conditions.

We just do not want to see our jihad become fruitless. We need to fight in areas where we can gain points toward the creation of the Caliphate-based state. A state which has the essential foundations to function and defend itself. If our state is not supported by the proper foundations, the enemy will easily destroy it.

Building a state without proper foundations is like building a house in the middle of a torrential stream. Every time the water destroys the house, we rebuild, then we rebuild until those who help us with the rebuilding give up on us. So, our state must be built on strong and proper foundations. Otherwise, the trust the mujahidin put in us to build a state will disappear.

The impact of losing a state can be devastating, especially if that state is at its infancy. The devastation would be even harder on those who had been directly involved in the building of that state.

The public often has all sorts of interpretations for the word failure. Nonetheless, the public does not like losers. The public is only interested in the results and it often ignores the details and conditions which led to one's success or failure. If the public stigmatizes a group, the group will likely fail to rally that public for support, be it to build or defend a state.

In Yemen, they often read a poem which says:

"If Ali Bin Salim wins, they say: He is a marvel!
And if Ali Bin Salim loses, they say: He is ignorant!"

The point is that people tend to be in favor of a winner rather than a loser. Accordingly, in the poem, people described Salim as a "marvel" because he had won and as "ignorant" because he had lost. Salim's characteristics in both situations, however, were the same. Salim cannot be both marvel and ignorant at the same time.

One must look closely at all requirements and suitable conditions. This is a very important and necessary step.

Accordingly, it appears to me that the requirements and suitable conditions for building a strong Muslim state have not been met in many of the Muslim countries.

Those requirements and suitable conditions will fall into place, however, only if America becomes weak. In other words, a weaker America means a weaker apostate regime in every Muslim country. The Mujahidin, then and only then, will be able to build a Muslim state and defend it. A state in which Muslims can live under the umbrella of a Caliphate-based authority.

Keep in mind that what the enemy fears the most is to see the Mujahidin succeed in creating a strong Caliphate-based state, in which God's code is being enforced.

The Muslim populations throughout the Muslim world will likely support the Mujahidin when they declare their intent about creating a new Caliphate-based state. The Muslim populations will see the Mujahidin as part of them. Some of the Muslim populations, however, may become subject to hostilities, due to their support for the Mujahidin. The worst part of those hostilities may include indiscriminate and persistent air strikes against their communities.

Again, the Mujahidin must have all the requirements and suitable conditions in place before attempting to declare their intent about building a new Muslim state anywhere. The Mujahidin cannot begin a new war in a country just because they hope that the population in that country will support them. If the Mujahidin only rely on that hope, they will likely fail in that country. This happened, for example, in Syria, Egypt, and Yemen.

In Yemen, the communist group failed there, because when they declared their new state in South Yemen they had not sought the support or approval of the local Yemeni tribes and communities. The communists had all the necessary institutions to run a government. The communists had the military, security forces, and major financial institutions on their side. The communists even had the political as well as the economic support from the

West (headed by America), and from the Arab world (headed by Riyadh). One of the reasons the communists rushed into declaring a new state was because their leaders were being assassinated, and fast. Some of those assassinations were carried out by the Mujahidin. Another reason was that the communists were paying too much money to the President, to buy his support.

We must not get involved in conflicts, especially conflicts which may drag us in deeper. If a few of our brothers happen to get killed in a given place by a given opponent (may God have mercy on the souls of all of our brothers), we are not to rush in and declare an all-out war in that area.

Again, the requirements and suitable conditions must be met before we get involved in any conflict and in any country.

Remember what Khalid had done during the Mu'ta battle, may God be pleased with him. Khalid withdrew his troops during the Mu'ta battle when the Muslims needed him most. Khalid even took with him a few of the Prophet's companions, may God be pleased with them all. Also, Khalid left behind Zaid (the Prophet's favorite), Jaafir (the Prophet's cousin), and among others, may God be pleased with them all.

The reason Khalid withdrew his troops from Mu'ta was to assist another Muslim army, the Companions Army, which was fighting the Romans. When Khalid got to the Companions Army, he helped them safely withdraw from the battle with the Romans.

Khalid's decision to withdraw from Mu'ta led to the rescue of the Companions Army. The Companions Army was too small compared to the army which the Romans had put forward on that battlefield. Indeed, without the help of Khalid, the Romans could have crushed the Companions Army.

The Prophet, peace be upon him, had instructed Khalid to go to Mu'ta. The Prophet never instructed Khalid to withdraw from Mu'ta or to help the Companions Army. The Companions Army, on the other hand, was unaware that Khalid was on his way to help them.

Based on the above, it appears that Khalid had defied the Prophet's instructions, but this was not the case. Khalid had made the right decision. This was what the Prophet, peace be upon him, said after everything was over and done with.

The Prophet, peace be upon him, said this about Khalid: "He won when he withdrew his army." Khalid had made the right decision, despite the possibility that the Muslims could have lost Mu'ta, and conditions worsened thereof.

Khalid saw a priority in rescuing the Companions Army, and that Mu'ta was important; but it was not a battle, if lost, which could bring devastating results upon the Muslims. Also, when he helped the Companions Army withdraw from that battlefield, he knew that the Romans were not dangerously close to vital Muslim positions. In the end, the Prophet praised Khalid and his troops for what they did. The Prophet said, "They withdrew, but they did not run away."

Khalid then participated in many battles which led to the defeat of the Romans in the Fertile Crescent region.

On the Day of Hudaybyah, when the Prophet heard that Othman, may God be pleased with him, had been killed, he said, "We will not rest until we punish the killers." The Prophet decided to go to war right there and then. When the Prophet came to Hudaybyah, he had no intention in going to war. On that day, the Muslims only had their swords, but no other fighting gear.

I say that this incident resembles an analogy with difference (TN: An "analogy with difference" is a jurist's term which means deduction by analogy based on two similar but different events. The second event being the incident with Khalid). The minimum requirement for the battle existed, which was the availability of fighters. On the day of Hudaybyah, the Prophet had a total of one-thousand four-hundred people. The unbelievers' army (who had been accused of killing Othman) had twice as many men as that of the Prophet's army. The Muslims were allowed to fight the unbelievers, and whoever agreed to fight the unbelievers had to take on ten men. Also, the Muslims had their swords, which were considered the fighter's main weapon.

I would like to say that the time to resurrect the Muslim state is getting closer. Also, the spread of our Jihad thought, especially among the younger generation, in comparison to other Islamic groups and movements, has been to our advantage. Other Muslim groups and movements have been unable to satisfy the demands of many of the Ummah's youth. Our Salafi jihad thought, on the other hand, has been appealing to the youth, simply because it tackles the Ummah's causes.

Many American reports, aside from stating the obvious, are talking about a decline in America's economic, military, and political powers. The decline of the United States, and the advance of the Mujahidin, God willing, will lead us to reach an equilibrium point with the enemy, during which time we could build and defend our state.

Based on the above, it is clear that the time to build the Muslim state is not here yet, because we still have other greater duties to complete, which include making suitable preparations for that future state. God willing, the state will be the nucleus for the Caliphate ruler-ship model.

It is also clear that the goal of the Islamic Maghreb's freedom-fighter Mujahidin, who are spread throughout the Islamic Maghreb, is to build the foundations for the Islamic state. The Maghreb Mujahidin should not, however, jump any of the stages. Also, the Maghreb Mujahidin should not get distracted by indulging in any conflict with the apostate governments.

The most important objective at this stage is:

To spread our ideas, especially important ideas on teaching fellow Muslims about Islam. People should understand what their religion says about the meaning of, for example, "there is no God, but one God." This should be the backbone to all of our appeals to the public. People should learn about how to avoid falling victim in the hands of the unbelievers. People should learn about what other Muslim groups think, and how they had given in to apostate leaders. People should learn about some of other Muslims groups' perspective on authority, which is in contradiction to the Islamic codes, as well as to the scholars' views on judgeship-and-jurisdiction (Hakimaya).

You should exercise caution, and calmly approach the public. You do not want to turn people off, especially people who may already think highly of other Muslim groups. We need to build wide public support, and as much as possible.

What we want is to resurrect a state which rules with the Almighty God's codes. You know how important it is to have public support if we are to accomplish this goal.

There has to be a wider and greater call for public support. For the most part, the call should be directed at people who appear to be far more accepting of our ideas.

We should not just seek the support of people who live in difficult terrains, which would be hard on the enemy to penetrate, but other areas as well.

You may want to find someone who enjoys doing call-to-Islam work (Da'wa). Ask this person to help you reach out to the public. You should use books, video, and audio material, and as needed, publish them in different languages, so you could reach all the populations of the countries in your region. The written material must be clear and in concise language, so the public can understand it. We must pay close attention to the Da'wa work, which is to explain to people the need to understand the Unity of God and other Muslim concepts.

This, for now, is our strategy for the area. Our work must focus on the long-term objective. A quick work might be fruitful in the short run, but it is not what we need to do. The outcome of any work must be viewed within the overall long-term plan. That plan is to create a Muslim state. So, the Da'wa work is a start toward that end, God willing.

For every country where the materials are to be disseminated, you should pay close attention to the overall public taste and opinions. The considerations to public taste and opinion must be weighed within the Islamic Law, however.

The Prophet, peace and blessings be upon him, had done the same thing. The Prophet said, "If it was not for the fact that your people have just emerged from the age of ignorance, I would have renovated the Ka'aba, and gave it two doors." (Narrated by al-Tarmathi).

All public announcements must be carefully evaluated. When issuing a public announcement, ask the question of what sort of positive or negative impact this announcement will generate for us? Being careful and considerate in our public announcements will also widen our appeal and boost our image among the Muslim populations. We want to ask the Muslim people to stop living in the shadow of the oppressive leaders.

The brothers must understand that their job is to educate the public, but not to incite it to a general call to arms. As you know, the situation in the mountains, particularly now, cannot take in more people, especially in greater numbers.

Having to bring in more people to the mountains, and now, will be a burden, rather than a help to the Mujahidin. So, those who sympathize with our views must be told that "we want what is best for you. Our most important message to you is to live a Muslim life, similar to the life which our most favorite generation had lived (the Prophet's companion generation.) You must stay put, and if we need you, we will call on you. For now, you should call upon God to help us, God willing."

View the list of countries which had deployed troops to Afghanistan, to help the Americans there. Then, kidnap citizens of those countries, especially diplomats. The kidnapping of diplomats of a country is far more embarrassing to that country than the kidnapping of ordinary citizens. The pressure on that country to free its diplomats is far greater than to free ordinary citizens.

The negotiation must be based on the demand: Withdraw your troops from Afghanistan, then we release the hostages. The intent is to leave America with as little support as possible, and, God willing, will push it to depart Afghanistan for good.

The announcements containing the terms of negotiations must be clear and concise, so that impartial and independent spectators judge for themselves. The announcements should also include the unjust acts which had been committed by those countries whose citizens are being held hostages, and that the hostages are servants of those countries. The announcements should also point out that a war is a joint responsibility, and that Muslims are not interested in harming anyone whose country was never involved in hostile activities against the Muslim people.

Other public announcements on operations which involve targeting Western interests should point out the unjust acts of Western countries in Afghanistan, too.

It is absolutely vital to study and analyze the Arab revolutions against the apostate governments in the region. The analysis should focus on the reasons behind the successes, as well as the failures of Arab revolutions. The majority of the revolutions that had succeeded in the area were secular. The secular revolutions succeeded because they had, for the most part, the support of the military. In any country, the military is considered to be a power breaker. The secular revolutions crept out of the military, then turned the military power to their advantage. The Islamic revolutions, on the other hand, mostly failed, because they had far fewer resources than their opponents. The Muslim Brotherhood in Sudan, for example, had the support of the army, and it was able to topple the government in a quo d'état. It soon became apparent, however, that only the army personnel had taken charge of the country, but not the Muslim Brotherhood.

Other examples of failed Islamic revolutions include the attempt made by Shaykh Marwan Hadid, may God have mercy on his soul, to topple the Syrian regime.

Hadid began his jihad life when he went to Jordan to train at one of the Palestinian Fida'in's camps. Hadid wanted to use his training to fight a jihad war against the Jews in Palestine. During his training, the September Event took place and the ruler of Jordan attacked the Fida'in camps, then killed a big number of them. The majority of the Fida'in left Jordan after most of their training camps had been destroyed. Hadid, may God have mercy on his soul, decided to go back to Syria.

Whatever military experience Hadid had learned in Jordan made him feel confident about himself. Hadid wanted to use his

training to do something for his religion. Hadid decided that
he could no longer live under the Syrian apostate regime. His
little experience and his age did not help him make the right
decision, however. Hadid was able to recruit a number of people,
so he could begin his work against the Syrian regime. Hadid did
not want to wait for the right time. Also, Hadid did not have
the essential resources to topple the regime. A few more people
joined his group, and among them were members from the Muslim
Brotherhood.

The Hadid group was able to assassinate a number of Syrian
officials. When the Muslim Brotherhood leadership found out that
some of its members had been involved with Hadid, they decided
to terminate their membership.

As Hadid succeeded in launching more operations against the
regime, the fear factor among his followers began to dissipate.
Even the Muslim Brotherhood started to take Hadid seriously, and
it thought of ways to turn his work into its advantage. The
Brotherhood felt that it, too, could help topple the Syrian
regime. The Syrian government, on the other hand, saw this as an
opportunity to demolish the Muslim Brotherhood, and forever.
That was what one of the Syrian officials said at the time.
Indeed, the Syrian government began a national campaign to
demolish the Brotherhood. The Syrian regime treated the
Brotherhood as if it was the one who assassinated its officials.
The regime knew though that it was not the case. The regime also
knew that the Brotherhood members who had joined Hadid had been
terminated by the Brotherhood's leadership.

The conflict then entered a new phase. The Brotherhood became
serious, and it called for the removal of the regime, and to
create an Islamic government. The Brotherhood never bothered to
calculate, however, what it needed to accomplish all of that.
The Brotherhood had not been realistic about its own resources,
and capabilities, in comparison to what the opponent Syrian
regime had. Even by looking at the number of people the
Brotherhood had compared to what the Syrian regime had, there
was a huge difference between the two.

The Almighty God says, "O Apostle! Rouse the Believers to the
fight. If there are twenty amongst you, patient and persevering,
they will vanquish two hundred: if a hundred, they will vanquish
a thousand of the Unbelievers: for these are a people without
understanding. For the present, God hath lightened your (task),
for He knoweth that there is a weak spot in you: But (even so),
if there are a hundred of you, patient and persevering, they

will vanquish two hundred, and if a thousand, they will vanquish two thousand, with the leave of God. for God is with those who patiently persevere." (65-66, al-Infal.)

The Brotherhood's calculations were unrealistic. The Brotherhood even thought that after it was able to topple the regime, it would take on Israel. Also, the Brotherhood did not have enough personnel who had the expertise or prudence to lead their military operations.

The Brotherhood went to war and it lost big. The Syrian regime used missile launchers to destroy the Brotherhood's threshold in Hama. The regime killed about twenty thousand people in Hama alone. Many people were arrested, including women and children. The regime had also used all sorts of torture methods against the Brotherhood. There is no might, nor power, except with God.

After that awful experience, many members of the Brotherhood went into shock, and jihad became their last resort. Many thought that they had to make the best of it while living under the regime.

The Brotherhood in Syria had lost an entire generation, which it could have wisely deployed for jihad work under better conditions and times. After the Hama experience, the Jihad work had totally stopped, and for twenty years. With the birth of a new generation, which had not lived that awful experience of Hama, a new light of hope emerged. We saw that most of the Syrians who joined the Mujahidin in Afghanistan and Iraq were young. Most of them had not experienced the Hama shock. Other older Syrians, who probably wanted to join the Mujahidin, could not do it because the Hama experience was still on their minds, even thirty years later.

One cannot ask people to bear more than what they can handle. Otherwise, the results might be devastating, and more people would fear going to jihad.

A Muslim movement, in particular, should not ask people to bear more than what they can handle, especially in areas where the movement is anticipated to be met with unrestrained violence from its opponents, just like what happened in Hama. Any movement must keep this in mind, either during the process of building a new Islamic state or afterwards.

The failure of the Brotherhood in Syria was not surprising, and that was the view of many experts. For example, experts like

Shaykh Abid al-Aziz Ali Abi Usama. Usama thought that the Brotherhood would fail to topple the regime. The Brotherhood, on the other hand, was in a dream world. The Brotherhood thought it could build a Muslim state which would become a model in the Fertile Crescent region.

There was also the Libyan experience. The brothers in Libya failed because, firstly, they did not listen to any of the advice they were offered. The al-Qa'ida advised them to wait, so did the Jihad Group and the Islamic Group. All the brothers advised the Libyan Mujahidin that they did not have the basic resources to topple the Libyan regime. Not to mention, the timing did not add up.

As you know, jihad is a duty, but it does not require Muslims to launch jihad battles everywhere and anytime. Also, jihad does not require Muslims to fight in areas where the conditions are obviously not in their favor.

Jihad is a means by which the sustainability of the religion is ensured. Jihad can be put aside as an option, due to lack of resources. Muslims, however, must continue to accumulate necessary resources until the conditions for jihad are improved.

The Shaykh of Islam -- Ibn Taymayah -- may God have mercy on his soul, agreed with the above view on jihad. Ibn Taymayah wrote, "… that is so, if the jihad experts agree that the conditions for jihad had not been met. Experts often analyze the jihad variables against these conditions, then draw conclusion to whether the outcome is positive or negative."

The excessive enthusiasm among the Libyan brothers about creating a Muslim state in Libya made them lose focus. Then, the Libyan brothers suffered tremendously as they entered into a conflict with the Libyan regime. Thousands of our Libyan brothers went to jail. Many of them were tortured and persecuted. May God grant our Libyan brothers a speedy release from prison.

(TN: End full translation)

In the name of God the most merciful

Honorable shaykh,

God's peace, mercy, and blessings be upon you

This is a letter from a loving brother whom you know and who knows you and who accompanied you on some business and programs, but conditions prevented us from communicating. My heart is full of love and appreciation to you; it gets happy for your happiness; and it hurts for your sadness; it longs to meet you, and still loves you in God. If we disagree on some of the issues, this disagreement should not keep us from communicating and offering each other advice. Instead, it should strengthen it and make offering advice an obligation.

Based on that, I wrote to you this letter, which I hope that you will receive with love, appreciation, and an open heart, especially when you know who the sender is. Regardless of the hardships and adversities, brotherhood in God will always grow stronger.

You know that previous crises showed that loyalty between the faithful continues, and admiration and forgiveness continue regardless of the differences in points of view.

Honorable Shaykh,

At this era, everyone knows about your unprecedented contributions and great efforts in the field of jihad, the revival of the spirit of jihad in the nation, and mobilizing its energy and cadres to carry out this obligation. You have indeed become the chief innovator in this field at this day and age.

Among the most prominent landmarks of accomplishment is breaking the American illusion, uncovering the truth about its fake strength, reviving the confidence of the nation in itself and its capabilities, and targeting with precision the greatest enemy and the head of the snake without getting distracted by opponents and enemies who are only some of the poison and secretions of that snake.

As your Eminence knows, the greatest thing that one can win in this life is God's pleasure; anything less than that would be considered limited gains that might have bad consequences. One does not leave his homeland, money, and family behind except for seeking God's pleasure. We consider you one of those who dedicated his life and his money for the sake of God, but God is the ultimate judge. Careful consideration, self-examination, requesting guidance from God, and striving to reach truth and virtue and abiding by them are among the greatest reasons for success.

Also among the great reasons for success are consulting others, getting to know their opinions, even if they different from yours, and considering those opposing opinions because some of them might lead to the right path and truth.

God said, "Consult with them on the matter." Here you notice that even the one who received the revelation and who communicated with the angel Gabriel ordered consulting others and seeking their opinion.

No doubt that one's distance (due to security situation and other reasons) from reality can weaken his precise vision, and it makes it harder for him to detect reality in a subjective manner, which sometime might affect the accuracy of his opinion.

The reason is that he bases his opinion on general information given to him by admirers and sympathizers who mix up wishful thinking and reality.

This is like asking people to give you their opinion regarding a specific event. They might give you the number and identities of those who agree with them and understate those who disagree with them. We have noticed something similar among those who agree with you and who inform you of the situation.

You can overcome this problem by listening to the opinions of those who are neutral on the issue or even those who disagree with you in order to get a clearer picture of people's points of view and evaluation of the event. Getting various vantage points is in our interest and can serve the decision, opinions, and positions that we form.

Being chased, besieged, and distant is not the best environment for thinking and for forming the right opinion and decision. In this case, one should seek the opinion of brothers who are outside of the hardship that he is in and should be wary of his own opinion, which could be subject to influences that he is not aware of. None of us believes that he is immune from making mistakes, and we should apply this belief by reexamining and reconsidering our opinions.

One can see his weakness and deficiency when he examines old decisions that were later proven to be mistaken or assumptions that turned out to be wrong. Returning to the truth and backing away from an opinion once you discover its falsehood is a reason to be proud and is honorable. That is the tradition of the companions of the Prophet, the faithful scholars, and leaders of our nation. Retraction does not take away from the person; to the contrary, it elevates him in this life and in eternity.

One can make a mistaken decision, but he will be excused for it. However, once he becomes aware of the mistake, but insists on his decision, there will be no excuse, and that might be a reason for his failure in what he does.

A quick review of the journey of work and the changes in it during the last twenty years reveals the effects of circumstances and variables that are out of one's control, but which one had to deal with based on the facts that were available to him at that time. Sometimes one makes the right decisions and sometimes does not, but one should benefit from this enormous experience (including the right and the wrong) in future work and correcting the course.

To complete the picture, here is a short review of the journey of work and the accompanying changes and transformations over the last twenty years.

-Work started with supporting the Afghani jihad, sacrificing everything, deploying youth to the fields of jihad, and placing great hope on the Islamic state in Afghanistan, which was considered a starting point for moving to all other countries in the world.

-After a period of Afghani jihad and the attrition of many of the cadre and money, the idea of establishing an international Islamic force, which is not only based in Afghanistan, and Afghanistan is not its top priority, came to being.

Most of the work in Afghanistan turned to the goal of luring and preparing youth.

-Then the Gulf crisis and Iraq's invasion of Kuwait took place. You offered your serves to Saudi Arabia to defend it in confronting the Iraqi regime in order to not use the foreign forces, and you asked the youth from the peninsula (Yemen, Saudi Arabia, and other Gulf countries) to return to their countries to participate in confronting the Iraqi invasion.

-After that phase, the goal became more precise and your approach and focus turned to attacking the head of the snake, America. You abandoned all jihadi work for the sake of this. America became the main enemy, and you declared a war against it and demanded it to get out of the lands of the Muslims and stop its dominance over Muslims.

-Immigrating to Sudan and calling on others to do the same and placing great hope on the Sudanese regime, which subsequently pressured you to abandon the political and jihadi approaches.

During this phase, your approach was:

--This phase was not conducive to jihadi work due to the many challenges, pressures, pursuits, and siege. Instead that phase was a phase of spreading the faith, building the culture, instilling the doctrine of "there is no god but God" in the hearts of the nation, and teaching renunciation of worldly things in order to prepare for jihad. Based on this conviction, the Association of Mus'ab Bin-'Umayr for Preaching was established and headquartered in Sudan.

--As pressure increased, you decided to move to Afghanistan. You were not keen on fighting alongside Taliban or supporting them until Taliban took control of Jalalabad, Kabul, and the rest of the country. You got to know them better, you accepted them and got comfortable with their approach, and pledged allegiance to Mullah 'Umar. That phase was the phase of working on completing the control over the rebellious north and deepening the roots of the infant Islamic emirate, which revived the ambitions that were on the verge of collapsing.

--Before the state was able to stand on its feet and complete its control of the entire country, you started to operate externally by targeting the head of the snake. You were moved by the youth who were gathering, eager, ready for sacrifice, and whose numbers at training camps were increasing. Then came the operations of Nairobi, Cole, and then 9/11, which ended the government of Taliban (the Islamic Emirate) on which many hopes were hanging.

These phases were accompanied by ideological changes and transformations that I do not wish to talk about or evaluate because this is not the place for that. My intention is to talk about the phase that we are in, which is the phase of work in Muslim countries in general and the Peninsula in particular.

Before I get into the details of the matter, I wish to ask a question here: Why the peninsula only? Do you only care to protect yourself and your security and let the entire world burn down?

I wish to say:

First: We think that you should not work inside Muslim countries, even if it is directed against the head of the snake, because this can cause great harm to Muslim people and can inflict great damage on various areas, including preaching, charitable work, dependence on God, and other areas. It also gives a chance for the head of the snake to get stronger and spread its poison in a greater manner.

Second: We think that the best places and most effective places for attacking the head of the snake are the locations in which it explicitly got involved militarily, such as Afghanistan and Iraq. Concentrating efforts in those areas is better than dispersing them and prevents the harm that could accompany them.

Third: There is no doubt that the peninsula is unique and different in terms of supporting jihad through cadre, financially, and morally. The peninsula is considered the rear base for all jihadi work in the world, starting from Afghanistan and Chechnya, all the way to Iraq and Palestine. Attacking this base has a very clear and apparent effect on all jihadi work.

Fourth: The best way to prevent the shedding of impermissible blood and not killing faithful people is to not work inside Muslim countries. I am sure that your Eminence knows that God said, "If it were not for faithful men and women among them, we would have punished them harshly." If faithful swords stopped fighting for fear of hurting the few faithful in the nonbeliever society, can you imagine the ruling when we talk about Muslim population in a Muslim society?

Fifth: Some of the brothers, who were among the veteran mujahidin and who dealt with some of the leaders of the organization, feared that the events in the peninsula might be influenced by anger, envy, and hatred toward citizens of the peninsula because of some past positions.

Sixth: When looking at the justification for the events, one has to wonder why this is not taking place in Pakistan in spite of the fact that it is closer geographically, easier to reach, known for its strict position toward the mujahidin, handed over some leaders and others to America, overtly supported the American occupation, and actively participated in toppling the Islamic emirate. I do not think that you should target Pakistan, but I am just saying that to make my point clear. Why didn't this take place in Kuwait and Qatar when they are the greatest agents and collaborators for the Americans?

The phase of working in the Arabian Peninsula:

It seems that those who know you well say that you did not support working inside until recently. Perhaps the start was based on personal efforts and initiatives that you were not aware of, especially because when we wrote to you in the past, you expressed that work inside would be inappropriate and would cause great harm. At any rate, events showed that it was a mistaken decision that had very dire consequences, including:

-Harming jihad and the mujahidin in all arenas.

--The nation lost many of the leaders and cadre who were killed or arrested because of these operations.

--Pressuring those who support jihad in Chechnya, Iraq, Afghanistan, Palestine, and other places and completely cutting off the funding, which caused great damage to jihad there.

--Banning youth from joining jihad and tightening the security on all passage points that lead to jihad, and arresting people going to jihad and returning from it.

--Detaining a large number of youth and sympathizers around them and exposing them to temptation that might be detrimental.

--Going after and perusing anyone who has ties to jihadi work.

--Suffering by many families of killed, detained, and wanted individuals.

--Banning any talk or promotion of jihad through lectures, sermons, and forums.

--People repulsed by the word jihad and its enemies continue to defame it.

--The jihadi stream lost many of its honest and faithful scholars and preachers who defended jihad and adopted it causes.

- Damaging the charitable work around the world and in all fields:

--Shutting down several charitable organizations that were carrying out relief work all over the Muslim world, such as al-Haramin Charitable Organization.

--Banning the collection of donations from individuals, organizations, and companies under any name and for any activity.

--Freezing bank accounts of charitable individuals and organizations. These accounts had great amounts of money that the poor were deprived of.

--Arresting anyone who is suspected of collecting money and supporting a charitable project that does not belong to an official organization.

--Stopping many charitable and relief efforts that were vital for needy Muslims all over the world (digging wells, building mosques, orphanages, education, health, clothing, and so on).

-Damaging the spread of the faith and fear of God.

-Giving an excuse to the deviated approaches to attack Islam in general and jihad in particular and push forward the projects of Westernization and secularism.

-Giving the enemy a chance to get involved more than before and pushing the state to jump into the lap of the enemy.

-Force official entities to deal with counter-terrorism in a much stricter way, change curriculums, and impose censorship on media in accordance with the so-called American campaign on terrorism.

-The great damages inflicted on Muslims' lives, properties, and freedoms.

Things are moving for people in a way that they did not want or seek. They even used to condemn people if they did any of the following:

You used to condemn any act that did not target the head of the snake and used to consider it unjustified and a waste of capabilities, but now because of the latest events, the battle has shifted from the head of the snake to its tail and from America to the regimes. This was a colossal strategic error that caused many losses in exchange for a very limited number of gains. These gains do not compare to what was sacrificed for them.

One can notice the lack of precision in predicting the position of scholars and the public toward the events inside. Perhaps the picture that is being conveyed to you is different from reality. I would like to say to you in all honesty, I do not know anyone who is a scholar, an intellectual, or a preacher who supports these actions or views them as legitimate. Many of the veteran mujahidin and the public stand against these actions. The most that is happening is some sympathy toward those who are innocent but were arrested and somehow hurt, or for believing that these youth were falsely accused of carrying out these actions.

The reality is that many of the actions of the youth and your statements, such as your call to target oil, turned people against you, especially scholars and intellectuals. If criticism against you would not be viewed as support to your crusader enemy, you would have seen much stronger open positions against you. Many of those who are quiet are doing so because they do not want to cause more problems.

Public opinion polls in the Muslim world prove that support to you among the Arab and Muslim people has shrunk after you targeted the peninsula.

It is not appropriate for an honest person to think that he is always right and that those who disagree with him are ignorant, hypocrites, or agents. Perhaps these people are correct on some issues.

Such belief leads a person to have hatred, bad intentions, and suspicion toward brothers. I told some brothers more than once, "You are more worthy of the accusations that you throw at those who disagree with you. You would not like it if those whom you insult for disagreeing with you, responded to you in the same way in terms of suspicion, insults, and accusations of being agents."

The solution:
Honorable Shaykh, I suggest that you get out of this crisis by conducting a review of this past experience and its apparent negative consequences.

You should go back to the principle from which you started and that is focusing on the head of the snake and targeting the greatest enemy of the Muslims, and not scatter the efforts and strength outside the target. The process of targeting should be governed and should not be conducted inside Muslim states in order to prevent the negative consequences I talked about earlier.

The regimes do not get hurt by targeting Americans in their countries. Instead, these attacks are confirmations that they are with the Americans and that they are working against the enemies of America and that they are being targeted like America.

As you know, one of the countries was about to be listed as a sponsor of terrorism and was about to be listed in what Bush calls the "Axis of Evil," but after the events, it went on to top the list of countries fighting terrorism and won the recognition and praise of the Congress for its efforts in this field.

Also, the political jurisprudence, which expanded to include dealing and having common interests with the Safawis who have a dangerous Persian project that threatens the presence and the future of the Muslim nation, will not be hampered by marginalizing and weakening the collaborating regimes that do not have any control. Any attacks on those countries negatively affect the Muslim people in the first place.

Some observers think that these acts help the interests of the head of the snake because they give legitimacy and justification to many of the projects that have been in the planning phase for a while and gives it (TN: the head of the snake) a chance to implement them. These acts convinced the world and the people that the American war on terrorism is just.

These acts did not only target infidels and enemies of Islam, but they target security and sources of energy. These sources of energy are one of the most important sources of income and source of prosperity that that Muslims in these countries enjoy. If these sources of energy are damaged, all people get hurt and their religious and worldly interests get damaged.

As for your statement about targeting oil because the ones who benefit from it are the enemy, it was not a good or an acceptable statement, unlike your statements and your talk in support of the persecuted and to incite attacks against the occupiers of Muslim lands.

Targeting oil can lead to great negative consequences, including:

1-It is the property of the nation and does not belong to a segment or even the ruling regime, for it is the main source of income. Establishing beneficial service projects for all Muslim people, hospitals, roads, communications, salaries, and infrastructure, depend on revenues from it. To make this picture clearer, you can compare between the infrastructure and prosperity in oil-producing countries and those in non-oil producing countries.

The enemy benefiting from oil and the regimes taking a large amount of the revenue from it are not a justification or a reason that would make the people accept and support targeting it.

2-The targeting of oil creates an excuse for foreign powers to intervene and impose international dominance over energy resources and get involved the country's security affairs and beyond, to include intellectual, cultural, minority, and sectarian affairs.

3-The damage inflicted on innocents working in these facilities and those around them in terms of their lives, property, and honor as result of targeting them was prohibited by God.

Therefore, I suggest to you:

1-Issue a clear and unequivocal statement to anyone who listens to you and accepts your opinion to direct the work and focus it on the head of the snake in its home or in areas that it occupies, such as Afghanistan and Iraq, and to dedicate all capabilities toward this goal. Also, stay away from operating inside Muslim countries in order to protect the reputation of the mujahidin, protect their acceptance within Muslim societies, prevent any harm to the mujahidin and supporters of jihad, prevent the secularists and liberals from exploiting these events, and direct the souls of the youth for the great battle against the head of the snake.

2-Issue your orders to your cadre to immediately abandon all work inside Muslim countries and move on to conduct jihad against the occupier in Iraq and Afghanistan.

3-Call on Muslims, especially the scholars, intellectuals, dignitaries, and businessmen, to stand beside the mujahidin against the great enemy that directly or indirectly stands behind every catastrophe inflicted on the Muslims.

This would also show the truth to all Muslims about the regimes that claim to be fighting terrorism because they are getting attacked and the regimes that pretend to be crying over the Muslim blood. This would place these regimes in a position where they will have to choose between standing in the trenches of the enemy and continuing to support them against the mujahidin or stand on the sidelines and open the way for the mujahidin to deal with their enemy.

In closing:

1-Hopefully God will give you honor in this life and in eternity and use you for improving the situation of the Muslims in general and the mujahidin in particular. I am writing to you based on my knowledge of you, your desire for the truth, and my intention to not see you accused or blamed by anyone. I pray to God to guide you because you went for jihad on His path, seeking His pleasure. God said, "We will show our paths to those who conducted jihad for us."

2-The mistaken decision by Khalid Bin-al-Walid (may God be pleased with him), which led the Prophet (peace be upon him) to say, "O God, I am innocent of what Khalid did," did not prevent Khalid from becoming God's sword against the infidels. Also, Khalid's stature did not keep the Prophet (peace be upon him) from criticizing him openly. Also, 'Usama Bin-Yazid, who made a mistake and the Prophet (peace be upon him) criticized him and scolded him, was later chosen by the Prophet (after making a mistake and admitting that he made a mistake) to lead the first army to leave Medina after the death of the Prophet (peace be upon him). The army included the shaykhs of immigrants and locals.

We salute those who help secure Muslims, keep harm and fear away from them, win their prayers, and support the oppressed and defend them from harm.

O God, the lord of Gabriel, Michael, Israfil, the creator of heaven and earth, you know the unknown, and you are the judge of your worshipers when they disagree with each other, guide us to the truth and to the right path.

I pray to God through His generosity to protect you, guard you, preserve you from the harm of the infidels, bless you wherever you are, use you to support His faith, and make you one of His victorious loyalists who have no fear or sadness.

The one who loves you,
Riyadh
14 September 2006

SOCOM-2012-0000019-HT

(TN: Religious opening, then:)

Dear Brother Shaykh Mahmud, God protect him,
Peace be with you, and God's mercy and blessings.
I hope this letter finds you, your family and all the brothers
well and in good health, and closest and most obedient to God
Almighty.

I begin this message with condolences for myself and you on the
death of our dear brother Shaykh Sa'id, God rest his soul. May
the Almighty honor him with what he desires, accept him as one
of the martyrs, and count his forbearance and steadfastness
among his good deeds.

God bless him, he spent nearly three decades in the theater of
Jihad aiding the religion of God.

(TN: Rest of paragraph is a eulogy of the life and deeds of the
above Shaykh Sa'id.)

I also offer condolences on the deaths of our dear brothers Abu-
'Umar al-Baghdadi and Abu-Hamzah al-Muhajir and those who waged
Jihad with them until they died. We ask God Almighty to
compensate us for our hardship and bring some good from it for
us, and that he

accept them among the martyrs and let them dwell in Heaven, for
He is most capable of that.

(TN: Paragraph seeking God's protection and guidance for all the
Mujahidin, then:)

In keeping with the words of the Prophet on forbearance, and to
fulfill our duties regardless of the hardship faced, I begin my
words with you on Jihad activities in general.

First, I wish to inform you that you have been appointed
successor to the departed Shaykh Sa'id for a period of two years
from the date on which you receive this letter. I ask Almighty
God to help you carry out this responsibility well, and augment
your success, forbearance, piety and good character which if the
leader possesses, his followers will benefit all the more so.

As you well know, the best people are the ones most agreed on by the people, and the key attributes that bring people together and preserve their staying behind their leader are his kindness, forgiveness, sense of fairness, patience, and good rapport with him, as well as showing care for them and not tax them beyond their ability.

What must always be in the forefront of our minds is: managing people at such times calls for even greater wisdom, kindness, forgiveness, patience and deliberation, and is a complex task by most any measure.

But, to begin again talking about Jihad activities:

We are now in a new phase of assessing Jihad activities and developing them beyond what they were in the past in two areas, military activity and media releases. Our work in these two areas is broad and sweeping, encompassing the headquarters and regional areas.

I put before you some ideas in my mind that time has enabled me to, so we can brainstorm and improve on them, in addition to a document that was attached to your message under the name "attachment for Shaykh Mahmud," which contained some of what I had sent to Shaykh Sa'id, God rest his soul, about this new stage.

Regarding military activities:

The conditions that grew more serious after the attacks on New York and Washington and the Crusader campaign against Afghanistan filled Muslims with sympathy toward their fellow Mujahidin, as it became patently clear that the Mujahidin are the vanguard and standard-bearers of the Islamic community in fighting the Crusader-Zionist alliance that has caused the people to endure various forms of pain and degradation.

One indication of that is the wide-scale spread of Jihadist ideology, especially on the Internet, and the tremendous number of young people who frequent the Jihadist websites—a major achievement for Jihad, through the grace of God, despite our enemies and their efforts.

On the other hand, after the war expanded and the Mujahidin spread out into many regions, some of the brothers became totally absorbed in fighting our local enemies, and more mistakes have

been made due to miscalculations by the brothers planning the operations or something that arises before it is carried out, in addition to some who have expanded the "barricade argument" (TN: on whether it is acceptable to kill Muslims being used as human shields by the enemy) which has resulted in the killing of Muslims (we ask God to have mercy on them and forgive them, and compensate their families). I reckon that the barricade argument was been debated centuries ago amid circumstances different from those of today, and it needs to be revisited based on the modern-day context and clear boundaries established for all the brothers, so that no Muslims fall victim except when it is absolutely essential.

Amongst the mistakes made were the killing of some, the Muslims did not understand the justification behind allowing their killing. As you may know, one of the principles of Shari'ah is to bring in the interests and repulse evil. This is what the Messenger of Allah, Peace and Prayers be upon him had done with the head of hypocrisy 'Abdallah Bin Abi; not to underestimate the fact that these issues, amongst others, led to the loss of the Muslims sympathetic approach towards the Mujahidin. What also led to the loss of the Mujahidin was exploitation of the foes to several of their mistakes and tainting their picture before the crowds of the nation; the purpose was to split them from their popular bases, and needless to say that this issue involving the loss of the nation's audience paralyzed the Jihadist movements.

Here is an important issue that we should pay attention to; carrying out several attacks without exercising caution, which impacted the sympathy of the nation's crowds towards the Mujahidin. It would lead us to winning several battles while losing the war at the end. It requires an accurate criteria for the ramifications of any attack prior to carrying it out; also weighing the advantages and disadvantages, to then determine what would be the most likely to carry out.

There is the need to collect anything within the capacity to collect - such as information, especially the Afghanistan commando operations carried out by the Mujahidin or others, the

Palestinian Liberation Organization; also to study the advantages and disadvantages as the study would include two aspects:

The aspect of the operational steps required to ensure the success of the operation, or the hindrances leading to its failure, as well as the impact on the foe.

The other aspect involves the impact on the nation's impression towards the Mujahidin and being sympathetic towards them. The operations that bear extreme negative impact on the partisans of the Jihad include targeting the apostates in mosques or nearby – such as the assassination attempt of Dustum during the holiday worship location, and the assassination of General Muhammad Yusuf in one of the Pakistani mosques. It is extremely sad for an individual to fall into the same mistake more than once.

I would also like to seek your advice on an opinion as follows: whatever exceeds our capability or what we are unable to disburse on attacks inside America, as well as on the Jihad in open fronts, would be disbursed targeting American interests in non-Islamic countries first, such as South Korea. We shall avoid carrying out attacks in Islamic countries except for the countries that fell under invasion and direct occupation.

There are two major reasons to avoid carrying out attacks in Islamic countries as follows: the first involves attacks amongst the Muslims which would increase the possibility of victims amongst them; even though the brothers were previously warned not to expand the shield issue (TN: possibly killing Muslims who are being used as human shields by the enemy), that was not made clear to them. The operational fact continues to expand in terms of the shield.

Firstly, it holds us responsible before Allah, praise and glory be to him, while in reality it holds us responsible for the losses and damages in the call to Jihad.

The second reason is the extremely great damage that impacts the brothers in the region where the work begins, following the alert of the state against the youths who are engaged in the Jihad work or even the preaching work. Tens of thousands are being arrested, similar to what happened in Egypt, and the arrest of thousands such as in the country of the two holy sanctuaries (TN: Saudi Arabia), while the issue is one involving time. The fact requires that we maintain the attrition of the head of disbelief (TN: Kufar) and the life artery of these apostate organizations on open fronts without bearing additional losses on the Jihad; by that, eliminating the ruler's despotism with these large numbers of devoted youths and Muslim prisoners.

When the global disbelief reaches the level of attrition, it would lead to its collapse; we would then engage in a conflict with the rulers, after they have been weakened following its weakness. We would then find the brothers there with their entire strength and energy.

Some of the disadvantages in carrying out attacks against the Americans in Islamic countries, where the components for success had not been prepared and the removal of the ruler is in an effort for the Americans not to accuse it of failing, the regime shall have a huge reaction towards the Mujahidin; this would lead to defending themselves and avenging the regime. The brothers and the regime would then engage in a war which we did not begin against it, because the power of the brothers is not ready for it, as such it would be one result.

The disadvantages in engaging as previously mentioned would change the general line - meaning to avoid wasting our energy with these regimes at this stage; that, in addition to losing the sympathy of the Muslims towards us.

This is when we lose the perception of the Muslims towards us, which is that we are the ones defending the Muslims and fighting their biggest enemy, the Crusader Zionist alliance - without killing those that the general public consider Muslims.

So, if we fight the rulers while being in this situation, and we do not respond other than with direct defense during their offense against us, and this issue is being repeated several times, it would appear that we are wronged and the rulers are the tyrants; it would increase the hatred of the people towards them and make them feel that the rulers did not defend our brothers in Palestine, Iraq and Afghanistan. They were not content with that, but they fought the Mujahidin that defend our people there.

However, if we engage in a fight against the rulers outside the direct defense, we would have eliminated the damage the rulers would have carried out in their fight against us; the reason is that it would reveal the truth, and the media shall demonstrate to the people that we are the ones fighting the government and killing the Muslims. Between the roar of the killing and the fight, the people shall forget who began the fight against the other – as such we shall lose the people and strengthen the stance of the government without cutting its hostility against us.

What aids the success of our fight against the Americans in non-Islamic countries and reducing its cost, is for limited groups, distanced from the Muslim and devout circles, to launch from countries with the Mujahidin presence without announcing their launching location; this is to avoid the reaction against the Mujahidin in that country. Given the potential for the foes to reveal that issue, it would be better for the training to be carried out and launched from the open fronts where naturally the foes would be exerting their utmost efforts.

Amongst the opportunities to be exploited in targeting the Americans is the state of security laxity found in countries where we had not carried out any attacks.

Given that the difference of the impact of attacks against the foes inside or outside of America is substantial, we need to confirm to the brothers that every effort that could be spent on attacks in America would not be spent outside of it.

The overflow of the work (TN: meaning attacks) outside of America and the work in non-Islamic countries could be spent in targeting the U.S. interests in the Islamic countries where we have no bases or partisans or Jihadist Islamic groups that could be threatened by danger. The Islamic groups there would express their stance against us and renounce us – a fact that would prevent the regime from retaliating against them following our attacks. The condition is to be extremely cautious and take necessary measures to avoid misleading the Muslims in these operations.

With respect to the media publications, I would say:
It is important for you to focus a portion of your interest on the Mujahidin publications; provide them with advice and guidance to avoid the mistakes that would impact either the reputation of the Mujahidin and the sympathy of the nation's masses or that would impact the mind and the character of the youths - who rely mainly in their culture on the publications

issued by the Mujahidin and their partisans. Needless to say, the substantial damages that this fact would have and the loss of great opportunities from a proper care and valuable guidance to millions of youths who listen to what the Mujahidin have to say in their lectures, movies and writings.

Based upon the aforementioned: I request that you prepare a memorandum that would include general guidelines on how the Mujahidin publications should be; focus on the basics and the Shari'ah literature (TN: rules) such as violation of the Muslim blood and their honor, as well as the importance in committing to the Hadith of the messenger of Allah, peace and prayers be upon him (not he who believes in stabbing, in blasphemy, the obscene, and the disgusting) as narrated by al-Bukhari.

Once the memorandum is prepared, we shall discuss it and send it to all the regions, along with sending the general policy in the military work. We shall then inform you of the committee that we are in the process of forming (I sent its formation to Shaykh Sa'id – May God have mercy on him); that committee will have the privilege of reviewing and postponing any publications assessed to be outside the general policy that we sought to keep in conformity with the Shari'ah teachings and which, God willing, would achieve the interest of Islam and the Muslims.

We ask every emir in the regions to be extremely keen and focused on controlling the military work and not to expand the barricade, due to the several attacks carried out by the Mujahidin whereby several Muslims had fallen; we could have reached the target without injuring the Muslims with some effort and deliberation. Also the need to cancel other attacks due to the possible and unnecessary civilian casualties – for example, the attacks targeting several infidel Imams during their visits to public locations where most of the Muslims are located, as they should be targeted away from the Muslims.

Making these mistakes is a great issue; needless to say, the greatness of the Muslim blood violation in addition to the damage impacting the Jihad. As a result, the alienation of most of the nation from the Mujahidin.

For the brothers in all the regions to apologize and be held responsible for what happened. They would be questioned about the mistake causing the flaw that occurred and about the measures to be taken to avoid repeating the same mistakes.

With respect to the human error outside the human will, as it is repeated in wars, the need to apologize for these errors and be held responsible, as the aspects of the flaw would be explained. Perhaps some of those killed and who were killed mistakenly were amongst the immoral; there is no need to reveal their immorality while the people are wounded and the foes are keen in demonstrating our indifference about them.

Should some of the brothers in the regions fail to carry out their duties in this respect, we should then assume the responsibility and apologize for what had happened.

The need to confirm to all the Mujahidin brothers the importance of clarity, honesty, loyalty and promises and be cautious of the betrayal.

The emirs in the regions would also be requested to task one of the qualified brothers with them, to follow up on the media section from all aspects as mentioned in the memorandum: from a Shari'ah standpoint - care for the general taste of the nation's crowds, so long as it does not conflict with the Shari'ah.

The same brother would be requested to always seek the development of his aptitude and his knowledge in all arenas associated with his mission, such as: reading books on dealing with the people because he would be largely dealing with the brothers, reading books concerning the production.

The purpose is for the Mujahidin publications to be a good potential for the competition and to gain the crowds. The main goal is to spread awareness amongst the people of the nation, to rescue them from the aberration of the rulers.

He, in turn, would seek to improve the aptitude of the brothers contributing in the media section; he would also provide advice in general for those issuing the statements, lectures, books, articles and those who comment on the Jihad films. He would be appointed as the Jihadist media individual in this region, characterized by objectivity and accepted by the people of the nation.

This brother would be in charge of the media as is the case in
the regions – otherwise the position of the General Manager of
the Media divisions would be updated in every region; no
publications would be made unless he reviews them, to include
the leadership speeches. He would have the right to stop any
publication that includes a term considered outside the general
policy, whether in the context or timing. The subject would be
reviewed with the individual who issued it, and he would be
informed of its conflict with the general policy; as well as the
dispersion of the nation's views from the larger Mujahidin
goals, such as the case of Palestine, while appointing the foe
to defame the reputation of the Mujahidin – therefore the fear
of the Mujahidin during this phase is substantial with respect
to their conduct and expressions.

Some of the examples to this was when the general populace were
in the peak of dealing with the Freedom Fleet heading towards
Gaza to break the blockade and deliver the civil relief to our
people there, and at the time when the Jews stopped it with an
armed force and killed several of those in it, activating Turkey
in this respect.

The Freedom Fleet attack dominated the media in a very large
way, as the western politicians were forced to discuss it; they
criticized the Israelis for publishing on one of the websites a
speech for the deputy of Abu Basir in Yemen, our brother Sa'id
al-Shahri. What was shown in the media was his speech concerning
the arrest of one of our sisters in the country of the two holy
sanctuaries and the Mujahidin demanding to carry out kidnappings
against the westerners, the princes of Al Sa'ud (TN: the Sa'ud
family) and the senior security employees in exchange for her
release.

Following the issuance of this speech, al-Arabiyah Television
channel exploited it widely and focused on it. It made it the
number one piece in its news reports and hosted men and youth
from the general populace on the streets as they had claimed.
That to include (TN: the hosting of) several ill-informed
scholars and state men – no doubt they accept each other,
especially those who ignore their status amongst the people; the
purpose was to discuss the tape, showing honesty and each
mentioning individually that the Mujahidin are not interested in
the Palestinian cause, and the blockade of our brothers in Gaza
– rather that their concern is to fight, corrupt and argue with
the security men and not with the usurper Jews.

No doubt, issuing this lecture was driven by jealousy of the
blood and honor of the Muslims; however it was not in
conformance with the events. The reason was because there were
one and half million Muslims at that time under siege, and most
of them were women and children. They have more than ten
thousand prisoners with the Jews, many of whom are sisters and
children in tragic circumstances. The issuance of this speech,
especially at this time, conflicted with our policy of focusing
on the bigger foe, and concealed our interest in the main issues
that were the main reasons in initiating the Jihad.

It announced to the people that we are in a fight and argument
with the rulers to avenge our brothers, those that were killed
and detained far from the cases and interests of the general
nation, due to which it held our brothers responsible for the
killing and imprisonment. It also gave the Muslims an impression
of us that we were overcome by the region-like command or
parties or both; they heard our brother talk about the sister
from the Arab Peninsula and from al-Qa'ida organization, but
they did not hear him talk about our sister in Palestine - this
is contrary to our reality and our general policy, as it weakens
our stance when we say that we are an international organization
fighting for the liberation of Palestine and all of the Muslim
countries to erect an Islamic caliphate that would rule
according to the Shari'ah of Allah.

This mistake was repeated, in a statement in which the brothers
in Yemen adopted the big operation, the operation of 'Umar al-
Faruq - May God release him when they said, it was a reaction to
the U.S. bombing of al-Mahfad; linking this large operation with
other than the Palestinian cause covers some of the stances that
show the victory of the brothers in Yemen for the Palestinian
cause. That, in addition to their absorption on a daily basis in
the fight against the Yemeni government and the strong focus on
the key figures of the Peninsula rulers in their lectures; it
drew the people's attention, that the first and biggest foe of
the Mujahidin in the Arab Peninsula are the rulers of Yemen and
the country of the two holy sanctuaries.

This was repeated in the comments of the brothers concerning the
attack of our brother Humam al-Balawi, may God have mercy on
him, when they mentioned it was a revenge for the murder of
Mahsud, may God have mercy on him. It was necessary to discuss
Palestine first.

In an effort to avoid such stances the international perception and the general policy should be present and clear in our minds; as such we would avoid being distracted or absorbed in its expansion at the expense of what is more of a priority and importance.

The priorities in the preaching work are to clarify the meaning of the term al-Tawhid (TN: monotheism) and its requirements and to warn the people from falling in its contradictions; that, to include the instigation of the Jihad against the Crusader Zionist alliance.

The priority in the military work is to focus and provide the lion's share for the head of international disbelief or to focus on the apostate and excessively talk about them which the people of the nation do not understand; consequently they would not react to it, as many of them would repel from it. This would make us the splinter in an environment that does not harbor the Jihadist movement, and does not provide us with support to pursue the Jihad and its continuity.

I believe there is a need to look into publishing pictures of the apostates' killing those of the apostate organizations who deal with the Americans against the Muslims.

Once the brothers in the regions are committed to the memorandum, it would be advisable for you and for Shaykh Abu Yahya to write some articles and provide advice to those working in the Jihad media in general to include the author partisans to the Mujahidin on the internet. Shaykh Yunis wrote to me about the importance of preparing a memorandum indicating our stance on the Takfir issue without the Shari'ah criteria. I wrote to him and told him I would send him what you had sent. I had attached it in the last letter, and asked him to follow up on sending his comments to you so you could write it in your style, in light of the fact that the foes know his true personality through the prisoners who also recognize his style when they peruse his articles on the internet.

Before concluding the discussion concerning the media publications, I would say:

We are in need of an advisory reading, with constructive
criticism to our entire policy and publications at the center
and in the regions internally; as such have two available
brothers ready for this mission.

From abroad, seek safe routes to achieve a contact with one of
the knowledge seekers so long as he is credible and trusted;
inform him that we are in a new phase of amendment and
development and require an advisory reading and development of
our entire policy and publication at the center and in the
regions. The purpose is to amend our mistakes and develop our
Jihadist work according to their suggestions and opinions,
especially in corresponding with the masses of the nation in
context and shape.

Taking into consideration the importance not to publish it and
the importance of the secrecy in all of that, as we ask God to
grant us success.

Important comment: After you provide me with your opinions and
suggestions, and after we consult amongst each other, we need to
send what we agree upon to the brothers, the leaders of the
regions and ask them for their responses to what we would be
sending them.

I intend to issue a statement, in which I would discuss starting
a new phase to amend what we have issued – as such we would
regain the trust of a large portion of those who had lost their
trust in the Mujahidin; we would increase the lines of
communication between the Mujahidin and their nation.

This would require, prior to telling and reassuring the people
that the intent from all aspects would have become clear to the
brothers in the center and in the regions – that it would be
established and implemented on the ground; the purpose is not to
contradict our statements with some of our conduct. First, for
all the brothers contributing in the media of al-Qa'ida in the
center, the need to commit to avoiding everything that would
have a negative impact on the perception of the nation towards
the Mujahidin; also ensure everything possible that would bring
the Mujahidin and their nation closer.

The basis for that is to take into consideration the general
opinion or the general taste within the Islamic Shari'ah
criteria; it is a very important issue that the Messenger of

Allah, peace and prayers be upon him had done – as was said in the Hadith (if your people were not newly ignorant, the Ka'bah would not have been destroyed and would only have two gates) narrated by al-Tarmazi.

The issues taking over the public opinion are the alienation from harshness and leaning towards friendliness and objectivity; also repulsion from repetition in lectures unless it is absolutely necessary.

It is therefore necessary to focus on expansion, and increase the knowledge in factual jurisprudence and developments of the events; the purpose is for our lecture to touch the crowds of the nation and their aspirations, while treating the important doctrinal issues.

In summary: committing to the general lines, designed according to the Shari'ah policy in our Jihadist operations and our media publications is an extremely important issue; it will achieve, God willing, great gains for the Jihadist movement – most importantly gain the crowds of the nation, correct the wrong impressions in the minds of the Mujahidin. Additionally, an increase in the attrition of the head of disbelief, because the plan was to focus more on it.

I add here two issues that appear important to me in the stability of the Jihadist work and its progress. I would like for you to research it amongst you- first: the need to circulate a new administration arrangement, sent to all the regions after we discuss it amongst us, and which would include the following points:

A. If any contingency situation results in the absence of the Emir from his leadership of the Mujahidin, the Deputy Emir will automatically and temporarily take on the responsibility of managing the affairs of the Mujahidin for several days, with his title being "Acting Emir". The Mujahidin in his territory will be informed of this, and he is not to be called "The Emir". Furthermore, he will not be announced in the meeting except after consulting with the brothers and gaining their agreement to that or some other action.

Consultation among brothers in any region will take place internally, though they will also consult with "Central al-Qa'ida). This term was coined in the media to distinguish

181

between al-Qa'ida in Afghanistan and Pakistan and al-Qa'ida in the other territories. In my opinion, there is no problem with using this term in principle in order to clarify the intended meaning.

B. The term of an Emir chosen by the influential people in each territory, in consultation with the central group, shall be two years, with the potential to be renewed. If there is delay in consulting with the central group due to a difficulty in communications, the term shall be one year, also with the potential to be renewed. It shall be taken into consideration that this term is most similar to the leadership of a Wali (TN: governor) in Muslim territories during the time of the caliphate, and is not like the grand imamate.

C. The Shura council in each territory will provide the Emir with recommendations and will write an annual report to be sent to the central group detailing the local situation, to include the progress of the local Emir in his activity and his dealings with the Mujahidin.

I also think that if the brothers in any territory deem to elevate the position of any of the brothers to a position of importance, such as First Deputy or Second Deputy, then that should be done in consultation with the central group. If there is a problem with communications, then the matter will be temporary until consultation can be completed.

This is with the stipulation that the CV of the brothers nominated to the position is sent.

Second: Attention should be paid to creating command structures and devising plans to develop and refine the energies called upon for Jihad. The Muslim Nation, in general, suffers from a lack of qualified leadership, and it comes as no surprise to you that the fields of Jihad are where leaders are made.

Finally: I want you to inform me of your recommendations that will help with elevating the level of activity on all fronts and in all territories. You no doubt understand the great importance of the progress of our work in the territories through general policies that are controlled by Islamic law in order to achieve our interests and reject corruption.

I reviewed your opinions regarding the issue of establishing an
Islamic state before the elements of success have been completed
and the issue of escalation in Yemen. I wanted to share with you
my opinion in these two matters in order to establish a fruitful
and constructive discussion, God willing.

However, talking about them brings sorrow, and I am compelled to
talk at length about them and their importance and the risks in
them. If I am unable to give these matters their due time within
these pages, then perhaps I can finish the discussion in the
next message. I'll begin with the matter of escalation in Yemen.
To begin I would say that Yemen is the Arab country most suited
to the establishment of an Islamic state, but this does not mean
that the necessary fundamental elements for

success for such a project have yet been realized. Henceforth,
we must increase our efforts to preserve Yemen and not drag it
into a war before the necessary preparations are made on a
number of important fronts. I anticipate that we will not
escalate in Yemen for the following reasons:

A. Escalation in Yemen would siphon off a large portion of the
energy of the Mujahidin without doing the same to the head of
the infidels (America) directly. Thus, the majority of harm
would be inflicted on the Mujahidin in general, and would impact
the greater war between the infidels and Islam. Yemen represents
an important center of gravity in supporting fronts with men,
and if war broke out there, then the supply lines to other
fronts would be disrupted or weakened.

Furthermore, Yemen represents a focal point in terms of
supplies, as a reserve force for the Mujahidin, and it has
become a proven fact in military science that in a war between
two sides, neither side should commit all its forces to the
fight; rather, it is important for a force to remain as a fork
with several prongs in reserve. It seems to me at this point
that Yemen remains a force of supplies and reserves for the
Mujahidin at the open fronts, and a powerful tool to restore the
caliphate when circumstances are conducive to doing so. Thus
far, circumstances are not yet suited to opening up a front in
Yemen that would bring about the desired results. The Islamic
nation, as an army, has several battalions. So when the enemy's
tanks advance, we need to advance anti-tank battalions, and when
the enemy's aircraft conduct raids, our anti-aircraft battalions
must show themselves, all the while camouflaging and concealing

our other battalions in order to protect them from being bombed, so as to not lose them.

So this is the state of things in our battle with the infidels of the world. We want to cause him to only bleed in this mission, while preserving the other armies as a reserve force that enters the battlefield at the appropriate time.

B. The emergence of a force in control of the Mujahidin in Yemen is a matter that provokes our enemies internationally and locally and puts them on a great state of alert, which is quite different from the emergence of the strength of the Mujahidin in any nation not in the heart of the Islamic world, despite the enemy's increased alert posture at the appearance of the Mujahidin in any location.

Thus, their situation in Yemen would be like that of anyone fighting for his life, for Yemen is the launching point toward all other oil nations. Control of these nations means control of the world, so they are willing to die and make every effort to break the backs of the Mujahidin there. At the same time, the capabilities of our brothers there are not yet such that they can enter this sort of struggle, neither in terms of their administration or their financial resources. The finances do not permit them to provide the basic life support services to whomever would take on the burden, whether they want to or not, particularly since Yemen is suffering from a food and health services crisis even before entering into a war, and all that this implies. The issue of providing for basic needs is a matter that must be taken into consideration before taking control of nations or cities. If a controlling force, that enjoys the support of the majority where it has taken control, fails to provide for the basic needs of the people, it will lose their support and will find itself in a difficult position that will grow increasingly difficult with each passing day. People will not bear seeing their children die as a consequence of a lack of food or medicine. This is in addition to providing necessities to fighters and what we call logistical support.

I would add that the initiative is in our hands, and we have the room to look for the appropriate time to begin Jihad in Yemen. In the words of Almighty God, "Against them make ready your strength to the utmost of your power, including steeds of war, to strike terror into (the hearts of) the enemies, of God and your enemies, and others besides, whom ye may not know, but whom God doth know. Whatever ye shall spend in the cause of God, shall be repaid unto you, and ye shall not be treated unjustly." (60). We still have a large force we are able to gather and prepare, and if we suppose that the suitable conditions for establishing an Islamic state in Yemen that can be preserved are realized in three years, for example, then beginning Jihad before that time is unwise because the forces would be squandered and it would take longer to prepare, all while not achieving their primary goal, which is to establish the religion.

It is our desire, and the desire of the brothers in Yemen, to establish the religion and restore the caliphate, to include all the countries of the Islamic world. God willing, that will be followed by other conquests that we are able to achieve by continuing to wage Jihad at the fronts that are prepared for combat, while holding off at the fronts that are not yet prepared, such as Yemen, until they become prepared and until combat at those fronts will produce results that aid in establishing a guided caliphate, God willing. What demonstrates the dangers in beginning a fight before the necessary elements have been put in place is the failure of the coup attempted by the socialists in Yemen, which was due to their haste in beginning before putting in place the elements necessary to success. These included securing the loyalty of the surrounding tribes and other such items, despite the fact that what pushed them to do this was the increase in assassinations among their cadre, be it assassination by way of murder at the hands of the Mujahidin or the assassination by granting money from the president, which drew them to him.

As you know, the duty of Jihad does not mean establishing it in every territory, including the territories in which the elements of success have not been achieved. Jihad is a means to establish the religion, and it might

be brought down by an inability to do so without being brought down by the preparation for it. This would be the case if most of those with experience in Jihad decided that the elements necessary for success had not been achieved such that the desired results could be realized.

By God's grace, Jihad is underway at several fronts, and these are sufficient, by His will and His glory, as well as by the steadfastness of the Mujahidin there, to perform the function of bleeding the head of the infidels, America, such that it is defeated, God willing. Then, the Islamic Nation will be able to expel that which has stricken it with weakness, servility, and degradation.

The interest of the Mujahidin in knowing that which effects the enlightenment of the people of the Islamic Nation and is met with acceptance by the people is sufficient, God willing, to rescue the nation from the oppression of the ignorant and the misled.

Thus, the plague that exists in the nations of Muslims has two causes: The first is the presence of American hegemony and the second is the presence of rulers that have abandoned Islamic law and who identify with the hegemony, serving its interests in exchange for securing their own interests. The only way for us to establish the religion and alleviate the plague which was befallen Muslims is to remove this hegemony which has beset upon the nations and worshippers and which transforms them, such that no regime that rules on the basis of Islamic law remains. The way to remove this hegemony is to continue our direct attrition against the American enemy until it is broken and is too weak to interfere in the matters of the Islamic world.

After this phase comes the phase in which the second cause – rulers who have abandoned Islamic law - are toppled, and this will be followed by the phase in which God's religion is established and Islamic law rules.

The focus must be on actions that contribute to the intent of bleeding the American enemy. As for actions that do not contribute to the intent of bleeding the great enemy, many of them

dilute our efforts and take from our energy. The effect of this on the greater war in general is clear, as is the resulting delay in the phases leading to the establishment of an Islamic caliphate, God willing.

Based on this, there is no overriding pressure or great need to exhaust and deplete the front in Yemen before the elements of success there have been achieved. Putting reserve forces and

upply lines for the Mujahidin into the quagmire is a difficult
hing, for the reasons I've already mentioned, including that
.he scope of the struggle will be greater than the capabilities
n a number of ways.

.o it seems to me that halting the escalation in Yemen is in the
general interest of the Mujahidin and is similar in many ways to
what took place in the Battle of Mu'tah, as the Prophet
described it, and the actions of Khalid Bin al-Walid. He
achieved victory when he withdrew the army; the victory in the
circumstances of that battle came in his rescuing the companions
(TN: of the Prophet Muhammad) from the destruction of their army
n the battle. Their army was completely outnumbered by the
Roman army, and there were no elements in place for success, and
.hey weren't on the verge of a complete disaster. They had the
ability to go and regroup, much like we do now. They even had
the ultimate Prophet, who eventually praised them, telling them
.hey were fighters, not fleers.

As for the matter of establishing the state before putting in
place the elements necessary for success:

A. It seems to me that being deliberate in this matter is a good
thing, and to explain further, establishing the state before the
elements necessary for success are put in place most often will
lead to aborting the effort wherever it takes place, because
establishing a state and then toppling the state represents a
burden that exceeds the energy of the people.

Weighing people down with something that exceeds their energies
is fraught with negative results and leads to the shock of Jihad
for the people of a territory in which the movement is
suppressed, and it may exceed them. This is true whether the
movement was suppressed after establishing the state or while it
seeks to do so, as was the case in Syria when the Muslim
Brotherhood tried to begin their Jihad and establish an Islamic
state before they were prepared to do so and before the elements
necessary for success were in place. This led to a shock for the
Muslims in Syria at the emergence of Jihad, and many people
decided it was less harmful to remain with the current regime
than what would happen to them if they took part in the Jihad.

Following this shock, Jihad lost a generation of men who had
been passionate about the victory of the religion, including men
who had given their lives for this cause. The winds of Jihad

were still for nearly twenty years in Syria until a new generation came along that had not experienced that shock. The overwhelming majority of those who answered the call to Jihad in Afghanistan and Iraq were those who had not witnessed the Hamah experience and the murder committed by the regime there.

B. Jihad as a means to bring down countries and to gain control of them does not require beginning such a plan based on the hope that people will fight to establish a nascent state. Instead, it requires close study and inspection and confirmation that the elements necessary to success are in place. And it requires searching for the appropriate time. So we cannot waste a golden opportunity, and we must not begin before the appropriate opportunity is at hand. A man might measure the results of establishing an Islamic state before toppling its enemies against the results of the fall of the Islamic emirate in Afghanistan, which we pray to God does not happen again. Such a comparison shows a big difference, due to a number of factors. The first factor is that the people of the Islamic world are divided into

two groups, the Arabs and the non-Arabs. Given that the enemies have knowledge of and experience with the Arabs and their history, they have learned that Arabs have dangerous qualities that make them suitable to quickly carry out the call to Jihad, and that the Qur'an and the Hadith are sufficient to justify that. On top of that is the speed with which they comprehend the texts of these without the need for translation. Based on this knowledge, the enemies have focused the bulk of their campaign against the Islamic world on the Arabs, particularly in the destructive media bombardment against Arab culture and their characteristics. This all serves the interests of the west; sufficient proof of this lies in the fact that the first language in which BBC broadcasts are transmitted after English is Arabic. This, when Arabs represent 2.5% of the world's population, while other people, including China by itself, represent a fifth of the world's population. The same is true for the Indian sub-continent, which represents another fifth of the population, while the number of Muslims in India is greater than the number of all the Arab Muslims. It was possible for the voice of the British Empire to reach 40% of the world's population through just its broadcast, but their primary concern was with destroying the Arabs via the media.

The second factor is the continued American occupation manifested in military forces on the ground. This is a very important factor in awakening people and inciting them to continue fighting, as opposed to the situation in countries in which the external enemy brings down the Islamic state established there without putting its military forces on the ground. Instead, they are satisfied to support the local or regional enemy, particularly if the country hasn't been destabilized by significant internal dispute, as is the case in Iraq.

The third factor is that the Afghan people are religiously devout by nature and live spartan lives. They are extremely sensitive to the presence of foreigners in their country, where there are many primitive villages in the mountains and rural areas cut off from the cities. The residents in such areas are aware of their freedoms and their strength, and know they are far from the control of the security forces that are weak even in the major cities.

These factors are important in completing the elements necessary for successfully establishing a Muslim state, but they do not apply to all countries in the region. The people in many of these countries are still not prepared to enter the fight against governments and to bring them down. Many people have no idea how they would respond, and those who do understand that or who want to do away with these governments for some other reason, such as poverty or administrative corruption, do not believe that the solution is to fight them and to bring them down, because America is the dominant force in the region and will bring down any state that is established after its representatives are toppled.

In this phase, Afghanistan, Iraq, and Somalia are exceptions to the countries in the region.

Here we have an important issue, which is that one of the most important factors that will aid in the success of Jihad and its continuation is calling on Muslims to fight the enemy whose hostility they know and whom they know it is permissible to fight against, as is the case with the American enemy. As for the local enemy, such as if the Yemenis were to begin a long battle against the security services, this is a matter that will weigh on the people. As time goes by, they will begin to feel that some of them have been killed and they will start to want to stop the fighting. This would promote the ideology of secular governments that raise the motto of pleasing all sides.

Our goal is not to expend our energy in Yemen, to use the greater part of our strength in supplies and reserves, and to wear down and ultimately topple an apostate regime, only to establish another apostate regime.

This is on the assumption that the people would revolt with us to topple that regime. However, while it is the nature of tribes to be daring in fighting among themselves, they are cautious and hesitant to enter a struggle against a sizeable opponent. (They will do so only) after they make sure that the force and timing sufficiently predicts that the revolution has a good margin of success. This is when one of the most important factors for establishing a stable Muslim country in Yemen is dependent on substantial tribal support and adoption and gaining their trust so that they enter the struggle and contribute to establishing the government and protecting it. It is worth mentioning here that the entity that the tribes are going to confront in their fight will be just the Yemeni government, it will be international and regional apostasy.

It is also worth mentioning that the situation on the ground imposes the importance of differentiating between the North and the South, as the situation in the South cannot wait any longer. This is due to the people's intense anger toward the government and the huge amount of injustice inflicted on the people by the government, in addition to the mobilization conducted by al-Hirak. These two factors made large sectors of the people in the South dare to revolt, prepare for armed confrontation, and fight against the government. As for North Yemen, I see that it is in the same condition as the rest of the countries in the region, as far as the people not being ready to fight against the government. So I see that we do not seek a truce in the South, as it goes against the fabric of the people in their movement to lift off the injustice put upon them. It will lead to us losing most of the government opponents; we should not follow their lead, but we benefit from the tense atmosphere in spreading our call to Allah among the Muslim ranks in the South.

This is because the current anger is led by al-Hirak, and it is allied to the United States and the Gulf states. Accordingly,

not declaring a truce does not mean that we escalate against the
government in the South and enter into a fight against the
military, as it would not bring the desired outcome. This is
because the sons of the northern tribes will be targeted in the
fight. The commoners in these tribes do not realize that the
military are apostates. So the tribes will think that we
increased the bloodshed, and people will talk among the tribes
saying that al-Qa'ida kills a lot. This would distance many
people from us and might lead to a tribal uprising to fight
against us in revenge for their sons. This also means that we do
not jump to establish an Islamic state in the South at the first
chance of the government losing control in the South. The reason
for this is what we mentioned earlier, that we are not yet ready
to cover the people with the umbrella of Islamic rule. The
reasons are that the people have needs and requirements, and the
lack of these requirements is the main reason for their revolt
against the ruler. We cannot provide for these needs in light of
the battle and siege of the whole world against us. It is human
nature that they will go with whoever better provides them with
these needs and requirements. The animosity of the world and its
siege against the Mujahidin is well known to the people, so no
matter how much they love the Mujahidin, they will not stand
beside them under these circumstances.

It is apparent from this that most people in Yemen, if given a
choice between a government formed by al-Qa'ida or a government
formed directly or indirectly by any of the Gulf states - such
as if they give support to 'Ali Salim al-Bayd or any other who
has administrative ability - they will choose the government
that is formed by the Gulf states, either in the North or the
South. The simple reason for this is

that they think that these are Muslim governments and that they
have the ability to provide them the necessities of their
livelihoods. These are the demands of the people.

To stay away from wishful thinking and hope, we have to look at
the people's revolution in the South like it is a boulder
rolling down the side of a mountain. It is a benefit to whoever
takes it; however, stopping it to our benefit is difficult, as
it naturally will end up with the person who has the ability to
control it, and who is at the current time, the Yemeni
opposition, which is supported by the Gulf states.

However, looking at the indications, it seems that at the time
the US is weakening - and accordingly, its agents are weakening
- the Mujahidin are preparing to cover the people with the
umbrella of the Caliphate. We will be the prime choice nearest
to them, as they are Muslims in Muslim countries, and it is
natural for that environment to receive the Mujahidin to
reestablish the Caliphate and rule with Allah's Shari'ah. This
is what scares the adversaries more than the Mujahidin; they are
scared of the rejectionists (TN: the Shi'a).

Based on the above, we should not begin to attempt to establish
a government in Yemen, even if the people revolted against
government and toppled it, either in South Yemen or in all of
Yemen. This is regardless of how bad the nominees to control
that government are, because the outcome will be worse on Islam
and Muslims if we start something that does not have all factors
of success put together. This would put us in trouble with the
people and put the Mujahidin forces in the sights of the enemy
fire. This is because in the view of the rulers of the Land of
the Holy (Mosques) (TN: Saudi Arabia), we are their worst
enemies and our presence in Yemen threatens their royalty's
existence, in addition to their abiding by the American wishes
for them to fight us, so they will pump huge funds into
recruiting the Yemeni tribes to kill us.

They will win over the swords of the majority, which will put
the Mujahidin force in Yemen under enemy fire and in a very
serious situation.

Miscellaneous Points:

1- Please give me the news about the condition of the sons of
our brother Shaykh Sa'id, Allah have mercy on his soul. (Tell
me) how he was martyred and how the enemy discovered his
location. I had been planning to mourn him and talk to the
nation about him; however, I did not get a confirmation of the
news from your side.

Please relay my regards and condolences to Shaykh Abu Muhammad,
and give me the news about his condition. For several months, I
have been sending messages to him, and Shaykh Sa'id told me that
he had not yet received a courier from him. It then became
noticeable that he has not been heard in the media in recent
times. I hope that the problem is something good, and I advise
that he get a companion (TN: bodyguard) from the Arab brothers.

2- I had mentioned in several previous messages to Shaykh Sa'id, Allah have mercy on his soul, the importance of the exit from Waziristan of the brother leaders, especially the ones that have media exposure. I stress this matter to you and that you choose distant locations to which to move them, away from aircraft photography and bombardment, while taking all security precautions. Also work on bringing out the brothers who have distinguished talents after they have been battle hardened, either by exposure to a big battle or by staying at the front for approximately one month.

3- It would be nice if you would send me the names of some who are qualified to be your deputy.

4- It would be nice if you would nominate a brother to be responsible for the general duty of the external work in all the regions. If it is not possible to nominate someone for this, then you take over that responsibility.

Knowing that Shaykh Yunis (Var: Younis) is the official responsible for external work in Africa and west Asia, please inform him of that.

I sent a message in the past to Shaykh Sa'id and to you about the importance of external work, I hope it has reached you. In any case, I have attached it to your messages.

5- It would be nice if you would nominate one of the qualified brothers to be responsible for a large operation in the US.

6- It would be nice if you would pick a number of the brothers, not to exceed ten, and send them to their countries individually, without any of them knowing the others, to study aviation. It would be better if they are from the Gulf states, as study there is at the government's expense. They have to be picked with the utmost care and with very accurate specifications, one of which is that they are willing to conduct suicide actions and are prepared to do daring, important, and precise missions that we may ask of them in the future.

So please pay top attention to this matter due to its utmost importance. Establish a mechanism to monitor and follow up on the brothers going to study aviation so that we reduce the chances of them slackening from conducting Jihad.

7- It would be nice if you would ask the brothers in all regions if they have a brother distinguished by his good manners, integrity, courage, and secretiveness, who can operate in the US. (He should be able to) live there, or it should be easy for him to travel there. They should tell us this without taking any action and also tell us whether or not he is willing to conduct a suicide operation.

8- It would be nice if you would send the message to the brothers in all regions, without exception, that whoever has an operation outside the region where he is located must coordinate with you. This is so there will no conflicts between operations or failures where the brothers could be exposed or captured.

9- It would be nice if you would send two messages - one to Brother Abu Mus'ab 'Abd-al-Wadud, and the other to Brother Abu Basir Nasir al-Wahishi - and ask them to put forward their best in cooperating with Shaykh Yunis in whatever he asks of them. Hint to the brothers in the Islamic Maghreb that they provide him with the financial support that he might need in the next six months, to the tune of approximately 200,000 euros.

These two messages are to be coordinated with Shaykh Yunis, and arrange a name for him that does not divulge his nationality. Arrange for a secure method of communications and coordination between them and Shaykh Yunis. Stress the utmost secrecy in work and restrict

the knowledge of Shaykh Yunis affair to the leadership in the regions in which he has to work with the brothers.

Also indicate to the brothers in Yemen when talking about coordination before conducting any work outside the peninsula, that working in the sea, even within the territorial waters of the peninsula, is to be considered external work that requires coordination with you.

Pay attention to explaining the importance of coordination, as well as the dangers of neglecting it, to all the brothers in all the regions. In general, it would be good to clarify the wisdom or the reason behind this in most of what we ask the brothers for, unless it exposes operational secrets.

10- Please write a report about Brother Shaykh Yunis at the first opportunity. Include (information on) his birth, education, social status, his best qualifications and experiences, as well as his manner and dealings with the Mujahidin and his relationship with them, the date of his becoming religiously adherent, and his joining Jihad. If it is not easy on you that the report be complete and comprehensive, it is alright to ask the brothers in the Islamic Maghreb for help after you send me whatever you already have.

11- In a previous message, we asked the security official, Brother Abu al-Wafa' and also his deputy for a report about the conditions on your side; however, we have not yet received them, it would be good if you would follow up on this matter.

12- Please report to me in detail about the financial situation on your side and about your vision and plans to improve it.

Your earmarking of the budget should set aside enough salaries for the brothers and the families for a year, regardless of the finical forecast for the coming days.

13- It would be good of you to provide us with detailed information about our brother Abu Bakr al-Baghdadi, who was appointed as a replacement for our brother Abu 'Umar al-Baghdadi, Allah have mercy on his soul, and his first lieutenant and deputy al-Nasir Lidin Allah, AKA Abu Sulayman. It would be better for you to ask several sources among our brothers there, whom you trust, about them so that the matter becomes clear to us. I also would like that you ask our brothers in Ansar al-Islam Organization where they stand on the new Emirs, Abu Bakr al-Baghdadi and his brothers.

I do remind you to put forward your maximum effort to achieve unity and resolve any conflicts between all of the Jihadi entities in Iraq.

In these efforts to achieve unity, there should be a special message directed to our brothers there that stresses the importance of unity and collectiveness and that they maintain a basic foundation of the religion, so it must get precedence over names, titles, or entities if they obstruct the achievement of that great duty.

14- I want to remind them of the importance of the people's first impression of who is addressing them, especially when he bears great responsibility. Since we carry the responsibility of a call that we want to deliver to the people, this takes care to find out what suits the people and the path from which you can reach them, deliver the faith to them, and convince them with it.

Part of this is to eliminate any strange appearance that will make them wonder and to adopt what they are used to, such as appearing in the media in true name, even if just a first name, and also appearing in Arab dress, as it is closer to the people than the dress of the people in these areas. (I also want to remind you that) people like short audio and video speeches and to disseminate what you can on the Internet.

These are just opinions and I am open to your opinion.

15- You should send (a message) to the brothers in all the regions saying that a minimum of two brothers should be sent for suicide operations; they should not send a single suicide brother. We have experienced this in many operations where the percentage of success was very low, due to the psychological effects that overcome the brother in such cases. The most recent of which was the operation in which our brothers targeted the British Ambassador in Yemen, and one of our brothers, Allah have mercy on his soul, conducted it. Regardless of the heroism of the brother and his steadfastness, the psychological factors that affect the person in such cases necessitate the presence of a companion that will support and bolster him.

Some people will say that some of the Prophet's companions conducted operations alone. This is a very different example: They were not suicide operations, and that is where the big difference lies.

16- I asked Shaykh Sa'id, Allah have mercy on his soul, to task brother Ilyas to prepare two groups - one in Pakistan and the other in the Bagram area of Afghanistan - with the mission of

anticipating and spotting the visits of Obama or Petraeus to Afghanistan or Pakistan to target the aircraft of either one of them. They are not to target visits by US Vice President Biden,

Secretary of Defense Gates, Joint Chiefs of Staff (Chairman) Mullen, or the Special Envoy to Pakistan and Afghanistan Holbrook. The groups will remain on the lookout for Obama or Petraeus. The reason for concentrating on them is that Obama is the head of infidelity and killing him automatically will make Biden take over the presidency for the remainder of the term, as it is the norm over there. Biden is totally unprepared for that post, which will lead the US into a crisis. As for Petraeus, he is the man of the hour in this last year of the war, and killing him would alter the war's path.

So please ask brother Ilyas to send to me the steps he has taken into that work.

17- It would be good if you coordinate with our brothers of the Pakistan and Afghanistan Taliban in regards to the external work, so that there is complete cooperation between us, and tell them that we started planning work inside America many years ago, and gained experience in that field, and we and they are brothers so we should not fall into the error that hurts the Muslims and benefits the enemy, due to lack of coordination between us. So, for example, the operation of brother Faysal Shahrazad, Allah release his imprisonment, was possible to avoid his capture and the errors that happened easily by one who had experience

in that area, so if a brother purchased the vehicle and then travelled from America to Waziristan before the operation, it would have made it difficult to capture the brother that fast, and based on that, draw their attention to the importance of cooperation among us and the possibility of the two sides adopting the operation reduces the possibility of these errors, after which the Americans commented that the Mujahidin have become unable to conduct a large operation that is well planned.

18- You have to keep in mind the possibility, though remote, that the journalists may be involuntarily monitored, in a way that we or they do not know about, either on ground or by satellite, especially Ahmad Zaydan, and it is possible that a tracking chip could be put into some of their personal effects before coming to the meeting place to conduct any business with them, or to conduct an interview with one of the brothers, and as you know Ahmad Zaydan has interviewed a number of the Taliban leaders and also with Shaykh Sa'id Allah, have mercy on his soul, and the Americans did not kill any of them or know his

location from surveying Ahmad Zaydan except that it may be a
matter that might attract their attention, as they identified
the house where the brothers Abu 'Umar al-Baghdadi and Abu
Hamzah al-Muhajir Allah, have mercy on their souls, were staying
in, across satellites, by monitoring some brothers who were
released from prison and who went to them after that.
And based on that, it would be prudent and a defeat to the enemy
to avoid any meetings with journalists.

And paying attention to aircraft and satellite surveillance
cannot be avoided with training on counter surveillance or
changing vehicles or conducting meetings with journalists in a
place away from the location of the Mujahidin, or bringing the
journalists by night so that they do not find the way and the
other procedures like that.

But you should use the secure means in contacting the media and
journalists which are using the mail.

So please inform our brothers of the Taliban in Pakistan and
Afghanistan about that for fear on their safety.

19- It is obvious that remaining on the same M.O. in
communications between us makes it weak from a security point of
view, as it makes it easy on the enemy to find out the method
that we use in communicating, so initially we have to employ the
following steps:

A- That the two brothers' couriers from my side and yours should
not meet to exchange messages except in a closed market or mall.
B- That the brother who is bringing the messages out of
Waziristan report to you after every trip to inform you if the
security situation is normal or elevated and changed, like
increased scrutiny, questioning, or photography, whether aimed
at specific persons or at all the passersby

or that the search elements have been replaced with elements
that are more alert and attentive.

20- Regarding our brother Abu Talhah al-Almani, Shaykh Sa'id
Allah, have mercy on his soul and accept him among the martyrs,
told me that the brother was on his way to a suicide operation,
so if he has executed the operation, we ask Allah to take him

among the martyrs and put him in paradise, and if his operation has been delayed and you see that he has a special talent that is lacking in the external work section, then it would be good to tell him that, and that if he postpones his desire to conduct a suicide operation that he write to me his vision of external work.

21- It would be nice to ask our brothers of Pakistan Taliban to deny their connection to the recent operation in Lahore against (phonetic: al-Briluwiyah). (TN: possibly referring to: (The News Online, 2 Jul) Lahore: Two back-to-back suicide bombings and a cracker blast killed at least 42 people and injured over 175 inside the crowded shrine of Data Gunj Bukhsh in Lahore on Thursday night.)

And also ask them about the truth in the news that talks about beginnings of negotiations and truce talks between them and the Pakistani government, and what is theirs and your opinion on that, knowing that much of what I have said about Yemen can be applied to the situation on your side.

22- It would be nice to inform us of the truth about what was mentioned of arresting our brother 'Azzam al-Amriki.

23- It would be nice if you can send us the book of Shaykh Abu Yahiya (Enemy Usage of Bystanders in Present Jihad), and his book (Studies in Decisive Unanimity) and it would be better that you provide us with each theological work published by you.

24-Enclosed is a message for Shaykh Yunis, please deliver it to him if he is on your side or if he has travelled, but there is a secure mode of delivering it; and if there is no secure method to deliver it, then please destroy it.

25- It would be nice to inform me of whom you have of the brothers who have no objection to accompanying me, and they are natives of this country and their situation is suitable for that matter. I asked Shaykh Sa'id Allah, have mercy on his soul, to tell me who he has and he mentioned some of the brothers, except that their situation, security wise, was not suitable to our conditions, and it seems that he had limited choices, so please continue the search and provide me with names and resumes of the brothers that you think are qualified. You know the features that they must have, like being tested until there is no doubt and that he is not wanted by the authorities for lawsuits or crimes, and that he owns an official ID card that is valid or can renew it if it has expired, and that he is able to rent houses and purchase requirements.

And that he be secretive even from his family and friends, and to be well-mannered, quiet, patient, aware, and knowledgeable of the enemy tricks, and able to stay away from his family if that becomes risky.

And that he is not from an area known to have many Mujahidin and that he does not inform you of his real name or the location where his family lives.

And please pay attention to that subject and inform me within two months, as the notice that my companion has given me is limited.

26- Brother 'Abdallah al-Halabi ('Abd-al-Latif) informed me that my family in Iran is on the way to come to the brothers in Pakistan or Waziristan, so as a precaution and to safeguard everyone, we have to assume that their arrival will be different than what we are used to when our brothers arrived who were coming from Iran in the past, for several reasons of which is that my son Ladin has been allowed by the Iranians to exit Iran and go to Syria as a show of good will to the rest of the detainees, and that they will be released, and he will be keen on informing the family that his brothers will be exiting soon from Iran. No doubt that such news will exchanged over the phone, while the phones are monitored, thus the information will be available to the adversaries. Accordingly, if the intelligence commander in the area is aware, he will think that they are headed to me and will survey them to find the place that they will settle in.

And regardless of the possibilities in monitoring them, we have to be on the cautious side and take the following steps to break the surveillance:

They will go to the tunnel between Kuhat and Peshawar, and arrange a meeting between them and another brother. The meeting must be precise in timing and it will be inside the tunnel, and they will change cars inside the tunnel, so they will ride in the car with the brother that they will meet instead of the car they were riding in, and the brothers who are going to drive the car must be instructed on the strict adherence to the timings.

After changing cars, the brother who is driving the car that is
subject to surveillance will drive to an area that is
unsuspected, and the people coming from Iran will go to
Peshawar, go to one of the closed markets, and change cars
again, then head to a safe place in Peshawar until we arrange
for them to come, with Allah's will.

The main thing about succeeding in avoiding surveillance is to
go to the tunnel and to move after getting out of it in overcast
weather, even if that would lead to them waiting for some time,
knowing that the Peshawar area and its surroundings is often
overcast.

They also should be warned on the importance of getting rid of
everything they received from Iran, like baggage or anything,
even as small as a needle, as there are eavesdropping chips that
are developed to be so small that they can even be put inside a
medical syringe; and since the Iranians are not to be trusted,
then it is possible to plant chips in some of the coming
people's belongings.

This process will be done only with Um Hamzah. As for my sons
'Uthman and Muhammad, it would be nice to arrange a safe place
for them in Pakistan.

And it is preferred that we communicate with the Iranians if
they release my family and do not release my daughter Fatimah,
as they promised that after the release of their prisoner with
us that they will release my family, which includes my daughter
Fatimah, and she is connected to her husband, and it is not fair
to separate women from their husbands, so she should be released
with her husband and his wife Um Hafs (TN: his other wife).

As for what concerns my son Hamzah, you had an opinion that the
arrival of the brothers to us be stopped due to the current
difficult situation, so after thinking it over, I sent to Shaykh
Sa'id Allah, have mercy on his soul, an opinion that he agreed
on with me, which is that we receive all the brothers arriving,
so that they remain as a lifeline and replenishment for what we
lose of talents and cadres, and to limit the time that they
remain in Pakistan to two or three weeks, whereby they are given
a quick training course that is heavy on ideology in addition to

weapons usage basics, and through that we get to identify the talents and abilities of the coming brothers, so that whom we find is distinguished and capable on call and recruitment. We will send him to his country to conduct specific missions like inciting for Jihad over the internet, collecting donations, or recruiting some distinguished brothers, and we will keep a limited number of them to develop their energy with you in Waziristan. As far as the rest of the youth, you send the ones that show toughness and discipline, and adherence to Islamic manners to the front with the Taliban, and you tell him that he will live like they live and those that you notice who do not have it, then you apologize to them and tell them that when the conditions improves, we will send a call out for him and his like to respond and join.

And based on that, there is an issue that I wanted to consult with you on, which is that my son Hamzah be sent to Qatar, where he studies religious sciences, and perform the duty of informing the nation and delivering some of what we ask him to deliver to the nation, spread the Jihad doctrine, and refute the wrong and the suspicions raised around Jihad within the freedoms allowed there.

There is no doubt that the nation needs to be approached and closely interacted with, and the knowledge of its realities and the approaches that need to be used in delivering the information, while the Mujahidin do not get that opportunity because of their distance and the apostates chasing them worldwide, which denies them the chance to find out the needs of the nation and to respond to these needs.

Except that Hamzah is one of the Mujahidin and he bears their thoughts and worries and at the same time he can interact with the nation, as it is difficult to indict him and to ask Qatar to extradite, him because he was imprisoned when he was a child, so there are no crimes outstanding against him.

27- In the past, I watched some of programs about me, the most recent of which was "al-Islamiyun" program (TN: the Islamists). In one of its episodes was a repeated matter that relied on incorrect information, and in some case inaccurate information, and as you know, if the person does not disclose his history then the media people and the historians will make up some history for him with whatever information is available to them, whether right or wrong.

So in order not have a mix-up on that subject, I thought that you could arrange with Ahmad Zaydan to prepare a program documented by us with real information, which I might send to you in a future message.

And part of the agreement is that the work would be joint between al-Jazeera and al-Sahab, so that they have the copyrights preserved to them.

In closing: We wait to hear your news and messages, and we pray to Allah to guide us all on what he likes and on what pleases him, and to get us together with his help and will, and cover us with his mercy, and praise Allah.

Your brother Zamrai.

--The attached is what Shaykh Yunis wrote:

Our status and the two pitfalls endangering us which we need to eradicate.

Presently we are experiencing the most favorable atmosphere in the history of the Islamic nation. There is a base of youths adopting our teachings and following our path without any efforts on our parts to teach them the faith. They are ready for anything posted for them on the "spider web" (TN: Internet), after validating the source.

It is the main principle of the empowerment strategy, as the saying goes; swords conquer and knowledge enlightens; and capturing the hearts comes before controlling nations. It makes the establishment of the religion easier; and the best example is the model of Fayruz al-Daylami, who accomplished his task without seeing the Prophet Muhammad. Also, because Fayruz knew in his heart what was needed to be done, and did it. Therefore, spreading our cause and simplifying its principles so it is easy to understand and clarify its applicability in answering all the mundane and religious questions. The model will speed up the conquering, the victory, and uncover any hidden surprises from the unexpected in our midst, which is a point realized by the enemy of God among the Christians. They have found a class of followers in our countries who are educated in their culture to work for them. It behooves us to facilitate the Jihad road before our ores in unimaginable, easy, and clean-to-achieve ways; and to protect against two dangerous pitfalls: one is security related and the other is inflexibility and narrow-mindedness, on which I will elaborate later.

Having the youth base represent the right soil for our cause, without having to publicize our activities. The leadership cadre here in Khurasan has been praised and trusted by everyone, and it is doing that on our behalf, allowing us freedom of movements and innovation in the methods, the ways of smuggling, and counterfeiting; and mastering these skills, will allow us to teach the art of mingling among the people executing our strikes and hiding without a trace.

Now the pitfalls:
1- Security pitfall: I will issue a small guideline, signed by the organization, for awareness and directions for anyone thinking about Jihad to prevent the brother from burning himself before burning the enemy. I will also add a suggestion to indicate they are preparing the stage for the coming nation, to

disguise our intentions from our enemy, leading him to thinking it is a dream attributable to the demise of our cadres and the adversity we are under. We will utilize the right individual at the right stage, either before or after the creation of the nation. The format of the guideline will be video, audio, written and translated to all languages available to us. It will save time in training and make any newcomer an arrow ready to fly.

2- We have to make our position unequivocally clear on the issue of inflexibility and narrow-mindedness; and must have concise, written instructions published for all of the awakening youths to know our stand. The benefits are undeniable on having a guideline to abide by, for ourselves as well as our friends, and to rid ourselves of the accusation of inflexibility and narrow-mindedness, and it will also broaden the horizons of our brethren. We are approaching a stage where narrow-mindedness is a killer, and ignorance of Shari'ah is damning. Lately, the term "the Salafist approach to Jihad" is spreading on the Internet, accusing individuals of not following the approach. It is a very dangerous situation, especially because it is attributed to us and the rise of new groups advocating for a stringent form of the faith.

The certainty in issues related to Jihad is mere guessing used to typify and classify people in a way that is not free from the hands and intervention of state security apparatus. It is a possibility that cannot be ruled out. This typifying (TN: religious stereotyping), boasting with titles, isolates and segregates us from the

nation. You have experienced it in Peshawar and have seen its outcome in Algeria. If this concept gains footing, it will put the individuals in a situation where they refrain from speaking the truth for the fear of typifying (TN: religious stereotyping). Therefore, it is a must to eliminate it while in its infancy, and expand peoples' horizons, guiding them gently to the truth. We are not monopolizing the Salafi way or any other doctrine, but we are members of the entire nation, reciting the words of its scholars on righteousness, and we do not hold any grudges or are unreachable by the followers of any dogma. We are all from one nation and we are all held by our words, and none but the ones descried in the Cow verse are left. The matter of the practical Jihad operations is vast, and the issues we are facing now are agreed upon by the prominent scholars of our nation.

We must avoid the stigma of being a one-dimensional sect, opposed to all others. We are Muslims following the teachings of Islam and we are not the owners of the Salafist way, and must avoid typifying (TN: religious stereotyping) each other. It is important to have a memorandum issued from Shaykh Abu-Yahya and Shaykh Mahmud clarifying the issues of penitence, atonement, and the virtue of patience; refraining from accusing and judging without being qualified to judge; in addition to expanding the awareness of the followers in the arenas of politics and Shari'ah, which I believe publishing a letter in the form of questions and answers well help greatly.

(TN: No signature, or date)

(TN: Blank)

Analysis: Letters from Abbottabad: Bin Ladin Sidelined?

Letters from Abbottabad: Bin Ladin Sidelined?

Nelly Lahoud
Stuart Caudill
Liam Collins
Gabriel Koehler-Derrick
Don Rassler
Muhammad al-`Ubaydi

HARMONY PROGRAM
THE COMBATING TERRORISM CENTER AT WEST POINT

www.ctc.usma.edu

3 May 2012

Foreword

The death of Usama bin Ladin one year ago understandably generated a significant amount of interest in the professionals who carried out the raid in Abbottabad, Pakistan, on the night of May 2nd. Lost in the focus on this single mission is the fact that United States Special Operations Forces (SOF) have conducted thousands of comparable missions in Afghanistan and Iraq since 2001. The success of "Neptune Spear" was the cumulative result of the experience, relentless focus and professionalism of a community that has been conducting these types of missions for over ten years.

A second feature of the raid and one much less apparent to the general public is that the professionals conducting this operation were trained to survey the site and collect any electronic media, papers, or pocket litter that might inform future operations. As discussed in the report, this process, known as F3EA (Find, Fix, Finish, Exploit and Analyze), has helped to revolutionize the fight against al-Qa'ida and created a cyclical operational process for combating networked actors. The end of the raid in Abbottabad was the beginning of a massive analytical effort as experts from across the Intelligence Community (IC) worked to exploit these captured documents, which in turn undoubtedly contributed to additional operations.

The Combating Terrorism Center, housed within the Department of Social Sciences at West Point, has long recognized that captured battlefield documents have enormous value to students of terrorism. Since 2005 the longstanding partnership between the CTC and our colleagues who manage the Harmony database has facilitated the release of hundreds of documents to the public, with the intention of advancing the study of terrorism and political violence. In its own small way, this report and the release of some documents from the Abbottabad compound to the public are simply a continuation of this partnership.

The CTC is proud to continue in this role by publishing these documents, and as with previous releases two cautions are worth highlighting. First and most importantly is that these documents likely represent only a fraction of the materials reportedly taken from the compound. If declassification of subsequent documents from Abbottabad or new caches of materials from other locations is forthcoming, this would inevitably necessitate additional analysis and reflection. Thus, the report that accompanies the documents must be understood as an effort to help reassess what we know about the group, but not as a definitive commentary on al-Qa'ida's evolution or the group's current status, and we should be extremely cautious of the notion that al-Qa'ida has been defeated. Rather, the problems presented by jihadism and violent extremism more broadly will continue to shift and mutate.

Second, as with all Harmony projects, analysis based on captured documents alone is fraught with risk. While they may offer unique insights, these are most valuable when contextualized with information drawn from other sources. It is our sincere hope that the initial commentary and the release of these documents will not be the last word on the subject but simply the opening foray into a much larger academic debate and discussion which will further our understanding of al-Qa`ida and terrorism more broadly.

The decision to release these documents to the CTC is an affirmation of the values of West Point and the Center's mission. It is my expectation that as long as the Center continues to focus on its core competencies — embracing the unique responsibility to prepare cadets to think critically about the challenges they will face during war and peace; producing academically rigorous and theoretically sound research; and leveraging its deep expertise to further the public's understanding of terrorism — it will continue as an enduring national resource for the study of terrorism.

Sincerely,

General (R) John P. Abizaid
Distinguished Chair, Combating Terrorism Center

Acknowledgements

While this report was authored by a small team of researchers at the CTC, we are conscious of the enormous debt of gratitude we owe to the "army" of supporters and institutions that helped make this project possible. We are indebted to Dr. Thomas Hegghammer who provided a masterful review and detailed critique of the draft in light of the documents. We are also grateful to colleagues and friends who provided internal reviews of the report: Lieutenant Colonel Jon Brickey, Brian Dodwell, Colonel Cindy Jebb, Colonel Mike Meese, Dr. Arie Perliger, Dr. Roland Rich, Major Todd Schultz and Rachel Yon. We are particularly thankful to Erich Marquardt who was peerless in his meticulous editing and proofing of the report.

Though self-evident, it is important to acknowledge that this project would not have been possible without the support of some larger institutional friends of the CTC. We are thankful to the office of the Director of National Intelligence for entrusting us with the analysis and release of these documents to the public for the first time. Thanks also to U.S. Special Operations Command (USSOCOM); to our colleagues who manage the HARMONY project; and to our friends at the Norwegian Defense Research Institute (FFI) for their support of the CTC and contributions to the study of terrorism.

Executive Summary

This report is a study of 17 declassified documents captured during the Abbottabad raid and released to the Combating Terrorism Center (CTC). They consist of electronic letters or draft letters, totaling 175 pages in the original Arabic and 197 pages in the English translation. The earliest is dated September 2006 and the latest April 2011. Some of the letters are incomplete and/or are missing their dates, and not all of the letters explicitly attribute their author(s) and/or indicate the addressee. In addition to Bin Ladin, the recognizable individuals who appear in the letters either as authors or as recipients are `Atiyyatullah and Abu Yahya al-Libi, both of whom are al-Qa`ida leaders; Adam Yahya Gadahn, the American al-Qa`ida spokesman and media advisor; Mukhtar Abu al-Zubayr, the leader of the Somali militant group Harakat al-Shabab al-Mujahidin; Abu Basir (Nasir al-Wuhayshi), the leader of the Yemen-based al-Qa`ida in the Arabian Peninsula (AQAP); and Hakimullah Mahsud, the leader of Tehrik-e-Taliban Pakistan (TTP). Given the small collection of documents released to the CTC, it is impossible to construct a coherent evolution of al-Qa`ida or its current state. "Letters from Abbottabad" is an initial exploration and contextualization of 17 documents that will be the grist for future academic debate and discussion.

In contrast to Bin Ladin's public statements that focused on the injustice of those he believed to be the "enemies" (a`da') of Muslims, namely corrupt "apostate" Muslim rulers and their Western "overseers," the focus of his private letters is Muslims' suffering at the hands of his jihadi "brothers" (ikhwa). He was at pains advising them to abort domestic attacks that cause Muslim civilian casualties and instead focus on the United States, "our desired goal." Bin Ladin's frustration with regional jihadi groups and his seeming inability to exercise control over their actions and public statements is the most compelling story to be told on the basis of the 17 declassified documents. The main points from each of the report's four sections are briefly summarized below.

Al-Qa`ida and Regional Jihadi Groups
Al-Qa`ida
- On the basis of these documents, the relationship between what has been labeled "al-Qa`ida Central" (AQC) under the leadership of Bin Ladin is not in sync on the operational level with its so-called "affiliates." Bin Ladin enjoyed little control over either groups affiliated with al-Qa`ida in name (e.g., AQAP or AQI/ISI) or so-called "fellow travelers" such as the TTP.
- The documents show that al-Qa`ida's relationship with its so-called "affiliates" is a contested one among the senior leaders, and three different positions exist

within al-Qa`ida on this subject. Some urge senior leaders to declare their distance, and even to dissociate themselves, from groups whose leaders do not consult with al-Qa`ida but act in its name. Others urge the opposite, believing that the inclusion of regional jihadi groups in the fold contributes to al-Qa`ida's growth and expansion. Bin Ladin represented a third position; he wanted to maintain communication, through his own pen or that of others in his circle, with "brothers" everywhere, to urge restraint and provide advice even if it fell on deaf ears, without granting them formal unity with al-Qa`ida.

The Affiliates

Rather than a source of strength, Bin Ladin was burdened by what he viewed as the incompetence of the "affiliates," including their lack of political acumen to win public support, their media campaigns and their poorly planned operations which resulted in the unnecessary deaths of thousands of Muslims.

- *Islamic State of Iraq/Al-Qa`ida in Iraq (ISI/AQI)*: The documents conclusively demonstrate that the failures of ISI/AQI weighed heavily on Bin Ladin, as he urged other groups not to repeat their mistakes. Adam Gadahn advised that al-Qa`ida should publicly dissociate itself from ISI/AQI.
- *Al-Qa`ida in the Arabian Peninsula (AQAP)*: While routinely described as "the most dangerous" al-Qa`ida affiliate, as of 2010-2011 Bin Ladin seemed to have spent more time worrying about this group than appreciating its contributions. In a strongly worded letter, the leader of AQAP, Nasir al-Wuhayshi, was directly warned against pursuing any expansionist plan, such as declaring an Islamic state in Yemen, and was urged to refocus his efforts on attacking the United States, not the Yemeni government or security forces.
- *Tehrik-e-Taliban Pakistan (TTP)*: The TTP seems to have come incredibly close to provoking a direct and public confrontation with al-Qa`ida's leadership. Its indiscriminate attacks against Muslims caused `Atiyyatullah and Abu Yahya al-Libi to write to TTP leader Hakimullah Mahsud to express their displeasure with the group's "ideology, methods and behavior." They also threatened to take public measures "unless we see from you serious and immediate practical and clear steps towards reforming [your ways] and dissociating yourself from these vile mistakes [that violate Islamic Law]."
- *Al-Shabab*: Bin Ladin appeared to have seen little practical value in formally recognizing the group's pledge of loyalty (*bay`a*). His motivations for withholding this recognition were largely pragmatic and reflected his concern over their poor governance and inflexible administration of *hudud* (deterrent penalties for certain crimes). He also wanted them to focus on "construction and

development" and feared that a formal merger with al-Qaʿida would prevent investment and foreign aid in Somalia.

- *Al-Qaʿida in the Islamic Maghreb (AQIM), the Taliban and Jaysh al-Islam*: While there is mention of these groups in the documents released to the CTC, these discussions are not substantive enough to inform an understanding of the relationship between al-Qaʿida's senior leaders and these groups.

Al-Qaʿida Ties to Iran and Pakistan?

While not extensive, the discussions of Iran and Pakistan in the documents suggest that al-Qaʿida's relations with both countries were fraught with difficulties.

- References to Iran show that the relationship is not one of alliance, but of indirect and unpleasant negotiations over the release of detained jihadis and their families, including members of Bin Ladin's family. The detention of prominent al-Qaʿida members seems to have sparked a campaign of threats, taking hostages and indirect negotiations between al-Qaʿida and Iran that have been drawn out for years and may still be ongoing.
- The discussion of Pakistan is scarce and inconclusive. Although references are made about "trusted Pakistani brothers," there are no explicit references to any institutional Pakistani support for al-Qaʿida or its operatives.

Bin Ladin's Plans

One of the 17 documents is a letter dated April 2011 authored by Bin Ladin in response to the "Arab Spring," which he considered to be a "formidable event" (*hadath haʾil*) in the modern history of Muslims. This letter reflected his intended strategy of responding to the new political landscape that was emerging in the Middle East and North Africa.

- In the Arab world, Bin Ladin wanted al-Qaʿida to focus its efforts on media outreach and "guidance." He believed that a media campaign should be launched to incite "people who have not yet revolted and exhort them to rebel against the rulers" (*khuruj ʿala al-hukkam*). But he also wanted to invest in guidance, "educating and warning Muslim people from those [who might tempt them to settle for] half solutions," such as engaging in the secular political process by forming political parties.
- In Afghanistan, Bin Ladin wanted jihadis to continue their fight against the United States. He believed that their efforts weakened the United States, enabling Muslims elsewhere to revolt against their rulers, no longer fearing that the United States would be in a powerful position to support these rulers.
- It is possible that Ayman al-Zawahiri is the author of one or more of the anonymous letters (see Appendix). Based on the 17 documents, ʿAtiyya was closest to Bin Ladin.

Introduction

"I plan to release a statement [announcing] that we are starting a new phase to correct [the mistakes] we made; in doing so, we shall reclaim, God willing, the trust of a large segment of those who lost their trust in the jihadis,"[1] wrote Usama bin Ladin in 2010. In contrast to his public statements that focused on the injustice of those he believed to be the "enemies" (*a`da'*) of Muslims, namely corrupt "apostate" Muslim rulers and their Western "overseers," the focus of Bin Ladin's private letters was Muslims' suffering at the hands of his jihadi "brothers" (*ikhwa*). He was at pains advising them to abort domestic attacks that caused Muslim civilian casualties and, instead, focus on the United States, "our desired goal." Bin Ladin's frustration with regional jihadi groups and his seeming inability to exercise control over their actions and public statements is the most compelling story to be told on the basis of the 17 declassified documents captured during the Abbottabad raid in May 2011.

This report is a study of these 17 documents, but it is by no means an exhaustive analysis of the information revealed in them. It consists of four sections. The first section describes the documents' format, the typical journey captured battlefield documents undergo before declassification, and the limitations imposed on assessing the state of al-Qa`ida today in light of these 17 documents alone. The second section argues that on the basis of these documents, the relationship between what has been dubbed "al-Qa`ida Central" (AQC) under the leadership of Bin Ladin is not in sync on the operational level with its so-called "affiliates." The third section discusses al-Qa`ida's relationship with Iran and Pakistan. With respect to Iran, the documents show that it is an antagonistic relationship, largely based on indirect and unpleasant negotiations over the release of detained jihadis and their families, including members of Bin Ladin's family. Relations with the Pakistani government are not discussed; the documents do not *explicitly* point to any institutional Pakistani support for Bin Ladin. The fourth section covers miscellaneous subjects raised in the documents that point to what the future might hold for al-Qa`ida, including Bin Ladin's response to the "Arab Spring" and how he planned to convert jihadi activities into missionary activities in the Middle East and North Africa, but not in Afghanistan, as well as the conspicuous distance of

---

[1] SOCOM-2012-0000019, 15. The pages of the documents received by the CTC are not all numbered in the original Arabic version. The English translation numbers the pages to correspond to the content of each page of the Arabic version. As a result, most Arabic pages take more than a single page when translated (except when the Arabic font is very large as with SOCOM-2012-0000016), so the reader will find that the page number of the Arabic version is included on a separate line in the text of the English translation. To avoid confusion, this report refers to the page number in the Arabic version so that the reader can easily find it in the English translation.

Ayman al-Zawahiri from Bin Ladin in the documents released to the Combating Terrorism Center (CTC) at West Point.

I- From Abbottabad to the CTC: The 17 Declassified Documents

It was reported that "thousands of items" were captured from Usama bin Ladin's compound during the Abbottabad raid.[2] To date, however, only 17 documents have been declassified and provided to the CTC, all of which are hereby released with the publication of this report.[3] They consist of electronic letters or draft letters, totaling 175 pages in the original Arabic and 197 pages in the English translation. They were written over several years. The earliest is dated September 2006 and the latest April 2011, a week before Bin Ladin's death. Some of the letters are incomplete and/or are missing their dates, and not all the letters explicitly attribute the author(s) and/or indicate the addressee. Given that they are all electronic documents presumably saved on thumb drives, memory cards or the hard drive of his computer, except for the letters addressed to Bin Ladin it cannot be ascertained that letters explicitly authored by him reached their intended destinations.

In addition to Bin Ladin,[4] the recognizable individuals who appear in the letters either as authors or as recipients of letters are Mahmud/`Atiyya[5] and Abu Yahya al-Libi,[6] both

---

[2] David Ignatius, "A Lion in Winter," *Washington Post*, 18 March 2012.

[3] The quality of the English translation provided to the CTC is not adequate throughout. When the translation was deemed inadequate, quotations cited in this report have either been amended or translated anew by Nelly Lahoud. Furthermore, the conversion of the dating of the letters from the Hijri to the Gregorian calendar is inaccurate in some places. The Appendix provides corrected dates to some of the letters, along with some pointers on how some letters relate to others.

[4] Usama bin Muhammad bin `Awad bin Ladin was born on 10 March 1957, in Riyadh, Saudi Arabia. He is the founder of Tandhim al-Qa`ida (al-Qa`ida Organization), which carried out the attacks on the World Trade Center and the Pentagon on 11 September 2001. The literature on Bin Ladin is extensive. For an informative account of his early life, see Jonathan Randal, *Osama: The Making of a Terrorist* (New York: Vintage, 2005). On 2 May 2011, President Barack Obama announced that Usama bin Ladin was killed in his compound in Abbottabad, Pakistan. For details, see "Remarks by the President on Osama Bin Laden," Office of the Press Secretary, 2 May 2011.

[5] He is also known by the alias Abu `Abd al-Rahman and `Atiyyatullah, and is one of the leading public faces of al-Qa`ida. His real name is Jamal Ibrahim Ishtiwi al-Misrati. He was born in 1970 in Misrata, Libya. `Atiyya pursued Islamic religious studies in Mauritania, then joined jihad in Algeria. He went to Afghanistan in the late 1990s and was killed in a drone strike in Pakistan on 22 August 2011. For details, see the biography Ayman al-Zawahiri provided in his eulogy for `Atiyya: "Risalat al-amal wa al-bishr li ahlina fi Misr," 8th episode, http://www.aljahad.com/vb/showthread.php?t=14008 (accessed 25 April 2012).

[6] Hasan Qa`id/Abu Yahya al-Libi is an al-Qa`ida leader and ideologue, as well as a former member of the Libyan Islamic Fighting Group. Al-Libi is believed to have traveled to Afghanistan in the early 1990s, then to Mauritania to study Islamic religious sciences before returning to Afghanistan. He was captured a

of whom are al-Qa'ida leaders; Adam Yahya Gadahn, the American al-Qa'ida spokesman and media advisor;[7] Mukhtar Abu al-Zubayr,[8] the leader of the Somali militant group Harakat al-Shabab al-Mujahidin — whose 2009 pledge of allegiance to al-Qa'ida was recognized by Ayman al-Zawahiri in February 2012;[9] Abu Basir (Nasir al-Wuhayshi), the leader of the Yemen-based al-Qa'ida in the Arabian Peninsula (AQAP);[10] and Hakimullah Mahsud, the leader of Tehrik-e-Taliban Pakistan (TTP).[11]

Before delving into an analysis of the documents, it is critical to address the academic limitations of studying declassified captured battlefield documents. Such a study is fraught with risks, not least because the academic community is not involved in the process of declassification and is therefore unaware of the larger classified corpus of documents. The academic community's access to captured battlefield documents is at the end of a journey that often starts with Special Operations Forces (SOF)[12] capturing

---

year after 9/11 by Pakistani authorities and handed to U.S. authorities. He was sent to Bagram prison from where he and several other high-profile captives escaped on the night of 10 July 2005. For details, see Michael Moss and Souad Mekhennet, "Rising Leader for Next Phase of Al Qaeda's War," *New York Times*, 4 April 2008.

[7] Adam Gadahn was born on 1 September 1978, in California. Gadahn converted to Islam in 1995 and subsequently traveled to Pakistan to study. Gadahn made his first public appearance as an al-Qa'ida member in a videotape in 2004 under the kunya 'Azzam al-Amriki. For details, see John M. Broder, "American Being Sought by the FBI Found his Place in Islam, Relatives Say," *New York Times*, 28 May 2004.

[8] His name is Ahmed Abdi Godane. For details, see "Who are Somalia's Shabaab?" BBC, 23 February 2012.

[9] Nelly Lahoud, "The Merger of Al-Shabab and Qa'idat al-Jihad," *CTC Sentinel* 5, no. 2 (2012).

[10] Nasir 'Abd al-Karim al-Wuhayshi is a Yemeni citizen and the leader of al-Qa'ida in the Arabian Peninsula. Al-Wuhayshi served as a private secretary to Usama bin Ladin for years in Afghanistan but left in 2001 and was soon arrested by Iranian authorities. Two years later, they transferred him to Yemen where he was imprisoned without charges. In February 2006, Nasir al-Wuhayshi was one of 23 Yemeni captives who escaped from custody from a maximum security prison in Sana'a and was acknowledged as the group's leader shortly thereafter. For details, see Gabriel Koehler-Derrick, ed., "A False Foundation? AQAP, Tribes, and Ungoverned Spaces in Yemen," *Combating Terrorism Center at West Point* (2011), 35, fn 82, 36.

[11] Zulfiqar Mahsud was born in 1981. He was elevated to the position of *amir* (leader) of Tehrik-e-Taliban Pakistan (TTP) after its previous leader, Baitullah Mahsud, was killed in a drone strike in August 2009. See "Profile: Hakimullah Mahsud," BBC, 3 May 2010.

[12] SOF is often confused with Special Forces (SF). The term Special Forces or SF applies to only a small subset of Special Operations Forces which consist of U.S. Army Green Berets. Special Operations Forces consist of forces from all four services including (1) Special Forces (SF), Ranger, Army Special Operations aviation, Special Operations MISO, and Special Operations Civil Affairs units from the Army; (2) SEAL, SEAL delivery vehicle, and special boat teams from the Navy; (3) Special Operations flying units (includes unmanned aircraft systems), special tactics elements (includes combat control, pararescue, weather, and select tactical air control party units), and aviation FID units from the U.S. Air Force; and (4)

them. The captured data is then passed to the intelligence community for (further) exploitation before it is declassified, in part or in its entirety, and released to the public or to an academic center such as the CTC to contextualize before its public release.

What then is the path that characterizes the journey of declassified captured battlefield documents?

Underlying the mystique that Navy SEALs and other SOF hold in the public's common perception is their superior ability to conduct "direct action" (DA) raids like the one carried out in Abbottabad to capture or kill Usama bin Ladin. In reality, direct action is only one of eleven core activities or tasks conducted by SOF. [13] Since 9/11, one of their major core activities has been counterterrorism operations, which include conducting sensitive site exploitation (SSE). An SSE is similar to gathering evidence during a domestic criminal investigation, although the period allowed for military forces to gather information is much shorter, consisting of minutes as opposed to hours, days or weeks. Much like a criminal investigation where the information is used to build a case against a suspect, the information gathered from a military target is analyzed for tactical, operational and strategic purposes. For example, the information may provide details on an impending attack, or specifics about the larger network that provides new leads or insight into the individual's or the organization's strategic plans.

The military in general and SOF in particular have always recognized the importance of capturing information about the enemy on the battlefield. Indeed, starting from the first operations in Afghanistan in October 2001, SOF built an SSE into every operation it carried out, seizing countless computers, phones, photographs, paper documents and other electronic media. When the SEALs conducted Operation Neptune Spear on 2 May 2011,[14] capturing or killing Bin Ladin was only one of their objectives; another main objective was the SSE of the compound to gather everything that could be exploited from an intelligence perspective.

The SSE often yields unique and valuable information. Sometimes the information can be exploited immediately, but often it will take additional time and capabilities in order

---

Marine Special Operations battalions. See Joint Publication 3-05, Special Operations, 18 April 2011, II-1, II-2.

[13] SOF Core Activities or Tasks include the following: direct action (DA), special reconnaissance (SR), counter-proliferation of weapons of mass destruction (CP of WMD), counterterrorism (CT), unconventional warfare (UW), foreign internal defense (FID), security force assistance (SFA), counterinsurgency (COIN), information operations (IO), military information support operations (MISO), civil affairs operations (CAO). See Joint Publication 3-05, Special Operations, May 5, 2011, II-5, II-19.

[14] It should be noted that the Abbottabad raid fell on May 1 in the United States and May 2 in Pakistan.

for it to be properly exploited. The collected data is then shared with the broader intelligence community for further analysis. Typically, the government agency that acquires the data effectively "owns" it and determines its classification, as well as controls its distribution and declassification. The standard procedure is to classify the data in the immediate phase following the SOF operation. From the intelligence community's perspective, many reasons justify immediate classification, including the possibility that its public release could cause other elements of the terrorist network to move or go into hiding, making it harder to locate and capture them. In the case of the Abbottabad raid, it is possible that declassification of additional documents or items is forthcoming. It is also possible that the remaining items are of no value to the public (e.g., books, movies, or grocery lists), and the intelligence agency that owns them made the decision that declassifying such items did not warrant the cost involved, or the time and energy of its staff.

It is only after the intelligence community has exhausted the data for tactical and strategic purposes that it is declassified. Therefore, when an academic center, such as the CTC, is provided declassified documents to study and analyze before releasing them to the public, its researchers have no part in the selection of documents to be declassified and are privy only to declassified documents. Like with any research project, a researcher does not always have at their disposal all the materials to study a given topic and must therefore extrapolate that which is *unknown* from that which is *known*. In some cases, such extrapolations may lead to firm conclusions. In other cases, however, conclusions reached on the basis of extrapolations — even when these are based on well-founded research — may need revision when previously unavailable materials are declassified. When scholars pursue a research topic that involves materials subject to classification by the government, they face what one may term the "(de)classification challenge." They have no choice but to wait for materials to be declassified, however frustrating the waiting period may be. The process of declassifying materials could occur all at once or in different stages; if it is the latter, it is even harder to reach firm or even plausible conclusions.

Whereas in the eyes of the SOF community the Abbottabad raid was successfully completed, the academic community studying al-Qa'ida has much work ahead before an authoritative study of al-Qa'ida can be expected. If the mission of the SEALs met all of its objectives – find, fix, finish, exploit, and analyze (F3EA)[15] – the academic community is still in the *find* stage of the necessary documents to accomplish its task.

---

[15] Michael T. Flynn, Rich Juergens and Thomas L. Cantrell, "Employing ISR: SOF Best Practices," *Joint Forces Quarterly*, no. 50 (2008), 56-61. F3EA describes the processes of *finding* a particular individual; *fixing*

From an academic perspective, in view of the thin volume of the documents and their spread over a period of six years, there is little hope of writing a coherent study of the *evolution* of al-Qa`ida since 2006 based exclusively on these letters. As it stands, analyzing the state of al-Qa`ida on the basis of the documents is like commenting on the tailoring of a jacket when only a sleeve is available. Although a sleeve cannot substitute for the remaining parts of the jacket, it can still offer important features about the overall jacket: it can indicate its color, its textile design, and most likely the quality of its stitches and lining.

II- Al-Qa`ida and Regional Jihadi Groups

To appreciate the new insights gained from the documents, it is helpful to place them in the context of what is previously known about al-Qa`ida as an organization through the lens of publicly available documents meant to be internal to the organization.[16] The founders of al-Qa`ida envisaged their organization as an international entity, serving as a "wellspring for expertise in military training and [the art of] fighting."[17] Al-Qa`ida's "by-laws" are explicit that this "wellspring of expertise" would also serve to enable other jihadi groups around the world, stating that "our relationship with sincere jihadi groups and movements is premised on cooperation [to advance] righteousness and piety."[18] In this collaborative spirit, when al-Qa`ida was operating in the open in the late 1980s and throughout the 1990s, it made its guesthouses (*madafat*) and its training camps in Pakistan and Afghanistan available to anyone who sought military training (*i`dad*) before engaging in fighting (*jihad*) either in Afghanistan or other locations. This, however, did not mean that those who received training in al-Qa`ida's camps

---

the precise location of the enemy target; *finishing* the target by either capturing or killing it; *exploiting* data or information on target or at a later date; and finally *analyze* the data, in combination with existing intelligence to identify new lines of operation and new starting points to continue the cycle.

[16] Following the U.S.-led invasion of Afghanistan in 2001, materials were captured on the battlefield and have since been stored in the Department of Defense's Harmony database. While they are illuminating, analyzing them is fraught with certain risks since it is difficult to assess how representative they are of the larger corpus of materials that exist.

[17] AFGP-2002-000078, page one of the Arabic document, but the document starts on page nine.

[18] AFGP-2002-600048, 4-5. Translation amended. It is worth noting that the by-laws state different types of relationships that al-Qa`ida can or cannot have: "our relationship with Islamic non-jihadi groups is premised upon love, friendship and advice; we acknowledge their good deeds but, if need be, make evident to them what we believe to be their shortcomings." Also see: "our position with respect to the idols, secular and national parties and their ilk is to dissociate from them and to declare our ongoing enmity against their unbelief until they believe in nothing but God. We shall not [compromise] with them on the basis of half-solutions, or [agree] to a dialogue with them or even flatter them [to further our agenda]."

automatically became members of the group;[19] by the same token, when al-Qa'ida assisted other jihadi groups it did not make its collaboration conditional on the group joining al-Qa'ida. In practical terms, the collaboration meant that al-Qa'ida and another jihadi group could come to a mutual agreement to carry out a joint operation or another militant activity together, yet the same jihadi group maintained its own autonomy, including its ideology (*fikr*) and activities.[20] The relationship between Indonesia's Jema'a Islamiyya (JI) and al-Qa'ida typifies this dynamic. In the words of a JI member who personally liaised with al-Qa'ida, the dynamic is like that of "a business affiliate, we can ask them (i.e., al-Qa'ida) for an opinion but they have no authority over us. We are free. We have our own funds, our own men. We are independent, like Australia and the U.S. But when it comes to an operation we can join together."[21]

Despite its collaboration with various jihadi groups around the world, al-Qa'ida did not seek to formalize these relationships into a unified command under its umbrella. Indeed, members of al-Qa'ida see themselves as part of a distinct entity that is separate from and even superior to other jihadi groups.[22] It was only when al-Qa'ida lost its sanctuary following the U.S.-led invasion of Afghanistan in 2001 that a trend of regional jihadi groups pledging allegiance to al-Qa'ida or acting in its name emerged. Paradoxically, this may have been due to the fame that the 9/11 attacks generated in the jihadi world and at the same time al-Qa'ida's inability to be in control of its organization after it lost its sanctuary. More precisely, it was in 2003 that the branding al-Qa'ida took off when Saudi militants adopted the name "al-Qa'ida on the Arabian Peninsula" (QAP).[23] In 2004, Abu Mus'ab al-Zarqawi's Jama'at al-Tawhid wa-al-Jihad group pledged allegiance to al-Qa'ida, and Usama bin Ladin publicly acknowledged the group as "al-Qa'ida in Mesopotamia," or al-Qa'ida in Iraq (AQI). Al-Zarqawi's group was the only regional group that Bin Ladin formally admitted into al-Qa'ida; others were later announced publicly by Ayman al-Zawahiri.[24]

---

[19] Fadil Harun, *al-Harb 'ala al-Islam: Qissat Fadil Harun* 1, 71. On the dynamics of collaboration but not union between al-Qa'ida and other jihadi groups, see Lahoud's forthcoming report that examines Harun's autobiography.

[20] Fadil Harun, *al-Harb 'ala al-Islam* 2, 426.

[21] Quinton Temby, "Informal Networks – Unraveling Al-Qaeda's Southeast Asia Alliances," IHS Defense, Security and Risk Consulting, March 2012. Nelly Lahoud is grateful to Quinton Temby for making his research available to her prior to its publication.

[22] Fadil Harun, *al-Harb 'ala al-Islam* 1, 9.

[23] Thomas Hegghammer, *Jihad in Saudi Arabia: Violence and Pan-Islamism since 1979* (Cambridge: Cambridge University Press, 2010), 37.

[24] In 2012, Ayman al-Zawahiri announced al-Qa'ida's merger with al-Shabab. See Ayman al-Zawahiri, "Bushra Sarra" (Glad Tidings), http://as-ansar.com/vb/showthread.php?t=55735 (accessed 26 April 2012). In November 2007, al-Zawahiri and Abu al-Layth al-Libi announced al-Qa'ida's merger with the Libyan

The proliferation of regional jihadi groups affiliating themselves with al-Qaʻida and the continued existence of core al-Qaʻida leaders believed to be based in Pakistan and/or Afghanistan led to the perception that al-Qaʻida was expanding. It was assumed that al-Qaʻida was able to rebuild across Pakistan's northwest frontier following the losses it suffered in the immediate aftermath of the U.S.-led military campaign in Afghanistan in 2001. Rejuvenated, al-Qaʻida is believed to have been able to "act as an organization,"[25] and the intelligence community labeled this revived entity "al-Qaʻida Central" (AQC) – both in reference to the geographical presence of the core senior leaders who were said to report to Bin Ladin to seek his approval for major decisions,[26] and also to indicate that there is at least a symbiotic relationship between "AQC" and regional jihadi groups, dubbed as AQC's "affiliates." According to this argument, AQC "gives strategic guidance to its regional affiliates" and it is assumed that the affiliates act largely in compliance with AQC's directives.[27]

The Construction of an "Al-Qaʻida Central"

The documents reveal a different story about the relationship between AQC and the affiliates, and about Bin Ladin's role in global jihadi activities. The documents show that this relationship is a contested one among senior leaders, and three different positions exist within al-Qaʻida on this subject. Adam Gadahn's letter to an unknown "shaykh" represented those who want to remain faithful to the principles for which they believe al-Qaʻida stands, and urged senior leaders to declare their distance or dissociate themselves from groups whose leaders do not consult with al-Qaʻida yet have the chutzpa to act in its name. Others, represented by an anonymous letter, urge the opposite, believing that the inclusion of regional jihadi groups in the fold contributes to al-Qaʻida's growth and expansion. Bin Ladin represented a third position, as he wanted to maintain communication, through his own pen or that of his inner circle, with

---

Islamic Fighting Group. See "Wahdat al-Saff," http://www.paldf.net/forum/showthread.php?t=185737 (accessed 26 April 2012). In May 2006, al-Zawahiri and Muhammad Khalil al-Hakaymah announced al-Qaʻida's merger with the Egyptian Islamic Group, "Communiqué from Those Adhering to the Covenant in the Egyptian Islamic Group," http://al-qimmah.net/showthread.php?t=6224&langid=2 (accessed 26 April 2012). In September 2006, al-Zawahiri announced al-Qaʻida's merger with the Salafist Group for Preaching and Combat (GSPC). See "Qadaya Sakhinah ma' al-Sheikh Ayman al-Zawahiri," http://www.tawhed.ws/r?i=efaperre (accessed 26 April 2012).
[25] Craig Whitlock, 'The New al-Qaeda Central," *Washington Post*, 9 September 2007. Whitlock based his argument on interviews he had with senior U.S. intelligence officials.
[26] Ibid.
[27] Eric Schmitt, "Jet Plot Shows Growing Ability of Qaeda Affiliates," *New York Times*, 31 December 2009. Schmitt based his article on interviews with U.S. counterterrorism officials.

"brothers" everywhere, to urge restraint and provide advice, without granting them formal unity with al-Qa'ida.

The documents show that some of the affiliates sought Bin Ladin's blessing on symbolic matters, such as declaring an Islamic state, and wanted a formal union to acquire the al-Qa'ida brand. On the operational front, however, the affiliates either did not consult with Bin Ladin or were not prepared to follow his directives. Therefore, the framing of an "AQC" as an organization in control of regional "affiliates" reflects a conceptual construction by outsiders rather than the messy reality of insiders. Judging by the letters, a relationship, at least via correspondence, clearly existed between Bin Ladin and regional jihadi leaders. But it is in the second half of 2010,[28] in a long and detailed letter addressed to 'Atiyya, that Bin Ladin, alarmed by the "increased mistakes" committed by the "brothers" who are spread over "many regions,"[29] sought to bring regional jihadi groups in line with al-Qa'ida's vision and code of conduct. The reader should note that when Bin Ladin used terms such as "brothers" (al-ikhwa) or "we," he was not always referring to members of al-Qa'ida. Except for the "apostates" (murtaddun), by which he meant Muslims who act as the West's agents (wukala') against the interests of the umma (global community of Muslims),[30] all Muslims were considered to be "we" in his eyes.[31] In the same spirit of unity, all jihadis were "brothers" in Bin Ladin's parlance — including those whose actions he chastised (e.g., TTP, AQAP),[32] and those whose request for formal unity with al-Qa'ida he denied (e.g., al-Shabab).[33]

---

[28] SOCOM-2012-0000019. The content of the letter makes it evident that it is authored by Bin Ladin. The letter, however, is not dated, but the author referred to a statement released by Sa'id al-Shihri concerning the arrest of Hayla al-Qasir in Saudi Arabia, who was accused of collecting money for the jihadis. The author also referred to the following report by the satellite channel al-'Arabiyya, which is dated 4 July 2010: "'Nisa' al-Qa'ida," al-'Arabiyya, http://www.alarabiya.net/articles/2010/06/04/110439.html (accessed 26 April 2012). Therefore, the letter must have been composed after 4 July 2010 but before 21 October 2010 because parts of SOCOM-2012-0000015 (which is dated 21 October 2010) follow up on issues raised in SOCOM-2012-0000019.

[29] SOCOM-2012-0000019, 3.

[30] See SOCOM-2012-0000016, 16, for an explanation of the connotation associated with the term "agents."

[31] In Islam, the spirit of unity among Muslims is an important tenet of the faith. That is why it is common for Muslims to highlight that believers are brothers in religion (cf. Q. 49:10). Thus, Bin Ladin's use of "brothers" is in reference to being brothers in religion, but not necessarily "brothers"/members in the same organization.

[32] See section below on the "Affiliates."

[33] SOCOM-2012-0000005, and discussion of al-Shabab below.

In 2010, Bin Ladin asked `Atiyya to prepare a memorandum of understanding (*mudhakkira*) that would require regional jihadi groups to consult with AQC before they act.[34] It is ironic that Bin Ladin deemed it fitting to appropriate the expression "AQC" from the media to clarify the plan he sought to implement. "This expression [AQC]," he wrote to `Atiyya, "is a technical term (*istilah*) used in the media to distinguish between al-Qa`ida in Afghanistan and Pakistan and al-Qa`ida in the rest of the regions (*aqalim*). I do not object to using it initially to clarify the objective [of the centralization endeavor]."[35]

Far from being in control of the operational side of regional jihadi groups, the tone in several letters authored by Bin Ladin makes it clear that he was struggling to exercise even a minimal influence over them. It is further evident that although he did not consider publicly dissociating (*tabarru' min*) himself and al-Qa`ida from the actions of regional groups, as Adam Gadahn strongly urged the senior leadership to do,[36] Bin Ladin largely disapproved of their conduct. High on his list of concerns was their flexible understanding of *tatarrus*, which resulted in the unnecessary deaths of Muslim civilians.[37] *Tatarrus* refers to special circumstances when it is permissible, from an Islamic law of war perspective, for a military commander to attack enemy territory, even if the attack may result in the deaths of non-combatants, including Muslim women and children.[38] In modern political parlance, it is comparable to civilians dying in war as collateral damage. Bin Ladin was concerned that regional jihadi groups had expanded the meaning of a classical legal concept meant to be applied in rare circumstances and turned it from an exception into the norm. As a result, the jihadis, he worried, have lost considerable sympathy from the Muslim public; this loss was compounded when "the mistakes of the jihadis were exploited by the enemy, [further] distorting the image of the jihadis in the eyes of the *umma's* general public and separating them from their popular bases."[39]

---

[34] SOCOM-2012-0000019, 9.

[35] Ibid., 17. Linguistically, the Arabic expression Bin Ladin uses for AQC is rather sloppy. He uses "al-Qa`ida fi al-markaz." A more appropriate designation would be 'Tanzim al-Qa`ida al-Markazi," or "Qiyadat al-Qa`ida al-Markaziyya."

[36] SOCOM-2012-0000004.

[37] SOCOM-2012-0000019, 4.

[38] See, for example, the discussion in Shaybani's Siyar in Majid Khadduri, *The Islamic Law of Nations: Shaybani's Siyar* (Baltimore: The Johns Hopkins Press, 1966), 101-102. The term *tatarrus* is not used in this classical text, but the context of the legal discussion is the same.

[39] SOCOM-2012-0000019, 4.

In practical terms, Bin Ladin wanted the memorandum to include broad guidelines concerning both the global military activities of the jihadis and their media releases. The two, he believed, should go hand in hand, so that "we do not violate our words with some of our practices."[40] The memorandum should then be sent to the regional leaders,[41] requesting their responses,[42] and ultimately demanding their "formal commitment" (*iltizam*).[43] As for the military activities, the memorandum should stipulate that every regional *amir* (leader) should take all necessary measures to maintain control and discipline over the military activities of his group and avoid a flexible approach to the question of *tatarrus*.[44] In the event that mistakes involuntarily occur and non-combatants die as a result, apologies and explanations should follow, even if those fallen are sinners (*fussaq*). Should the regional leaders fail to apologize, "it would be necessary for us [presumably AQC] to take responsibility [for their errors] and apologize for what happened."[45]

As for media releases, Bin Ladin wanted the memorandum to include a commitment to centralize all jihadi media releases. The importance of having a sophisticated and coherent media strategy was critical for Bin Ladin, believing it to be "a principal element of the battle."[46] In a different letter, he (and possibly `Atiyya) stressed that winning "the media occupies the greater portion of the battle today," wittily adding that "the satellite channels today are worse than the satiric poets (*shu`ara' al-hija'*) of the pre-Islamic era."[47] The poetic genre of *hija'* to which he is referring had a powerful

---

[40] Ibid., 15.
[41] Ibid., 9.
[42] Ibid., 15.
[43] Ibid., 14.
[44] Ibid., 9.
[45] Ibid., 10.
[46] SOCOM-2012-0000015, 5.
[47] SOCOM-2012-0000016, 18. This letter may not have been authored by Bin Ladin. It may be helpful to understand it in the context of the following: SOCOM-2012-0000015, authored by Bin Ladin, noted on page 5 that he is enclosing a file consisting of parts of a letter that he would like `Atiyya to edit for the purpose of sending to Abu Basir (Nasir al-Wuhayshi), the leader of AQAP. He indicated that `Atiyya is better placed than him to draft it because he knows the "brothers" there in Yemen. He also asked him to share with him the final format of the letter. SOCOM-2012-0000017 consists of many paragraphs and notes that do not form an internally coherent essay/letter. Some of these are identical to paragraphs included in Letter 13. It is therefore possible that SOCOM-2012-0000017 was the draft that Bin Ladin enclosed to `Atiyya; in turn, `Atiyya used parts of SOCOM-2012-0000017 and transformed them into a coherent letter to Abu Basir, and this coherent letter is SOCOM-2012-0000016 – which is not signed – to share with Bin Ladin before sending. It is not clear whether Bin Ladin wanted `Atiyya to sign it in his or Bin Ladin's name. The line on "hija" is not included in SOCOM-2012-0000017; if it is `Atiyya who edited it, then this would be his colorful language, not Bin Ladin's.

resonance in that distant era, and Arabs today understand too well the connotations it imparts. In the words of Pellat, the purpose of *hija'* "was to stigmatize the failings that were the antithesis of the qualities glorified."[48]

Bin Ladin explained to `Atiyya that "we are in need of sincere internal advice and a constructive critical evaluation of all our politics and [media] releases be they from AQC or from regional groups." He advised that two "competent brothers," internal to the organization, should devote all their energy to this task and also seek help externally to find a trusted and learned person to assist in "correcting and developing" our politics.[49] Bin Ladin was not alone in being concerned about the mediocre state of jihadi media. Adam Gadahn was highly critical of the inadequate level, even vulgarity, he found to be characteristic of jihadi media. In a letter composed in early 2011 and forwarded to Bin Ladin,[50] Gadahn wrote about jihadi forums with utter disdain, believing them to be "repulsive to most Muslims" and a liability to al-Qa`ida. He argued that most of their participants are characterized by religious fanaticism and biases, and therefore "distort to some extent the image of al-Qa`ida."[51]

Beyond centralizing jihadi releases, Bin Ladin was keen to create a credible jihadi media so that it becomes a reference point for mainstream Muslims interested in learning about jihad and jihadis. It bothered him that he watched a television program on al-Jazeera, *al-Islamiyyun*, which ran an episode littered with factual errors about him.[52] Although Bin Ladin did not generally come across as egotistical, in this instance it is clear that he worried about his legacy. "He who does not make known his own history

---

[48] Ch. Pellat, "Hidja'," *Encyclopedia of Islam,* second edition. There is also a poetic genre for the purpose of glorification, the genre of *"madh."*

[49] SOCOM-2012-0000019, 15.

[50] SOCOM-2012-0000004. This letter does not explicitly indicate who the author is or to whom it is addressed. Since the author remarked that the American television channel ABC broadcast a part of a statement he gave on the fourth anniversary of 9/11, this suggests that it was authored by Adam Gadahn who did indeed release a statement then, part of which was broadcast on ABC. The content suggests that it was not addressed to Bin Ladin since Gadahn refers to him in the third person. It is also not dated, but it must have been authored either in January 2011 or soon thereafter, since the author referred to the resignation of Keith Olbermann from MSNBC on 21 January 2011. The letter is in essence responding to many of the requests/queries that Bin Ladin made in SOCOM-2012-0000015, particularly those concerning a media strategy for the ten year anniversary of 9/11. It is likely that `Atiyya shared SOCOM-2012-0000015 with Gadahn, and SOCOM-2012-0000004 basically addressed the questions in SOCOM-2012-0000015.

[51] SOCOM-2012-0000004, 4.

[52] Bin Ladin is referring to a program on *al-Jazeera*. The specific episode to which he is referring is entitled "Man huwa Bin Ladin" (Who is Bin Ladin). It may be viewed at http://www.youtube.com/watch?v=0Yd2NPKuJJA (accessed 30 April 2012).

[to the world]," he wrote to `Atiyya, "[runs the risk that] some in the media and among historians will construct a history for him, using whatever information they have, regardless of whether their information is accurate or not."[53]

Bin Ladin clearly sought to centralize global jihadi activities so that AQC could oversee the affairs of regional groups and, if needed, veto certain decisions. It is possible that he wanted to make the most out of a bad, perhaps even doomed situation that al-Qa`ida was confronting after almost ten years of war. Indeed, the letter in which he proposed a blueprint for centralization is one of two letters that stand out for their reflective tone.[54] Not only is it the longest, consisting of 44 pages, but also because Bin Ladin comes across as someone taking stock of world events since the 9/11 attacks, burdened by the plethora of mistakes committed by regional jihadi groups, and eager to engage in a serious "assessment of jihadi activities" (*taqyim al-`amal al-jihadi*) as well as ways to ensure its sound "development/evolution" (*tatwir*).[55]

It is also possible that Bin Ladin may have had other strategic considerations in mind, namely to find an alternative framework for mounting operations from outside Afghanistan and Pakistan. That is because the year 2010, during which he put these reflections in writing, witnessed the deaths of numerous senior al-Qa`ida leaders in Afghanistan and Pakistan. The same letter in which Bin Ladin proposed centralization was also a letter of condolences to `Atiyya whom he notified of several leadership appointments, including his own as the successor of Mustafa Abu'l-Yazid.[56] Abu'l-Yazid had served as the operational leader of al-Qa`ida in Afghanistan,[57] and had recently been killed in May 2010.[58]

This must have been a particularly tough period for al-Qa`ida because another letter that Bin Ladin wrote to `Atiyya shortly after also started with lines of condolences, indicating additional losses.[59] Thus, the losses al-Qa`ida suffered in 2010 in Waziristan and the poor conduct of regional jihadi groups compelled Bin Ladin to reassess existing

---

[53] SOCOM-2012-0000019, 44.

[54] The other letter is SOCOM-2012-0000010 in response to the Arab Spring, likely the last one he wrote.

[55] SOCOM-2012-0000019, 3.

[56] SOCOM-2012-0000019, 1-2.

[57] He was announced as leader of al-Qa`ida in Afghanistan in 2007. See the following report about him by *al-Sharq al-Awsat*, 25 May 2007.

[58] Frank Gardner, "Death of Mustafa Abu al-Yazid 'Setback' for al-Qaeda," BBC, 1 June 2010. It was reported that a U.S.-operated unmanned aerial vehicle (UAV) killed him in Pakistan's North Waziristan tribal area.

[59] SOCOM-2012-0000015, 1.

strategies. Two major concerns seem to have preoccupied him. First, he was keen for the talented "brothers" either to be evacuated safely from Waziristan or, if they must stay, to take stringent measures to avoid being captured or killed.[60] Bin Ladin's letter was littered with detailed instructions to be followed to ensure the safety and security of the remaining "brothers" even if the work "should proceed at a slower pace during this period."[61]

Bin Ladin's second main concern was to find alternative places outside Afghanistan and Pakistan to mount "external operations." He had received a letter from a "Shaykh Yunis" presenting him with a strategy on how al-Qa`ida could focus on putting together a secret operational force that could evade the eyes of the authorities. It is not clear whether this operational force was already in existence or whether it was meant to be a new one that Yunis developed and Bin Ladin should work on establishing. This force, Yunis explained, required coordination between AQC leaders and leaders of jihadi regional groups, but such a plan, he added, involves positive and negative consequences. On the positive front, the coordination between the leadership in Khurasan/Waziristan and the leaders of jihadi regional groups could yield productive results in operational terms.[62] In Yunis' words:

> We (i.e., the operational force) do not need to claim/announce our [jihadi] activities – i.e., the activities that we carry out. There is a side [by which he implicitly refers to Bin Ladin] that is the focus of the eyes and hearts' attention...that could claim [our jihadi activities]; alternatively you could advise [jihadi leaders] in the regions to claim it...this would allow the party involved in the [operational] work the freedom of movement, not to mention [the possibility] of perfecting means and ways of forgery (*tazwir*) and smuggling (*tahrib*) to become proficient in such skills. [We would also] train members to blend in with the public. All of this would allow us to melt/disappear (*dhawaban*) whenever we want, and this would have a more profound impact on covering our tracks after [we carry out] attacks.[63]

---

[60] Ibid., 2.

[61] Ibid., 3.

[62] The term Khurasan is often used in jihadi literature to designate Central Asia, but it is also used to refer to Afghanistan. See the discussion: al-Malahim wa-al-Fitan, "Khurasan: hal hiya Afghanistan?" http://alfetn.net/vb3/showthread.php?t=17231 (accessed 26 April 2012). Although it could not be asserted, the location of Yunis was likely Waziristan.

[63] SOCOM-2012-0000019, 46.

Yunis then added some concerns. The first concern pertained to some of the "brothers'" unproductive enthusiasm for jihad which causes failures in security; the other pertained to extremism and fanaticism in religion by some "brothers" who claim to be affiliated with al-Qaʿida. Yunis was referring to *takfiris*, i.e., jihadis who readily declare fellow Muslims to be unbelievers liable to be killed if they disagree with them over religious doctrines.[64] "You [i.e., Bin Ladin] experienced this problem [first hand] in Peshawar [in the 1980s] and you [also] saw its outcome in [Algeria],"[65] he warned Bin Ladin. In other words, Yunis warned Bin Ladin that unless the enthusiasts and religious extremists are brought in line, they would be a liability for such a strategy.

Shaykh Yunis is probably Yunis al-Muritani who was captured in Quetta, Pakistan, in September 2011.[66] He is reported to be in his mid-30s, and if he is indeed the same "Shaykh Yunis" it suggests that al-Qaʿida has managed during the past decade to attract jihadis who are distinguished by their strategic and operational visions. Yunis' letter clearly left a powerful mark on Bin Ladin; Yunis' strategic operational vision and his erudition, evidenced by citing examples from Islamic history in the appropriate places, must have immediately impressed Bin Ladin. He referred to Yunis as "shaykh," not "brother" (*akh*), bestowing upon him a seniority status that Bin Ladin seemed to reserve for leaders of AQC, compared with the brotherly language he used when referring to regional jihadi leaders. He further shared Yunis' letter with ʿAtiyya and instructed him to let Yunis know that he is to be dispatched to Africa and West Asia and be responsible for the "external work"[67] to be carried out "inside Western countries."[68]

Bin Ladin's appointment of Yunis to head al-Qaʿida's "external work" is a testament to his appreciation of Yunis' letter. It is remarkable that Bin Ladin, who did not take appointing leaders lightly, nominated Yunis to a highly sensitive post even though he appeared to have known little about his background. In the same letter where he asked

---

[64] On the liability of *takfiris* to jihadism, see Nelly Lahoud, *The Jihadis' Path to Self-Destruction* (New York/London: Columbia University Press/Hurst, 2010), 1-14.

[65] SOCOM-2012-0000019, 48. For an expanded discussion of al-Qaʿida's ideology as understood by its members in comparison with the rigid/extremist religious ideology as espoused by other jihadi groups, see Nelly Lahoud's forthcoming CTC report based on Fadil Harun's autobiography al-Harb ʿala al-Islam (The War Against Islam: The Story of Fadil Harun).

[66] "Al-Qaeda Chief Younis al-Mauritani Held, Says Pakistan," BBC, 5 September 2011; Mazin Aman, "al-ʿArabiyya tazur usrat ʾYunis al-Muritaniʾ," al-ʿArabiyya, 7 September 2011; "Iʿtiqal fi Pakistan maʿ ʿUnsurayn Barizayn bi-al-Tanzim," al-ʿArabiyya, 5 September 2011.

[67] SOCOM-2012-0000019, 31.

[68] SOCOM-2012-0000015, 5. This reference suggests that Bin Ladin is clarifying what he wrote before, which suggests that the document was composed after SOCOM-2012-0000019.

`Atiyya to appoint him to head the "external work," he also asked him to send "at the earliest convenience a report about Shaykh Yunis that would include his date of birth, upbringing, academic studies, social status, experiences and skills; and also include [description] about his character and his manner of dealings with the jihadis and his relationship with them; and also the date when he joined [al-Qa`ida] (*dukhulihi ma` al-multazimin*) and when he began to take part in jihad [on the battlefield] (*nafiruhu liljihad*)."[69]

Other letters authored by Bin Ladin suggest that he was quite selective in his choice of leaders. It seems that Abu Basir (the alias of Nasir al-Wuhayshi) had suggested Anwar al-`Awlaqi to be his replacement as the leader of AQAP in Yemen, but Bin Ladin politely rejected the suggestion. If ever a slap and a kiss could be combined, Bin Ladin's response to Abu Basir could count as one. He complimented Abu Basir on being "qualified and competent" to manage the affairs of Yemen, but added that although his "positive attestation of al-`Awlaqi is duly acknowledged, we would like further assurances; for example, over here we are generally assured after people go to the battlefield and are tested there."[70] Despite the preoccupation with al-`Awlaqi among U.S. analysts and the intelligence community, this in itself does not appear to have earned him recognition in Bin Ladin's mind. Bin Ladin, wanting more evidence about al-`Awlaqi's suitability, asked that Abu Basir, Abu Sufyan, Sa`id al-Shihri and al-`Awlaqi write him separately with a "detailed conceptualization" of the way they each conceived of the events in Yemen. It is as if Bin Ladin was getting his red pen ready to grade, and even fail, the essays of each of these leaders.

How might centralization of global jihadi media and operational activities serve Bin Ladin's strategy? The plethora of mistakes that Bin Ladin enumerated about the conduct of regional jihadi groups suggests that he would partner with them only if they agreed to play by AQC's rules, hence the need for a memorandum. Bin Ladin perhaps reasoned that he would withhold the symbolic public blessing that seemed to matter to regional leaders in return for their compliance; since he was prepared to apologize for mistakes such as unintended civilian casualties, he may have even been willing to bestow the brand "al-Qa`ida" publicly if they would commit to the memorandum in writing.

The documents suggest that Bin Ladin also needed regional groups to give cover to al-Qa`ida's "external work" since the landscape of Waziristan was too closely monitored

---

[69] SOCOM-2012-0000019, 33.
[70] SOCOM-2012-0000003, 2.

by U.S. intelligence to permit the safe work of the "brothers." Bin Ladin, therefore, looked for alternative geographical arenas to facilitate either the continuation of "external work" in Western countries, with the United States on the top of his list, or start a new initiative. His immediate plan was to dispatch Yunis either to Yemen or Algeria or the surrounding areas of these two countries and wanted the leaders of AQAP, Nasir al-Wuhayshi, and AQIM, Abu Mus`ab al-Wadud, to give Yunis their full cooperation. Specifically, Bin Ladin instructed `Atiyya to write to these two leaders asking them "to make their utmost efforts to cooperate with Shaykh Yunis in everything he asks of them," and further asked the "brothers in the Islamic Maghrib to provide Yunis the financial support he needs, which may reach 200,000 euros in the next six months."[71] The request for such a sum may suggest that AQC's financial situation was not self-sufficient if it needed to seek the assistance of the "affiliates," and it may also suggest that Bin Ladin had a specific operation in mind that he wanted Yunis to carry out.

If the above speculations are plausible, the documents suggest that an AQC in sync with the affiliates on the operational level was being forged in 2010 to advance al-Qa`ida's "external operations." Even if the speculations are not entirely plausible, AQC and the affiliates appear to have had more differences than commonalities.

It is difficult to speculate on the prospects of Bin Ladin's strategy. Still, even if its chances of success are slim, Bin Ladin's strategy to centralize the public statements and activities of regional jihadi groups in the interest of efficiently advancing "external operations" is carefully considered. This strategy, along with Bin Ladin's detailed instructions on the kind of measures the "brothers" must adopt to evade the authorities, are far more developed than the explicit operation he outlined to assassinate President Barack Obama and/or General David Petraeus who, at the time, was serving as the NATO commander of the International Security Assistance Force. Bin Ladin had asked `Atiyya's predecessor, Mustafa Abu al-Yazid, to task Ilyas, presumably Ilyas Kashmiri, to set up two units, one in Pakistan and another in Bagram, Afghanistan, to target airplanes known to be carrying President Obama and/or General Petraeus on their visits to these areas. He only wanted President Obama and General Petraeus to be targeted. He explained that the death of President Obama would see the "utterly unprepared" Vice President Joe Biden automatically assume the presidency, which would cause the United States to enter into crisis mode, and "the killing of Petraeus would have a serious impact on the course of the war," as Bin Ladin considered him to be "*the* man of

---

[71] SOCOM-2012-0000019, 32.

this [critical] phase."[72] Bin Ladin did not explain, however, why he did not want "Secretary of Defense Gates or the Joint Chiefs of Staff Mullen or the Special Envoy to Pakistan and Afghanistan Holbrooke" to be targeted.[73] It is possible that Bin Ladin had prepared a more detailed plan in a previous letter, which might explain why the brief description available reads as an amateurish plot or just wishful thinking.

The Affiliates

The documents show that the so-called "affiliates" have not just been a problem for al-Qa'ida in terms of harming its image in the eyes of the majority of Muslims who have been the primary victims of their attacks, but the affiliates have also caused internal debates among the senior leadership. A panoramic view of the documents points to three different positions within al-Qa'ida on the subject. There are what one may term the "principled," represented by Adam Gadahn, urging senior leaders to declare their distance and even to dissociate themselves from groups whose leaders do not consult with al-Qa'ida yet still act in its name. There are those represented by an anonymous author urging the opposite, believing that the inclusion of regional jihadi groups into the fold contributes to al-Qa'ida's growth and expansion.[74] Bin Ladin represented a third position. Bin Ladin wanted to maintain communication, through his own pen or that of 'Atiyya, with "brothers" everywhere, at least to urge restraint and provide advice even if it fell on deaf ears, but without franchising the brand.

The groups for which there is enough substantive content in the documents to gain a meaningful understanding of al-Qa'ida's relationship with them are: Islamic State of Iraq (ISI/AQI), al-Qa'ida in the Arabian Peninsula (AQAP), Tehrik-e-Taliban Pakistan (TTP) and to a lesser extent al-Shabab. AQIM is mentioned in a number of letters, but not as a separate subject of discussion that discerns how Bin Ladin viewed the group. There is also a letter dated 2006 forwarded to a certain 'Abd al-Hamid. The actual letter was addressed to 'Atiyya, consisting of legal questions from the group called Army of Islam (*Jaysh al-Islam*) based in Gaza.[75] The gist of the letter makes it known that the group is in need of financial assistance "to support jihad," and the questions largely

---

[72] SOCOM-2012-0000019, 35-36.

[73] Ibid.

[74] SOCOM-2012-0000006, 1.

[75] SOCOM-2012-0000008. The letter is forwarded to a certain 'Abd al-Hamid. Jaysh al-Islam emerged on the political scene in 2006 when it mounted a joint operation (with the support of the military wings of both Hamas and Fatah) that resulted in the kidnapping of the Israeli soldier Gilad Shalit. See the analysis by Marwan Shehade, "Jaysh al-Islam al-Filastini 'ala Khuta al-Qa'ida al-'Alami," *Majallat al-'Asr*, 5 July 2006. Their relationship with Hamas quickly deteriorated and their questions to 'Atiyya makes this clear; their global religious ideology was not compatible with Hamas' nationalist focus.

pertain to the permissibility of accepting financial assistance from other militant Palestinian groups that are not purely fighting to establish God's Law in the eyes of Jaysh al-Islam (e.g., groups that are nationalists or supported by Iran).[76] The significance of the letter pertains to 'Atiyya's legal knowledge, but it does not point to a firm relationship between al-Qa'ida and Jaysh al-Islam.[77] 'Atiyya comes across as cordial but distant. He responded strictly to the questions posed but refrained from giving any strategic advice. It is possible that Jaysh al-Islam was "testing the water" to see whether al-Qa'ida would lend them financial support, not least because Hamas was fighting against them.[78]

Given that the documents leave out many jihadi groups, the rest of the discussion in this section is thus limited to ISI/AQI, AQAP, TTP and al-Shabab.

Islamic State of Iraq/AQI

It should not come as a surprise to learn that Bin Ladin's public admission of Abu Mus'ab al-Zarqawi's group in Iraq[79] into the al-Qa'ida fold in December 2004[80] referred to in the secondary literature as AQI, became a liability, not an asset.[81] Al-Zarqawi's group launched several indiscriminate attacks against Shi'ite civilians, and when Iraqi Sunni militants disapproved of his tactics he turned against them.[82] The group's

---

[76] SOCOM-2012-0000008, 1.

[77] It is noteworthy that 'Atiyya refrained from answering questions that he did not deem himself qualified to address, such as whether it is lawful to invest money in the stock market if the profit is used to advance the cause of jihad. 'Atiyya confessed that this question required expertise he lacked and advised them to seek the opinion of learned legal scholars who specialize in these technical issues. He did not suggest the names of any legal scholars who have the necessary expertise, which may be an additional indication that he wanted to maintain a cordial but distant relationship with the group.

[78] See, for instance, Hamas's actions against Jaysh al-Islam over the kidnapping of the BBC reporter Alan Johnston, whose release Hamas secured. "Hamas Arrests over BBC Reporter," *BBC*, 2 July 2007.

[79] Al-Zarqawi's group was called Jama'at al-Tawhid wa-al-Jihad; when it was admitted into al-Qa'ida, it became known as al-Qa'ida in Mesopotamia. After he was killed in 2006, and Abu Hamza al-Muhajir and Abu 'Umar al-Baghdadi succeeded him, the group declared itself as the Islamic State of Iraq. The new name was highly controversial in jihadi circles.

[80] Usama bin Ladin, "Risala ila al-Muslimin fi al-'Iraq Khasatan wa-al-Umma al-Islamiyya 'Ammatan," December 2004 (CTC Library).

[81] See, for instance, Ayman al-Zawahiri's letter to Abu Mus'ab al-Zarqawi, http://www.ctc.usma.edu/posts/zawahiris-letter-to-zaraqawi-original, and 'Atiyyatullah al-Libi's letter to al-Zarqawi, http://www.ctc.usma.edu/posts/atiyahs-letter-to-zarqawi-original.

[82] The Islamic Army of Iraq, "Rad al-Jaysh al-Islami fi al-'Iraq 'ala Khitabat al-akh Abi Omar al-Baghdadi," http://www.arab-eng.org/vb/showthread.php/50571-رد-الجيــش-الاســلامي-فـي-العــراق-على- القاعـده?s=26ba96a7fa433f7ed50ff41cd2654c96 (accessed 25 April 2012). See the discussion in Nelly Lahoud, *The Jihadis' Path to Self-Destruction*, 205-211.

indiscriminate attacks did not improve with al-Zarqawi's death; Abu ʿUmar al-Baghdadi and Abu Ayyub al-Misri, who succeeded him and declared an Islamic State of Iraq (ISI), were perceived by jihadi leaders to be more repulsive and dangerous than al-Zarqawi.[83] By 2007, Bin Ladin was publicly expressing his disappointment with jihadis in Iraq, urging them to form a unified front.[84]

The documents confirm and provide additional insight into the grief ISI/AQI caused in many jihadi circles. A letter dated 28 March 2007,[85] addressed to a legal scholar by the name of Hafiz Sultan,[86] and authored by someone who is clearly of Egyptian origin,[87] shows that the author was alarmed by AQI's conduct and urged Sultan to write to its leaders to correct their ways: "I fear for the brothers from committing political mistakes, you have no doubt heard Abu ʿUmar [al-Baghdadi's] recent speech; in my view, it contains obvious mistakes." In his mind, not only was the speech unfitting for a leader to make, but it also revealed that "they are extremists (*mutashaddidun*)...[and that his speech] is repulsive and lacks wisdom."[88] The author was by no means a distant or otiose observer; he assured Sultan that "I [already] wrote to them and rebuked them." He was appealing to Sultan because he knew him to be respected by and possibly related to "al-Karrumi," presumably Abu Hamza al-Muhajir/Abu Ayyub al-Misri, and wanted Sultan to exert pressure on him.[89]

The author of the letter also urged Sultan to respond to the letters and grievances of "our brothers [Jaysh] Ansar al-Sunna, for they await your correspondence and responses to their complaints and letters."[90] It seems that Ansar al-Sunna, the temporary

---

[83] SOCOM-2012-0000011, 1. This letter is incorrectly dated in the English translation as 28 March 2011. It should be 28 March 2007. It was composed a few months before Ansar al-Sunna formed an alliance with other Sunni militant groups excluding AQI. The new alliance was formed in July 2007.

[84] Usama bin Ladin, "Ila Ahlina bi-al-ʿIraq," http://www.iraqipa.net/10_07/21_25/News/a1_25okt07.htm (accessed 13 April 2012)

[85] SOCOM-2012-0000011.

[86] Hafiz Sultan is probably the same person who wrote articles for the magazine *Vanguards of Khurasan*. The magazine can be accessed on Minbar al-Tawhid wa-al-Jihad at http://www.tawhed.ws.

[87] SOCOM-2012-0000011. The author uses Egyptian colloquial terms, such as "aw haddi min ikhwanina," and "ma ykhissinash."

[88] Ibid., 1.

[89] Abu Hamza al-Muhajir/Abu Ayyub al-Misri is not reported to be known by the name al-Karrumi. However, since his name is used in the same sentence as Abu ʿUmar al-Baghdadi and since he is presumed to be in a leadership position, it would not be farfetched to assume that al-Karrumi is the same man.

[90] SOCOM-2012-0000011, 1.

name of Ansar al-Islam,[91] had threatened to denounce AQI, and the author wanted to prevent this by asking Sultan to write to them, sympathize with their concerns, but also warn them that *fitna* (sedition/division) is worse and they must therefore stick with their fellow jihadis. His concerns were well placed. Within a few months of his letter, Ansar al-Sunna returned to using its original name Ansar al-Islam and formed an alliance with other Sunni militant groups, an alliance that excluded AQI.[92]

A few months before Hafiz Sultan was urged to write to and counsel the leaders of AQI, it seems that a dispute was raging among religious scholars in Saudi Arabia. The dispute is discussed in one of the letters authored by an intermediary between some of these scholars and `Atiyya, to whom the letter is addressed.[93] The letter was authored in early 2007 shortly after private meetings the intermediary held with several religious scholars during the Hajj (December 2006-January 2007). What is known publicly is a statement released in November 2006 and signed by 38 Saudi scholars in support of Iraq's Sunnis. It is characterized by a highly sectarian tone, accusing the Twelver Shi'ites of Iraq, whom they consider to be *rafida* (rejectionists), of "embracing the Crusaders and protecting their backs," putting into practice their "hateful creeds" (`aqa'iduhum al-baghida*) against Sunnis.[94] This was followed by a statement that `Atiyya released praising these scholars, taking it to mean support for jihadis, and singling out two of them, `Abd al-Rahman al-Barrak and `Abdallah al-Ghunayman. `Atiyya then added what was missing in their statement, calling on Sunnis in Iraq to join and support the

---

[91] The group is based in Kurdistan. According to Abu `Abdallah al-Shafi`i, the leader of Ansar al-Islam, the group was established in 2001, but it had to change its name to Ansar al-Sunna because it was the target of U.S. occupation forces in 2003. For some time, he explained, the group changed its tactics and expanded its operations to cover all of Iraq, and as of November 2007 the group resumed using its original name, Ansar al-Islam. The changing of its name in 2007 may have been to signal its separation from AQI. His statement is available on *Archive al-Jihad*,
https://www.jarchive.net/b/details.php?item_id=3511 (accessed 22 April 2012). He was reported to have been arrested by the U.S. Army in May 2010. See Shirzad Sheikhani, "Za`im 'Ansar al-Islam' Yantahi fi Qabdat al-Jaysh al-Amriki," *al-Sharq al-Awsat*, 5 May 2010.
[92] Brian Fishman, *Dysfunction and Decline: Lessons Learned from Inside al-Qa`ida in Iraq*, Combating Terrorism Center at West Point (2009).
[93] SOCOM-2012-0000014.
[94] "Nida' li-Ahl al-Sunna fi al-`Iraq wa-ma Yajibu `ala al-Umma min Nasratihim," *al-Muslim*, http://almoslim.net/node/46629 (accessed 22 April 2012). The term *rafida* is literally "those who reject." It is used in a pejorative way against Shi'ites to denote that they reject the legitimacy of the first three caliphs the Sunnis consider to have been lawful. The Twelver Shi'ites consider that `Ali (the fourth caliph from the Sunnis' perspective) to have been the first lawful imam. For an academic study of the evolution of sects in Islam, see Patricia Crone, *God's Rule - Government and Islam: Six Centuries of Medieval Political Thought* (New York: Columbia University Press, 2005), chapters 2-11.

Islamic State of Iraq (i.e., AQI). [95] The Islamic State of Iraq also released its own statement "blessing" the scholars' statement.[96]

According to the account of `Atiyya's intermediary, the meeting during which Saudi scholars signed the statement was attended by 70 scholars, 32 of whom abstained from signing. Some, he related, disagreed with its wording, while others cited their fear of being suppressed or closely monitored by the authorities to justify their abstention.[97] More importantly, `Atiyya's intermediary was told that the statement originally included four additional lines that were critical of the Islamic State of Iraq, declaring it to be unlawful. However, a group of scholars, led by al-Barrak, insisted on deleting these lines, which forced others to concede in view of the importance of releasing the statement against the "Rafida" and ensuring that al-Barrak was among the signatories to the statement.[98]

A biography of al-Barrak available on the internet indicates that he is a retired professor of religious sciences, who supervised many doctoral and masters' theses, but refused several offers to become a member on the council that delivers formal legal opinions.[99] The explicit reference to his refusal is another way of making known that he refuses to hold an office that might compromise his principles and render him accountable to the ruling Saud family. In his meeting with `Atiyya's intermediary, al-Barrak expressed that he was touched and honored when `Atiyya singled him out in his statement and prayed for "victory for and consolidation of the Islamic State of Iraq."[100] `Atiyya's intermediary could not meet in person with `Abdallah al-Ghunayman, the other scholar singled out in `Atiyya's statement, but he met with one of his students. He was told that al-

---

[95] `Aityyatullah, "Tabshir Qulub al-Mujahidin bi-Talahumi ahli al-`Ilmi wa-al-Mujahidin," *Multaqa Hadramut,* http://www.hdrmut.net/vb/t227524.html (accessed 22 April 2012).

[96] Islamic State of Iraq, "Dawlat al-'Iraq al-Islamiyya tubarik bayan 'Nida' li-Ahl al-Sunna fi al-'Iraq wa-ma Yajibu 'ala al-Umma," http://www.alaqsagate.org/vb/showthread.php?t=726&s=0c7651228409936e43d02f96df7fc84b (accessed 26 April 2012).

[97] A number of the scholars who signed the statement are reported to be imprisoned by Saudi authorities. See Minbar al-Tawhid wa-al-Jihad.

[98] SOCOM-2012-0000014, 4. This is a highly difficult text to read in Arabic; it was written in a hurry, it is littered with spelling mistakes and it lacks clarity in several critical places.

[99] "Nabdha Mukhtasara `an al-Sira al-Dhatiyya li-al-Sheikh `Abd al-Rahman al-Barrak Hafizahu Allah," http://www.saaid.net/Warathah/1/albarak.htm (accessed 22 April 2012). For informative background on the role of al-Barrak and other Saudi scholars in supporting jihadis, see Stephane Lacroix, *Awakening Islam: The Politics of Religious Dissent in Contemporary Saudi Arabia* (Cambridge: Harvard University Press, 2011), particularly chapter 5. Also see Hegghammer, *Jihad in Saudi Arabia,* particularly chapter 7.

[100] SOCOM-2012-0000014, 4.

Ghunayman had made a promise not to publish his books during his lifetime, but happily changed his mind when one of his students suggested that he should publish them and donate the proceeds to the jihadis.[101] Al-Ghunayman is a renowned religious scholar, having occupied several prestigious faculty positions, and his classes are reported to be highly sought after.[102]

It is not clear from the letter if the support of these religious scholars extended beyond preaching and writing in support of jihadis. Yet the letter points to a certain "Shaykh Abu Zifr/Zafr" who is clearly in contact with `Atiyya on a more operational level through a different intermediary. His relationship with `Atiyya must have involved sensitive matters because he complained that the current intermediary through whom he communicated with `Atiyya was not trustworthy and could not be trusted with secrets if arrested.[103] He also indicated that of the 38 scholars who signed the statement in support of Iraq's Sunnis, they do not all deserve to be praised, remarking that they are likely to "turn against you"; however, he did not object to singling out al-Barrak and al-Ghunayman, both of whom are deserving of his praise.[104] Shaykh Abu Zifr/Zafr's name does not appear in the statement; it is possible that it is an alias and that is why he could not be identified.

Three years after these debates, Bin Ladin remained concerned about divisions among jihadi groups in Iraq and hoped that they would re-unite after the killing of Abu `Umar al-Baghdadi and Abu Ayyub al-Misri. He asked `Atiyya to write him a report about Abu Bakr al-Baghdadi and his deputy, Abu Sulayman al-Nasir, the new leaders of AQI.[105] He further added that "I would like for you to ask our brothers in Ansar al-Islam about their stance vis-à-vis the new leaders...and remind them to exert their utmost efforts to seek unity and resolve differences between the different jihadi entities in Iraq."[106]

In view of AQI's liability to the image of jihad generally and of al-Qa`ida in particular, it stands to reason that it should serve as a point of contention among senior AQC leaders. No one among the main personalities who star in the documents comes across

---

[101] Ibid., 5.

[102] `Abdallah bin Muhammad al-Ghunayman, http://www.alukah.net/Web/goniman/CV/ (accessed 22 April 2012).

[103] SOCOM-2012-0000014, 1-2.

[104] Ibid., 2.

[105] SOCOM-2012-0000019, 34. They were announced as leaders on 15 May 2010. See al-Shumukh, http://www.shamikh1.info/vb/showthread.php?t=62187 (accessed 12 April 2012).

[106] SOCOM-2012-0000019, 34.

more righteously critical than America's own Adam Gadahn. Gadahn's letter was meant to respond to Bin Ladin's queries about an effective media strategy, including engineering a way that would get American television channels to broadcast a speech by Bin Ladin on the tenth anniversary of 9/11.[107] Among the reasons Bin Ladin wanted a new strategy was to "make known the justice of our cause" to the world.[108] Gadahn capitalized on the "justice of our cause" and used it as an opening to highlight the injustices he believed the jihadis are committing, with AQI and TTP occupying the lion's share of his criticism.

Gadahn had planned to prepare an Arabic statement addressed to Christian Arabs. He wanted to warn them against collaborating with "the enemies of Islam," invite them to join Islam, and welcome today's "Islamic conquest," presumably by the jihadis, just as their ancestors did when the second Caliph `Umar conquered Jerusalem.[109] In the collective memory of Muslims and Arab Christians, `Umar is reputed for his respect of the religious rights of Christians. It is reported that on his tour of Jerusalem, `Umar visited Christian churches but refrained from performing the Muslim prayer in one of them, likely the Holy Sepulcher, lest it be turned into an Islamic shrine after his death; he thus prayed outside the church where al-Aqsa Mosque was later built.[110] Gadahn wanted to invoke the spirit of Islamic tolerance that `Umar's reign evokes. His plan was thwarted, however, when a Catholic church in Baghdad was attacked by AQI, the organization "that we support and which – like it or not [...] – is known to the people as an Iraqi branch of the organization of al-Qa`ida."[111] He thus cancelled his plan because his appeal to Arab Christians would have no credibility in view of ISI/AQI's attacks targeting Christian churches.[112] He compared AQI's policy to that of President George W. Bush, who, in his mind, repelled the Europeans and the intellectuals of the world. In a perhaps constructive criticism of Bin Ladin, and to highlight the need for al-Qa`ida to dissociate itself from ISI/AQI, Gadahn passionately asked: "is this the justice that we preach and that Shaykh [Bin Ladin] preaches in his statements and letters?"[113]

Gadahn was clearly highlighting to AQC's leaders that they were just as guilty of the double standards they accused the West of perpetuating in the Muslim world. He was

---

[107] SOCOM-2012-0000004.

[108] SOCOM-2012-0000015, 8.

[109] SOCOM-2012-0000004, 6.

[110] S.D. Goitein, "al-Kuds," *Encyclopaedia of Islam*, second edition, online edition (accessed 28 April 2012).

[111] SOCOM-2012-0000004, 6.

[112] Ibid. On attacks against churches in Iraq, see Anthony Shadid, "Church Attack Seen as Strike at Iraq's Core," *New York Times*, 1 November 2010.

[113] SOCOM-2012-0000004, 7.

alarmed by the gap between "the statements of our leaders and religious scholars and the actions of those who are said to be affiliated to or allied with them."[114] He thus advised that al-Qaʿida should take decisive public measures to dissociate itself from the "ignorant/ungodly criminality" (*al-ijram al-jahili*) of jihadi groups.[115] In his words, al-Qaʿida should publicly:

> ...declare its disapproval of these and other actions that the organization so-called the Islamic State of Iraq (i.e., AQI) is carrying. [It should be made clear that AQI's actions are being taken] without the orders of or consultation with al-Qaʿida. I believe that sooner or later – hopefully sooner – it is necessary that al-Qaʿida publicly announces that it severs its organizational ties with the Islamic State of Iraq, and [to make known] that the relationship between its leadership and that of the State [i.e., ISI/AQI] have not existed for several years, and that the decision to declare a State was taken without consultation with the leadership, and this [ill-considered] innovation (*qarar ijtihadi*) led to divisions among jihadis and their supporters inside and outside Iraq. [Thus] all that remains between al-Qaʿida and the State (i.e., AQI) is the tie that unites Muslims on the basis of faith, namely Islam, which makes it incumbent upon us Muslims to give advice [to our fellow Muslims when we deem it necessary], to command right and forbid wrong, and support and encourage doing good deeds.[116]

To date, none of the senior leaders have followed Gadahn's advice, and it seems that he would not act unilaterally. He assured the person to whom he addressed his letter that "I only discuss this subject with shaykhs like you and occasionally with my brothers at al-Sahab."[117] By April 2011, it does not look like progress was made on the Iraq front. Bin Ladin was eager for ʿAtiyya to inform him about "correspondence with the brothers in Iraq, the details of its progress and the reasons behind its scarcity."[118] It is possible that this scarcity was due to security constraints facing AQI in Iraq. Alternatively, communicating with AQC leaders may not have been a priority for the "brothers" in Iraq, or they may have responded but ʿAtiyya did not share their letters with Bin Ladin.

---

[114] Ibid., 8.
[115] Ibid., 18.
[116] Ibid., 8.
[117] Ibid., 5.
[118] SOCOM-2012-0000010, 4.

AQAP

If the criticisms of AQI in the documents are not particularly surprising, the concerns Bin Ladin expressed about AQAP will no doubt be revealing to many.[119] It is widely believed that AQAP is a success story from al-Qa'ida's perspective, especially since it is regularly described by senior U.S. government officials as the "most dangerous" of al-Qa'ida's affiliates.[120] Yet the documents show that at least in 2010 Bin Ladin was far from being impressed with the "brothers in Yemen." He comes across as critical of both their words and deeds, in particular the group's attacks in Yemen, its lack of acumen to win the Yemeni people's support, and the ill-advised public statements of its leaders. In fact, with the possible exception of AQI, none of the other "affiliates" appear to be more of a source of concern for Bin Ladin than AQAP.

To start with, Bin Ladin was anxious that AQAP was attempting to accomplish more ambitious actions than it was capable of sustaining. Even before the protests of February and March 2011 paralyzed the country, as thousands of Yemenis inspired by events in Tunisia and Egypt took to the streets,[121] AQAP was feeling emboldened. It appears that Abu Basir (Nasir al-Wuhayshi) had sent a letter either to Bin Ladin or 'Atiyya in which he wrote that "if ever you wanted Sana'a, today is the day,"[122] by which he meant that AQAP was ready to declare an Islamic state in Yemen and was possibly seeking a public blessing from AQC for its takeover plan. It also seems that Abu Basir had requested that a senior leader be dispatched to Yemen to help in the operational work.[123] Before responding to Abu Basir,[124] Bin Ladin had written at length to 'Atiyya about Yemen and told him that, in his mind, such an Islamic state, if prematurely declared before developing a firm foundation, is doomed to fail[125] and is likely to lead "to aborting the work [of jihad]."[126] At the time Bin Ladin was writing, in 2010, he believed that the circumstances were not yet ripe for declaring an Islamic state;

---

[119] For further discussion of AQAP in light of the "documents," see forthcoming CTC paper by Gabriel Koehler-Derrick.

[120] "CIA Chief: Yemen Qaeda Affiliate Most Dangerous," Reuters, 13 September 2011.

[121] These events culminated in former President Salih's formal ceding of power in late November 2011 in a deal negotiated by the Gulf Cooperation Council (GCC). See Brian Whitaker, "Yemen's Ali Abdullah Saleh Resigns—But it Changes Little," *Guardian*, 24 November 2011.

[122] SOCOM-2012-0000016, 1. The letter is authored either by Bin Ladin or 'Atiyya and the way it is composed makes it evident that the author was responding to several queries already put to him by Abu Basir in a letter that is not available.

[123] Ibid., 4.

[124] SOCOM-2012-0000016 is a letter addressed to Abu Basir, but it cannot be ascertained whether the letter reached him or not.

[125] SOCOM-2012-0000019, 19.

[126] Ibid., 23.

instead, Yemen should serve as a reserve and support base for jihadis engaged in warfare on the open fronts (i.e., occupied Muslim countries such as Iraq and Afghanistan).[127]

Underlying Bin Ladin's concern was a seeming distrust of AQAP's competence as a jihadi entity, not least its lack of a sound understanding of politics. It is possible that the 2003 premature campaign in Saudi Arabia by QAP — the group that merged with the Yemeni group in 2009 to form AQAP — weighed on his mind.[128] It would be naïve to assume, Bin Ladin wrote to `Atiyya, that the general public would be prepared to fight simply because a group declared jihad to bring down the regime/state. Unless the timing is correct and the jihadis are capable of governing, he warned, a fragile Islamic state would let people down, "burdening them with pressure they cannot handle," and expecting them to suffer this pressure would have grave consequences.[129] People are likely to fight, Bin Ladin explained, when there is an external enemy, whose enmity they understand, occupying their country. Absent that, the tribal character of Yemen and the tribes' disposition to fight among themselves makes it highly likely that a civil war would erupt if AQAP entered into a long fight with the government.[130] AQI's loss of the tribes' support in Iraq appears to have been on Bin Ladin's mind. The 2003 U.S.-led occupation of Iraq saw Iraqi tribes joining forces with AQI to fight against the Americans, but when AQI began targeting members of the Anbar tribes, Bin Ladin lamented, the tribes turned against AQI with a vengeance.[131]

The Saudi government's response to an Islamic state in Yemen was an additional risk that entered Bin Ladin's calculations. Saudi rulers, he wrote to `Atiyya, are already concerned about the jihadis' presence in neighboring Yemen, believing them to be "their worst enemies." Should the jihadis go on to declare an Islamic state, Saudi rulers would interpret such a declaration to be a threat to their stability; accordingly, they are sure to "pump vast amounts of money to mobilize Yemeni tribes to fight against us."[132] The documents make clear that as of 2010, Bin Ladin believed that AQAP had neither the financial resources nor the manpower to withstand a sustained assault from the Yemeni government, Saudi money, and U.S. support. In the end, an ongoing civil war,

---

[127] Ibid., 19.
[128] Ibid., 6.
[129] Ibid., 23-24.
[130] Ibid., 26-27.
[131] SOCOM-2012-0000016, 12.
[132] SOCOM-2012-0000019, 29-30.

he feared, would make secular governments appealing to the general public since they promote the slogan of compromise to appease the interests of all parties.[133]

Beyond domestic considerations, Bin Ladin was worried about the amateurish, ill-advised and badly timed public statements released by AQAP's leaders, which is one of the reasons he suggested centralizing media releases. He was particularly disappointed with a public statement by one of the deputies of Abu Basir, Sa`id al-Shihri (known as Abu Sufyan al-Azdi), in which he demanded the release of Hayla al-Qasir who was arrested in Saudi Arabia for collecting money — more than $500,000 according to media reports — to support jihadis.[134] Bin Ladin did not object to al-Shihri wanting to protect jealously the honor of Muslim women, but he was furious that al-Shihri chose to release his public statement at the same time the "Freedom Flotilla" was heading to Gaza to break Israel's blockade and bring aid to the people of Gaza. When Israeli forces killed some of the activists onboard, Bin Ladin observed, "Western politicians were forced to talk about this and criticize the Israelis."[135] In Bin Ladin's mind, the cause al-Shihri was voicing, notwithstanding his "praiseworthy jealousy," should not compete or even compare with the plight of a million and a half Palestinians in Gaza, many of whom are women and children, in addition to the 10,000 prisoners in Israeli jails.[136]

On the basis of Bin Ladin's concerns and possibly those of `Atiyya, the letter addressed to Abu Basir[137] is unambiguous and somewhat condescending in its tone. On the question of declaring a state, the author wrote: "[of course] we want [an Islamic state] in which we would establish God's Law," but only if "we are capable of holding on to it."[138] As if AQAP does not follow the news, the author deemed it necessary to explain the basics, namely that the United States, "despite it being weakened militarily and economically before and after [the attacks of 9/11], continues to have capabilities that would enable it to bring down any state that we might establish, even if the United States is incapable of maintaining the stability [of the countries it invades]."[139] The author reminded Abu Basir that if jihadis were unable to hold on to Afghanistan as an Islamic state in the face of the U.S.-led invasion in 2001, the chances of jihadis holding on to Yemen are even slimmer. The author warned that if jihadis do not learn from their

---

[133] Ibid., 26.
[134] Nasir al-Haqabani, "Hayla al-Qasir tajma` al-tabarru`at li-al-Qa `ida wa-ta'wi al-matlubin wa-tujannid al-Nisa'," al-Hayat, 4 June 2010.
[135] SOCOM-2012-0000019, 12.
[136] Ibid., 11-13.
[137] SOCOM-2012-0000016.
[138] Ibid., 1.
[139] Ibid., 2.

past mistakes, it "would make us like he who builds [a building] on the path of a torrential stream. If the building is swept away by the torrent and the owner decides to rebuild it on the same path, the people would run away."[140] As to Abu Basir's request for a senior leader to be dispatched to Yemen to assist in the operational work, this was politely denied, citing security related reasons that necessitated the avoidance of any movement except under special circumstances. This denial is quite telling. Although Bin Ladin was planning on dispatching Shaykh Yunis to the region and wanted him to link up with AQAP's representatives so that they would give him money, Bin Ladin was not prepared to compromise the autonomy of Shaykh Yunis' mission and ask him to "work" with them.

In practical terms, the letter to Abu Basir (Nasir al-Wuhayshi) advised him to reach, through the mediation of scholars and tribal leaders, "a fair truce to bring stability to Yemen,"[141] without agreeing to being disarmed.[142] It is possible that the author feared that in the event that AQAP agreed to be disarmed, the group might be tempted to turn itself into a political party.[143] In reality, the author of letter 13 is not optimistic that such a truce would be successful; in fact, he is confident that `Ali `Abdallah Salih, Yemen's president until 27 February 2012, would not agree to it. The intent, however, was to show the Yemeni public that jihadis seek peace and stability unlike the Yemeni government. More precisely, the author of the letter was confident that external pressures on the Yemeni government, particularly from the United States, would make it prone to making more mistakes, especially in its dealings with the tribes; thus, if jihadis forge good relationships with the tribes, they would stand to gain from the government's losses.[144]

In the meantime, and on the domestic front, jihadis should devote their energy not to jihad but to i`dad, or "preparing for jihad," and the longer the regime clings to power and fails the people, the more time jihadis have for i`dad and to win the sympathy of the public.[145] At the same time, work must continue "to exhaust [economically and militarily] America from outside Yemen"; in this respect, Yemen would serve as a base from where jihadis could leave to mount "external operations."[146] Lest he is misunderstood, the author of letter 13 specifically warned against targeting the Yemeni

---

[140] Ibid.
[141] Ibid., 3.
[142] Ibid., 5.
[143] Ibid., 18-19.
[144] Ibid., 14.
[145] Ibid., 3.
[146] Ibid.

army and its police force: "The Americans are our desired goal,"[147] he stressed, and any work that is not directed against them weakens the mission. The author patiently explained this strategy to Abu Basir, using the metaphor of a tree:

> The enemies of the *umma* today are like a malignant tree: it has a 50 cm American trunk and branches that differ in sizes, consisting of NATO members and many [apostate] regimes in the [Middle East and North Africa] region. We want to bring down the tree by sawing [its trunk], but our force and capability is limited. Thus, the sound and effective way to bring the tree down would be to focus our saw on its American root. [To be precise] if while [our energy] is focused on the trunk and we reach say 30 cms into its depth, should the opportunity of sawing into the British branch of the tree presents itself, we would not take it. [That is because preoccupying ourselves with the branches] would disrupt our efforts and energy; that is why we should stick to sawing the American trunk, for when the trunk is [sawn], the [branches] would all fall, if God so pleases.[148]

The fact that AQAP continues to mount attacks against the Yemeni army and police since the letter was composed suggests that al-Wuhayshi either did not receive the letter or, if he did, was displeased with its content and ignored its directives.[149]

Despite the clarity of Bin Ladin's (and possibly `Atiyya's) strategic vision, there is an aura of insincerity or perhaps partial amnesia to the claim that al-Qa`ida has always focused on mobilizing the jihadis' energy exclusively against the United States. While it is true that on the operational level al-Qa`ida's attacks focused on the United States (e.g., 1998 East Africa embassy bombings, 2000 USS *Cole* bombing, the 9/11 attacks), Bin Ladin's public statements have often called on the youth in Muslim countries to rebel against their rulers, and jihad inside Saudi Arabia was the focus of one of his most aggressive statements. In December 2004, Bin Ladin confronted the "ruling family" directly, accusing it of "oppressing every reformist movement...on behalf of America and its allies." He proceeded to say that "it is not permitted for Muslims to agree to be governed by such rulers," concluding that the solution to the situation, "as explicitly stated in [God]'s Law," entails "deposing the ruler." If the ruler refuses to step aside, Bin Ladin explained, "it would be necessary to rise up against him with arms to depose

---

[147] Ibid., 4.
[148] Ibid., 7.
[149] For attacks in Yemen since then, see, for example, Robert Worth, "Chaos in Yemen Creates Opening for Islamist Gangs," *New York Times*, 27 June 2011; Laura Kasinof, "Death Toll Rises in Attack on Yemeni Army Base," *New York Times*, 5 March 2012.

him." He further encouraged the jihadis to focus their attacks on what hurts most, namely oil infrastructure in the region.[150]

One of the letters (document 15) dated September 2006 from a "loving brother" addressed to Bin Ladin is a serious rebuke of this policy, including the December 2004 statements that focused on Saudi Arabia, the place where the author of the letter was residing at the time (Riyadh).[151] The author included all the necessary respectful rhetorical tools, referring to Bin Ladin as "Honorable Shaykh," acknowledged that Bin Ladin's gift to and precedence in the field of jihad "does not escape anyone during this era," and expressed his "continued love and appreciation" despite circumstances preventing "ongoing correspondence" between the two.[152] The author's tone quickly changed, however, as he alerted Bin Ladin that when one is distant from reality, as Bin Ladin was because of security measures he was forced to take, the soundness of one's judgment was bound to be impaired.[153] In a more aggressive tone, the author asked Bin Ladin about the rationale of focusing his energy on "Islamic countries in general and the Arabian Peninsula in particular." The author reminded Bin Ladin that the Arabian Peninsula has a number of features that distinguish it, not least its financial support of the jihadis, serving "as the rear base of all jihadi activities around the world, from Afghanistan to Chechnya, Iraq and Palestine."[154] Among the numerous negative consequences of engaging in jihad inside Saudi Arabia, the author informed Bin Ladin that people are now repulsed by the technical term "jihad" and it is even forbidden to use it in lectures. The author strongly advised Bin Ladin to change his policy, consoling him that even the seventh century commander Khalid bin al-Walid erred; in other words, Bin Ladin would still be in good company but only if he took measures to rectify his recent mistakes.[155]

Despite its damning critique of his policy, Bin Ladin kept the letter.[156] While the anonymous author's advice is echoed in Bin Ladin's letters composed in 2010, the letter did not cause him to alter his public statements and does not explain the inherent

---

[150] Usama bin Ladin, "Risala ila Ahl Bilad al-Haramayn Khasatan wa-Bilad al-Muslimin 'Ammatan'," 16 December 2004 (CTC Library).
[151] It is difficult to guess the identity of this "loving brother." Is it possible that he might be AFGP-2002-003251 (Harmony document), Abu Hudhayfa, 'ila al-Akh al-Fadil al-Sheikh al-Jalil Abi `Abdallah, dated 20 June 2000. He has a similar style: cordial but does not hesitate to criticize in a blunt manner. Regardless, the author clearly knows Bin Ladin well.
[152] SOCOM-2012-0000018, p. 1.
[153] Ibid.
[154] Ibid., 4.
[155] Ibid., 8.
[156] Unless the document was deleted and recovered.

contradiction between his earlier speeches and his disapproval of rebelling against the Yemeni government as the letter to Abu Basir makes clear. That is because as late as 2009, almost three years after receiving this letter, Bin Ladin continued to call on people to depose their rulers. In March 2009 and in a statement he released about Palestine, Bin Ladin warned that "unless we understand that our countries are occupied in the interests of the rulers and their mandators/overseers (*muwakkilihim*)," by which he meant Western powers, "and unless we work to uncover the truth of [these rulers], fight against them, depose them and liberate ourselves from their dominion, we shall never be able to liberate Palestine."[157]

One cannot help but wonder whether Abu Basir responded to Bin Ladin's (or `Atiyya's) letter, if he ever received it. If he did not receive it, the public release of the letter with this report might give him the opportunity to reflect not just on Bin Ladin's inconsistencies, but also on how little the "shaykh" thought of AQAP. It was probably the lack of discipline among AQAP's members and the enthusiasm and ignorance of "the new generations of young men who joined the path of jihad"[158] that caused Bin Ladin to conclude that AQAP could not be trusted to mount qualitative attacks inside Yemen without massive civilian casualties.

TTP

Tehrik-e-Taliban Pakistan (TTP) is believed to be one of al-Qa`ida's primary partners in that region. Although the TTP has not pledged allegiance to al-Qa`ida, it is reported that al-Qa`ida fighters active in the Waziristan region have had operational ties to factions of the TTP and have conducted joint operations in Afghanistan.[159] Al-Qa`ida leaders active in the Waziristan region have also operated in the same social orbit as former TTP leader Baitullah Mahsud (and, after his death, current leader Hakimullah Mahsud) and worked together to address disputes.[160]

Letters authored by Bin Ladin did not discuss at length his views of the TTP, but the few scattered references in which he mentioned the group are far from flattering.[161] The documents make it clear that Bin Ladin was not informed of the TTP's planned

---

[157] Usama bin Ladin, "Khutuwat `Amaliyya li-Tahrir Filastin," March 2009 (CTC Library).

[158] SOCOM-2012-0000016, 6

[159] For example, see "Hearing to Continue to Receive Testimony on the Situation in Afghanistan," Senate Armed Services Committee, 16 June 2010, 14.

[160] For example, see Joby Warrick, *The Triple Agent: The al-Qaeda Mole who Infiltrated the CIA* (New York: Doubleday, 2011), 72.

[161] For further analysis of the TTP in light of the "documents," see forthcoming CTC paper by Don Rassler.

bombing of Times Square in New York City, a failed attack on U.S. soil attempted by Faisal Shahzad in May 2010. Bin Ladin was following Shahzad's trial in the news and was disappointed by his performance, which he thought distorted the image of jihadis:

> You have perhaps followed the media trial of brother Faisal Shahzad, may God release him, during which the brother was asked to explain his attack [against the United States] in view of having taken an oath [not to harm it] when he was awarded his American citizenship. He responded that he lied [when he took the oath]. It does not escape you [Shaykh `Atiyya] that [Shahzad's lie] amounts to betrayal (*ghadr*) and does not fall under permissible lying to [evade] the enemy [during times of war]...please request from our Pakistani Taliban brothers to redress this matter...also draw their attention to the fact that brother Faisal Shahzad appeared in a photograph alongside Commander Mahsud. I would like to verify whether Mahsud knew that when a person acquires an American citizenship, this involves taking an oath, swearing not to harm America. If he is unaware of this matter, he should be informed of it. Unless this matter is addressed, its negative consequences are known to you. [We must therefore act swiftly] to remove the suspicion that jihadis violate their oath and engage in *ghadr*.[162]

This is not the only instance that Bin Ladin worried about jihadis violating their oaths. The letter addressed to Abu Basir in which he is asked to focus on operations inside the United States (instead of Yemen) alerted him to focus on Yemenis "who hold either visas or U.S. citizenships to carry out operations inside America as long as they did not take an oath not to harm America."[163] Underlying Bin Ladin's thinking is a distinction between a visa (*ishara*), acquired citizenship — which involves taking an oath (`ahd) — and citizenship by birth — which does not entail taking an oath. From an Islamic law perspective, it is not lawful to violate one's oath (*naqd al-`ahd* or *naqd al-mithaq*). Accordingly, Bin Ladin wanted to promote the image that jihadis are disciplined and conform to Islamic Law. Faisal Shahzad's boasting that he lied during his oath not to harm the United States, therefore, is antithetical to the image of jihadis that Bin Ladin wanted the world to see.[164]

---

[162] SOCOM-2012-0000015, 7.

[163] SOCOM-2012-0000016, 4.

[164] Bin Ladin may also have had in mind the debate between Ayman al-Zawahiri and his former mentor, Dr. Fadl. The latter reneged on his jihadi views and among the accusations he made was that the 9/11 hijackers violated the terms of their visa, interpreting it as a form of *aman* (safe passage) from an Islamic law of war perspective. Thus, from Bin Ladin's perspective, it is only when a Muslim takes an oath that he must be bound by it; a visa and citizenship by birth do not qualify as an oath.

It is not just the lapses in the public statements of TTP that worried Bin Ladin. The group's indiscriminate attacks against Muslims are also a subject of concern that he raised with `Atiyya. In particular, he drew his attention to an operation the TTP carried out against one of the tribes on the basis that the tribe was against the Taliban. "Even if this were to be proven, it does not justify the operation in view of the non-combatants who died, for that would contradict the [Islamic] legal basis of our politics," Bin Ladin wrote. "I therefore urge you to continue advising TTP [to reform their ways]."[165] This TTP attack was not an isolated incident; their indiscriminate attacks, including targeting Muslims in mosques, is the subject of a long list of serious concerns that Adam Gadahn enumerated in his letter.[166]

It was left to `Atiyya and Abu Yahya al-Libi to write a letter addressed to the "respected brother" Hakimullah Mahsud, the leader of the TTP. Its content hardly reflected any respect for Mahsud. The authors did not mince words, explicitly stating their dissatisfaction with the TTP's "ideology, methods and behavior." These, they stated, are marred with "clear legal errors and dangerous lapses," and unless the group changes its ways, its errors would be a "cause of great corruption of the jihadi movement in Pakistan." News had reached `Atiyya and al-Libi that Mahsud had declared himself to be "the singular leader to whom everyone must pledge allegiance and declaring anyone who rebels against him (*kharij `alyhi*) or is not in his Tehrik to be a rebel (*baghi*)."[167] In classical Islamic political parlance, dissenters (*khawarij*) and rebels (*bughat*) who renounce the authority of the legitimate imam are subject to jihad and liable to be killed. Thus, Mahsud's announcement amounted to declaring himself to be the great imam with political authority over all Muslims, so `Atiyya and al-Libi found it necessary to point out to him that there is a difference "between the [minor] position of leader of jihad and that of great imam," a distinction with which Mahsud should familiarize himself.[168]

It also seems that Mahsud or members of his group had referred to al-Qa`ida as "guests." In response, `Atiyya and al-Libi explained to Mahsud that "we in al-Qa`ida (Tanzim Qa`idat al-Jihad) are an international Islamic-jihadi organization, we are not bound by country or race. In Afghanistan, we pledged allegiance to the Commander of the Faithful Mullah Muhammad `Umar, [we recognize him to be] a mujahid and the

[165] SOCOM-2012-0000010, 9.
[166] SOCOM-2012-0000004, 11-13.
[167] See Khadduri, *Islamic Law of Nations*, 230, footnote 1.
[168] SOCOM-2012-0000007, p. 1.

commander of the faithful of the Islamic Emirate of Afghanistan. From his side, it is permitted for us to be involved in general jihadi work...we would like to make clear to you that this description [of 'guests'] lacks a legal basis, and that Muslims are brothers in religion."[169] The letter concluded with an unambiguous threat: "unless we see from you serious and immediate practical and clear steps towards reforming [your ways] and dissociating yourself from these vile mistakes [that violate Islamic Law], we shall be forced to take public and firm legal steps from our side."[170] 'Atiyya's and al-Libi's letter was not the first warning issued to the TTP by the leadership of al-Qa'ida. In light of its rebuking tone, an examination of some of 'Atiyya's and Mustafa Abu'l-Yazid's statements a year prior to the drafting of the letter makes it clear that their condemnation of the indiscriminate targeting of Muslims in mosques and marketplaces was an implicit criticism of the TTP.[171] It is either that the TTP was too slow to understand that these public statements were implicitly criticizing their actions or simply pretended that they did not understand.

Al-Shabab

Al-Shabab is not extensively discussed in the documents, but there are enough references that reflect Bin Ladin's displeasure with the group's style of governance. There is also a letter authored by Bin Ladin and addressed to the leader of al-Shabab, Mukhtar Abu al-Zubayr. It seems that Abu al-Zubayr had sent a letter to Bin Ladin in which he requested formal unity with al-Qa'ida and either consulted him on the question of declaring an Islamic state in Somalia or informed him that he was about to declare one.

On the question of formal unity with al-Qa'ida, Bin Ladin politely declined, although he acknowledged that this is a "legal duty" (*wajib shar'i*), by which he meant that such a duty is incumbent upon all Muslims to work towards and implement when circumstances are conducive. Bin Ladin cited two reasons to explain why he discouraged formal unity. First, he indicated that it would give the "enemy" the excuse to mobilize its forces against Somalia; further, without formal unity, it would remain feasible for foreign aid to reach Muslims in need in Somalia.[172] The second reason Bin Ladin cited is the extreme poverty in Somalia as a result of ongoing wars. He further wanted to promote economic development to enhance people's lives. "I am

---

[169] Ibid.

[170] Ibid., 2.

[171] Mustafa Abu'l-Yazid, "Blackwater and the Peshawar Bombings," al-Sahab, 11 November 2009; "Statement by Shaykh Atiyatallah about the Peshawar Bombings," November 2009 (Released by Al-Fallujah Islamic Forum in January 2010).

[172] SOCOM-2012-0000005, pp. 1-2.

determined," he wrote to Abu al-Zubayr, "to urge merchants in the Gulf states in one of my public statements to [invest] in effective and important developmental projects. These would not be too costly, we have already tested such projects in Sudan. Thus the absence of a public affiliation between the jihadis [in Somalia] with al-Qaʻida would strengthen the position of merchants who desire to help their [Muslim] brothers in Somalia."[173]

On the question of declaring a state (*dawla*), Bin Ladin advised against it. Yet if al-Shabab believed it was necessary to formalize their authority in Islamic terms, Bin Ladin suggested that the group declare an *imara*, an emirate/province, not a state, and call it "the Islamic Emirate of Somalia."[174] In Islamic political parlance, an *imara* is part of a broader Islamic state/dynasty; it is headed by an *amir* who is a representative of the caliph/greater imam. As with Yemen, Bin Ladin urged Abu al-Zubayr to restrain his ambitious plans. He concluded his letter to Abu al-Zubayr with gentle advice on governance: "[just as] I urge myself, I urge you to hold on to piety, patience, and perseverance and to adhere to noble characters, those to which when an *amir* adhere, the affairs of his citizenry would improve." He further explained to Abu al-Zubayr that the leader's wisdom is manifest through "his forgiveness, justice, patience and good relationship with his citizenry."[175] Bin Ladin's advice is not for stylistic flourish; it is intended to signal to Abu al-Zubayr that his leadership is ultimately measured by how well Somalis are governed and their needs met.

Bin Ladin's concern over al-Shabab's mode of governance was explicitly articulated in a letter to ʻAtiyya. He asked ʻAtiyya to enquire from "the brothers in Somalia" about the economic situation of the states under their authority: "it does not escape you [Shaykh ʻAtiyya] that attending to people's livelihood is an important objective, according to the Law, and it is one of the most important duties of the leader. It is therefore necessary to seek to create an economic force [in Somalia towards achieving this end]." Bin Ladin had apparently sent ʻAtiyya some suggestions on how to improve the economy, but ʻAtiyya either ignored them or had not attended to them.[176]

In addition to al-Shabab's neglect of building a viable economy, Bin Ladin was also worried about the group's rigid approach to Islamic Law, specifically its inflexible

---

173 Ibid., 2.
174 Ibid., 1.
175 Ibid., 3.
176 SOCOM-2012-0000010, 5.

application of the *hudud,* or deterrent penalties for certain crimes.[177] He must have thought that the group was applying penalties with excess and asked `Atiyya to write "to our brothers in Somalia with some advice on how to deal with those whose offenses are ambiguous (*al-mushtabah bihim*) so that they may heed the prophetic hadith 'avert the *hadd* penalties by means of ambiguous cases' (*idra'u al-hudud bi-al-shubuhat*)."[178] Bin Ladin was referring here to a hadith, a report attributed to the Prophet Muhammad, which has served as a basis for jurists to avoid the imposition of severe penalties.[179]

Bin Ladin's letter to Abu al-Zubayr has echoes of the "it's not you, it's me" excuse. Why should he deny al-Shabab official membership in al-Qa`ida yet still honor Abu al-Zubayr with a personal and cordial letter that he could have asked `Atiyya to write on his behalf? It is possible that he had been sending personal letters to other regional leaders, believing that even though he could not control them, it was still his duty to continue to advise them to change their ways, in which case his letter to Abu al-Zubayr would fit this pattern. It is also possible that Bin Ladin's reasoning may not have been entirely noble; it may be that al-Shabab was trying to *purchase* its way into al-Qa`ida. In what was probably his last letter, Bin Ladin asked `Atiyya to inform him of the "sums of money in support of jihadis coming from inside and outside Pakistan, and to itemize separately the sums arriving from each region; and of these to explain what happened with respect to the sum from the brothers in Somalia mentioned in your letter."[180] In itself, the reference to a distinct sum from Somalia is obviously not conclusive that al-Shabab was attempting to *purchase* use of the brand, but it may suggest that the sum from Somalia stood out in relation to others. If this is a plausible observation, then it might explain Bin Ladin's position: although he was not prepared to "franchise" al-Qa`ida's brand, fearing that al-Shabab's shortcomings would be a liability, he still deemed it necessary to be cordial to the leader of al-Shabab to ensure the group's continued financial support of jihadi activities, (mis)leading Abu al-Zubayr to think that al-Shabab could eventually be granted membership. Nine months after Bin Ladin's death, Ayman al-Zawahiri delivered to al-Shabab what Bin Ladin had denied them. Al-Zawahiri and Abu al-Zubayr released a public statement announcing the union

---

[177] On al-Shabab's rigid application of the *hudud,* see Al-Qimmah Islamic Network, "Tatbiq Hadd al-Rajm wa-Hadd al-Harabah bi-Wilayat Shbili al-Wista al-Islamiya," http://al-qimmah.net/showthread.php?t=24727&langid=2 (accessed 26 April 2010).

[178] SOCOM-2012-0000010, 5.

[179] See E.K. Rowson, "Shubha," *Encyclopaedia of Islam, Second Edition* (Brill, 2012). Edited by: P. Bearman; Th. Bianquis; C.E. Bosworth; E. van Donzel; and W.P. Heinrichs.

[180] SOCOM-2012-0000010, 8.

between the two groups as a testimony that the "jihadi movement is growing with God's help."[181]

Bin Ladin's decision not to grant al-Shabab a public union with al-Qa'ida is intriguing in another respect. A close reading of a related letter may suggest that Bin Ladin's denial was the subject of internal debate within al-Qa'ida and possibly behind his back.[182] The author of the letter was concerned with the content of another letter to which he was made privy. He referred to it as the "letter of our friend" (*risalat sahibina*) and explained that:

> ...it is possible that the reason behind it is the fear of those brothers from the expansion and growth of the size of al-Qa'ida, with God's grace and power. They believe that being burdened by this expansive body is weighty on their neck and their capability cannot sustain it. It would make them liable to problems with many sides, especially since they desire or hope to pursue the path of construction and development. That is why they are satisfied with those who seek them, but do not see [the need] to go beyond that...That is why I believe it is necessary to affirm al-Qa'ida's ties to its branches and make it public as a fait accompli and useless to deny...Therefore, I hope that you would reconsider your decision of not declaring publicly the union with the brothers in Somalia simply because we might be pressured in the future to declare that we are not affiliated with them or others.[183]

This letter suggests that Bin Ladin's position was subject to internal criticism. The pursuit of "construction and development," which Bin Ladin outlined in his letter to Abu al-Zubayr was atypical al-Qa'ida discourse and was not welcomed by the author of this letter. Furthermore, it suggests that some were frustrated with Bin Ladin's reluctance to welcome publicly groups pledging allegiance to al-Qa'ida, accusing him of "being burdened by this expansive body" instead of seeing it as a sign of "God's grace." The only regional jihadi group that Bin Ladin publicly granted a formal affiliation is al-Qa'ida in Mesopotamia (AQI); all other groups that were formalized to be in the fold of al-Qa'ida were announced by Ayman al-Zawahiri.

---

[181] "Bushra Sarra," *Shabakat Shumukh al-Islam*, http://www.shamikh1.info/vb/showthread.php?t=148330 (accessed 30 April 2012).

[182] See Appendix for alternative readings of this letter.

[183] SOCOM-2012-0000006, 1.

If Bin Ladin was in charge of AQC, the content of his correspondence suggests that he did not enjoy a symbiotic relationship with the affiliates on the operational front. The documents reveal that Bin Ladin was burdened by what he viewed as the affiliates' incompetence: specifically a lack of political acumen, an inability to win public support, and most importantly poorly planned operations that resulted in the deaths of thousands of Muslims. If AQC lacks the ability to exert control over its supposed affiliate groups — whether distant groups like AQAP or so called "fellow travelers" like the TTP that are active in the geographical space where it is based — it stands to reason that the power and clout AQC is meant to exert over the global jihadi landscape is most doubtful.

III-   Al-Qaʿida Ties to Iran and Pakistan?

While the documents speak volumes about Bin Ladin's dwindling control over the movement that he helped to cultivate and inspire, they are less clear on the role of two powerful regional actors, Iran and Pakistan, frequently accused of enjoying ties to the group. Nonetheless, given the limited amount of reliable available information on this issue, the documents shed some light on how al-Qaʿida viewed these two key actors. Relations between al-Qaʿida and Iran appear to have been highly antagonistic, and the documents provide evidence for the first time of al-Qaʿida's covert campaign against Iran. This battle appears to have been an attempt to influence the indirect and unpleasant negotiations over the release of jihadis and their families, including members of Bin Ladin's family, detained by Iran. References to Pakistan are much too scattered to provide a coherent presentation of al-Qaʿida's relationship with the Pakistani government, but the few mentions of the Pakistani security forces in the document do not *explicitly* point to any institutional Pakistani support to Bin Ladin.

Iran

The relationship between al-Qaʿida and Iran is one of the least understood aspects about al-Qaʿida's history. Due to the scarcity of reliable public information to elucidate the nature of this connection, theories vary widely.[184] The Western frontier of

---

[184] One of the earliest reported links between al-Qaʿida and Iran comes from the testimony of Jamal al-Fadl – a former member of al-Qaʿida who defected and became an informant for the U.S. government. During his trial testimony (against Bin Ladin) in February 2001, al-Fadl described contact that four al-Qaʿida members – Abu Talha al-Sudani, Abu Jaffar al-Misri, Sayf al-Misri (see below), and Sayf al-ʿAdl – allegedly had with Hezbollah operatives in Lebanon in the 1990s. To the authors' knowledge, this information has not been corroborated. See *USA v. Osama bin Laden*, et. al., United States District Court Southern District of New York, 6 February 2001, http://cryptome.org/usa-v-ubl-02.htm. For background

Afghanistan bordering Iran was considered by al-Qa'ida strategists as an alternative base for their activities to escape and evade the intrusion of U.S. Special Operations Forces that were targeting them prior to the U.S.-led invasion of Afghanistan in 2001. Sayf al-'Adl, one of al-Qa'ida's tier-one leaders, related in his publicly available writings that the choice of this geographical location was due to its close proximity to the safest route available to the "brothers," namely Turkey-Iran-Afghanistan. "Pakistani authorities," he explained, "were beginning to exert pressure on us and closely monitor our movements, making it very difficult for Arab brothers and others to reach Afghanistan via Pakistan." Al-'Adl further related that they established links with some supporters in Iran, but not with the Iranian government; some "brothers" from Gulbuddin Hikmatyar's Islamic Party (al-Hizb al-Islami) made available to them some apartments and farms that they owned in Iran. Many families, he wrote, headed to Iran following the U.S.-led invasion in 2001 presumably expecting to be left alone, but before long Iranian authorities, pressured by the U.S. government in his view, began a campaign of arresting people and deporting them to their home countries.[185]

When he wrote this article, al-'Adl himself was believed to be detained by Iranian authorities, and this may have constrained his ability to provide elaborate details as to the Iranian regime's rationale with respect to detaining jihadis. Nevertheless, his account provides a plausible rationale as to why al-Qa'ida would look to Iran, namely as a passage or a base that appeared to provide safety for its members or other jihadis. Al-Qa'ida did not appear to have looked to Iran from the perspective that "the enemy of my (American) enemy is my friend," but the group might have hoped that "the enemy of my (American) enemy would leave me alone." Al-'Adl's explanation about the clampdown by Iranian authorities, however, is not satisfactory because they did not deport all jihadis, and the documents reveal that Iran was releasing jihadis and their families as recently as 2011.

The documents provide insights on al-Qa'ida and Iran starting in 2009. In a letter dated 11 June 2009, authored by 'Atiyya and addressed to "our venerable shaykh," Bin Ladin or possibly another senior leader, he wrote that "I am delighted to inform you that the Iranians released a group of brothers in several batches last month."[186] The list included

---

on these debates, see Bruce Riedel, "The Mysterious Relationship between al-Qa'ida and Iran," *CTC Sentinel* 3, no. 7 (2010).

[185] Sayf al-'Adl, "Tajrubati ma' Abu Mus'ab al-Zarqawi," *Minbar al-Tawhid wa-al-Jihad*, http://www.tawhed.ws.

[186] SOCOM-2012-0000012, 1. The names of the released and their profiles are as quoted in the letter: "'Abd al-Muhayman al-Misri and his family; Salim al-Misri (of the Jihad Group) – the term used for "of" (amta') could mean "of the baggage" – which could imply a pejorative sense) – and his family; Abu Suhayb al-

a number of legacy al-Qa'ida members (described as mid-level brothers) whose ties to the group stretch back to the 1990s.[187] In the document, 'Atiyya further indicated that the Iranians told the person liaising between the two parties that they would soon be delivering to him the family of "Azmarai" (Bin Ladin), "perhaps even within a week."[188] The initial promise was that they would release "the family (women and children, excluding the men)."[189] The Iranians also leaked to those whom they released that they planned to free more prisoners in the near future.[190]

Makki (of Yemeni origin: during the Crusader campaign, he served as the bodyguard of Shaykh Abu Suleiman al-Makki al-Harbi) and his family; al-Zubayr al-Maghribi (a brother who used to work with the Libyan Fighting Group) and his family; on his way (he might be in Quetta or thereabout, importantly, he crossed the Iranian border, and may God deliver him [safely] is Khalifa al-Misri and his family."

[187] SOCOM-2012-0000012, 2; According to Fadil Harun, *al-Harb 'ala al-Islam*, p. 374, 'Abd-al-Muhayman's family was chosen to be among those families to live in the newly constructed compound in Kandahar, Afghanistan, in 1998, illustrating that he has been associated with the group since at least that time. See also Harmony document AFGP-2002-600046, 2. Salim al-Misri was an explosives trainer at al-Qa'ida's Jihad Wal camp in the late 1990s. He was also one of the al-Qa'ida members believed to have received training from Hezbollah in explosives. See *USA v. Osama bin Laden*, et. al., United States District Court Southern District of New York, 6 February 2001, http://cryptome.org/usa-v-ubl-02.htm. In 1996, Salim al-Misri lived in Saudi Arabia and members of his family in Sudan. See Harmony document AFGP-2002-000232, 9 (of the original Arabic); Abu Suhayb al-Makki (Muhammad Ali Qasim Yaqub) was detained by Pakistani authorities in Karachi several weeks after Bin Ladin's death. According to press accounts, Abu Suhayb al-Makki is "said to have worked directly under the al-Qaida leadership along the Pakistan-Afghanistan border." See Declan Walsh, "Pakistan Hones in on Osama bin Laden Network with Arrest of al-Qaeda Man," *Guardian*, 17 May 2011.

[188] Although this cannot be ascertained, it is possible that Ezedin Abdel Aziz Khalil (aka Yasin al-Suri) and/or Salim Hasan Khalifa Rashid al-Kuwari helped to facilitate the transfer and travel of these individuals from Iran to Pakistan. See "Treasury Targets Key Al-Qa'ida Funding and Support Network Using Iran as a Critical Transit Point," 28 July 2011.

[189] SOCOM-2012-0000012, 2.

[190] According to 'Atiyya, the next group would include Abu Hafs al-'Arab, Abu Ziyad al-'Iraqi, and Abu 'Amru al-Misri. See SOCOM-2012-0000012, 2. In an interview conducted by *al-Hayat*, a former al-Qa'ida member "Muhammad al-Tamimi" mentioned the name Abu Hafs al-'Arab as one of the leaders of the Egyptian Jihad Group who was among those he met in al-Dahhak house in Kandahar in December 2001. See http://www.jammoul.net/forum/showthread.php?t=1628 (accessed 30 April 2012); Abu Hafs al-'Arab's name is also mentioned in a captured document that summarizes the interrogations of several Arabs detained by al-Qa'ida and the Taliban on suspicions that they were spying for foreign intelligence services during the late 1990s. The document suggests that Abu Hafs al-'Arab had a relationship with Sayf al-'Adl and could have been involved in security issues. See Harmony document AFGP-2002-800775, 75. Two other Harmony documents identify Abu Hafs al-'Arab as a member of al-Qa'ida. See AFGP-2002-600046, 2 and AFGP-2002-600177, 2. Abu Ziyad al-'Iraqi's name appears in a letter sent from 'Abd al-Wakil al-Somali to Abu al-Faraj. In the letter, Abu al-Faraj is informed that Abu Ziyad will be coming to his area per the direction of "Shaykh Abu Hafs" (likely a reference to Abu Hafs al-Misri). The document suggests that Abu Ziyad knew Abu Hafs or worked on his behalf. See Harmony document AFGP-2002-800636, 1. For additional background on other al-Qa'ida members believed to be in Iran, see

If `Atiyya's explanation is credible, then the Iranians were not releasing jihadi prisoners to forge a bond or strengthen an existing one with al-Qa`ida. Rather, `Atiyya was of the view that "we believe that our efforts, which included escalating a political and media campaign, the threats we made, the kidnapping of their friend the commercial counselor in the Iranian Consulate in Peshawar, and other reasons that scared them based on what they saw [we are capable of], to be among the reasons that led them to expedite [the release of these prisoners]."[191] The commercial counselor at the Iranian Consulate to whom `Atiyya was referring is Hesmatollah Atharzadeh-Nyaki; he was kidnapped in Peshawar in November 2008[192] and released in March 2010.[193] A few weeks before he was kidnapped, Abdul Khaliq Farahi, the Afghan consul general in Peshawar, was also kidnapped. Six months into his ordeal, he found himself sharing a room on and off for a year with none other than Atharzadeh. Farahi believed that his kidnappers were al-Qa`ida, and they seemed to have had links with Pakistani militants.[194]

It is significant to note that the Iranians do not appear to have made direct contact with al-Qa`ida, at least not in the initial stage. `Atiyya's frustration could not be clearer: "But the criminals did not send us any letter, nor did they send us a message through any of the brothers [they released]! Such behavior is of course not unusual for them; indeed, it is typical of their mindset and method. They do not wish to appear to be negotiating with us or responding to our pressures, as if to suggest that their actions are purely one-sided and based on their own initiative."[195]

Bin Ladin was equally distrustful of the Iranian regime. The release of his family was fraught with hurdles and did not materialize "within a week," as `Atiyya was led to believe. A seemingly authentic letter authored by Bin Ladin's son Khalid addressed to Iranian Supreme Leader 'Ali Khameneii in January 2010 has been published. In it, Khalid made known to Khameneii that numerous letters requesting the release of members of his family were ignored by the Iranian government. It appears that the

---

Christopher Boucek, "Examining Saudi Arabia's 85 Most Wanted List," *CTC Sentinel* 2, no. 5 (2009). Iran has also "released" Mustafa Hamid (Abu Walid al-Misri), who is not believed to have been an al-Qa`ida member but historically an advisor and trainer for the group.
[191] SOCOM-2012-0000012, 2.
[192] Jane Perlez, "An Iranian Diplomat Is Abducted by Gunmen in Pakistan," *New York Times*, 13 November 2008.
[193] Alan Cowell, "Iranian Diplomat in Pakistan Is Freed," *New York Times*, 30 March 2010.
[194] Carlotta Gall, "Afghan Tells of Ordeal at the 'Center of Al Qaeda," *New York Times*, 2 March 2011.
[195] SOCOM-2012-0000012. 2.

escape of his sister Iman to the Saudi Embassy in Tehran forced the Iranian government to admit the presence of Bin Ladin's family in Iran. His brother, Sa`d, also "managed to escape by himself and he related to us the truths of what was happening, that they had repeatedly asked to leave Iran but they were beaten and suppressed."[196] Sa`d was reported to have been killed in 2009,[197] and in his last letter Bin Ladin indicated to `Atiyya that he was about to send him a copy of a letter Sa`d wrote before he died to be included in al-Sahab's archive "in view of the important information it reveals about the truth of the Iranian regime."[198]

It appears that the Iranians promised to release Bin Ladin's family in exchange for the release of Atharzadeh, but they seem to have kept one of his daughters and her husband. In the second half of 2010, Bin Ladin asked `Atiyya to correspond with the Iranians (not clear if directly or indirectly) to tell them that "they promised that upon releasing their captive, they would release my family, which includes my daughter Fatima who [should naturally stay in the company of] her husband. It is not fair to separate women from their husbands; it is therefore necessary that they release her and her husband along with his [second wife] Umm Hafs."[199] Despite the many hurdles al-Qa`ida faced from the Iranian regime, the release of detainees in 2010 was timely. As noted earlier, Bin Ladin urged `Atiyya to move the "brothers" out of Waziristan, fearing for their security. He therefore saw the detainees released by Iran as a "lifeline" to compensate for those who were getting out or being killed. Not all the released detainees seem to have been known to al-Qa`ida, for Bin Ladin suggested that they should be given an intensive course not exceeding three weeks with a heavy emphasis on ideological instruction and some basic military training. He further remarked that this should serve as a testing course "through which we get to know their capabilities." Once the talents of the "brothers" were identified, they would be assigned appropriate tasks, such as sending them to their home countries to preach, recruit, raise money; others were to be kept in Waziristan to develop further their capabilities, and those who are disciplined could be sent to the frontlines to fight alongside the Taliban.[200]

Although the documents make it clear that the relationship between Iran and al-Qa`ida is antagonistic, it is difficult to explain Iran's rationale for detaining en masse these jihadis for years, without due process. One plausible explanation that has been

---

[196] Khalid bin Ladin, "Min Khalid Bin Usama bin Ladin ila Murshid al-Thawra `Ali Khameni'i," http://hanein.info/vb/showthread.php?t=162003 (accessed 23 April 2012).
[197] Eric Schmitt, "U.S. Officials Say a Son of bin Laden May Be Dead," *New York Times,* 24 July 2009.
[198] SOCOM-2012-0000010, 10.
[199] SOCOM-2012-0000019, 42-43.
[200] Ibid., 43.

advanced is that Iran held them "in part as a deterrent against a Qaeda attack on Iranian soil."[201] Another widely reported explanation is that Iran was holding al-Qa'ida members "as a bargaining chip in its war of nerves with the US, and will only allow their extradition in return for substantial concessions."[202] Whether Iran was aware of it or not, al-Qa'ida had plans to put the released detainees to "work."

Pakistan

Unlike the explicit and relatively substantive references to the Iranian regime, the documents do not have such references about Pakistan. Although there are notes about "trusted Pakistani brothers," there are no *explicit* references to any institutional Pakistani support. The one instance Pakistani intelligence is mentioned is not in a supporting role: in the course of giving detailed instructions about the passage his released family from Iran should take, Bin Ladin cautioned 'Atiyya to be most careful about their movements lest they be followed. More precisely, he remarked that "if the [Pakistani] intelligence commander in the region is very alert, he would assume that they are heading to my location and he would monitor them until they reach their destination."[203] This reference does not suggest that Bin Ladin was on good terms with the Pakistani intelligence community. Another reference worth highlighting in this regard, is that Bin Ladin did not appear to enjoy freedom of movement with his family. In his long list of security measures to be followed by the "brothers" to evade the eyes of the authorities, he wrote to 'Atiyya that it is most important not to allow children to leave the house except in emergency situations. For nine years prior to his death, Usama bin Ladin proudly told 'Atiyya that he and his family adhered to such strict measures, precluding his children from playing outdoors without the supervision of an adult who could keep their voices down.[204] Bin Ladin, it was said, could run but he could not hide. He seems to have done very little running and quite a lot of hiding.

Rather than outright protection or assistance from states such as Iran or Pakistan, Bin Ladin's guidance suggests that the group's leaders survived for as long as they did due to their own caution and operational security protocols.[205] While the release of new documents may necessitate a reevaluation of al-Qa'ida's relations to Iran and Pakistan, the documents for now make it clear that al-Qa'ida's ties to Iran were the unpleasant byproduct of necessity, fueled by mutual distrust and antagonism. The limited discussion of the Pakistani military does not lend itself to any final determination on

---

[201] Eric Schmitt, "U.S. Officials Say a Son of bin Laden May Be Dead."

[202] Dan De Luce, "Iran Holding al-Qaida Men 'as Bargaining Chip with US'," *Guardian*, 7 August 2003.

[203] SOCOM-2012-0000019, 41.

[204] SOCOM-2012-0000010, 8.

[205] See forthcoming article by Liam Collins to be published in the *CTC Sentinel*.

ties between Bin Ladin and the Pakistani state or actors within it, but Bin Ladin's emphasis on security precautions suggests that fear and suspicion dominated his calculations.

IV-   Bin Ladin's Plans

Among the documents, Bin Ladin's last private letter is dated 25 April 2011. By then, events in the world, as he was observing them on his television screen, were unfolding at a pace that caused him to reassess his worldview. He saw the revolutions sweeping the Arab world to represent a "formidable event" (*hadath ha'il*), a turning point in the modern history of the *umma*. At the time he was writing, the presidents of Tunisia and Egypt, Zein al-`Abidin bin `Ali and Husni Mubarak, had fallen. Bin Ladin was convinced that their fall was bound to trigger a domino effect, and "the fall of the remaining tyrants in the region was inevitable." Thus, "if we double our efforts towards guiding, educating and warning Muslim people from those [who might tempt them to settle for] half solutions, by carefully presenting [our] advice, then the next phase will [witness a victory] for Islam, if God so pleases."[206]

In line with al-Qa`ida's traditional stance, Bin Ladin dismissed the Muslim Brotherhood (*Ikhwan*) and similar Islamist groups, accusing them of being in pursuit of "half solutions" (*ansaf al-hulul*). This, in his parlance, means that although they raised the banner of Islam in their political discourse, they deviated from its teachings when they agreed to pursue their objectives through the electoral process. This is the spirit that underlies the statements made by al-Qa`ida's leaders when they accuse Islamists of compromising God's Law when they form political parties and contest elections that are regulated by positive law (*qawanin wad`iyya*). Nevertheless, Bin Ladin believed that, in recent years, some among the *Ikhwan* have been spreading the "correct understanding" of Islam, which caused him to anticipate that their return to "true Islam" (*al-islam al-haqq*) is merely a matter of time.[207]

Thus, within a week of his death, Bin Ladin envisaged two different strategies to be deployed in two geographical zones respectively. The first strategy pertains to the Arab

---

[206] SOCOM-2012-0000010, 1.

[207] Ibid., 2. Bin Ladin's cause for optimism that the Ikhwan may eventually return to "true Islam" is largely based on a long question that was addressed to "Abu Muhammad" (Ayman al-Zawahiri). Bin Ladin was most likely referring to al-Zawahiri's 2008 "al-Liqa` al-Maftuh," an online interview that was referred to in the press as the "Town Hall" meeting. It consists of two parts. The question that Bin Ladin was likely thinking about is the one posed by a certain "Sayf al-Islam" and it is in the second part. See "al-Liqa' al-Maftuh ma` al-Sheikh Ayman al-Zawahiri," *Minbar al-Tawhid wa-al-Jihad*, http://www.tawhed.ws/r1?i=7534&x=1502092g (accessed 2 April 2012).

region undergoing revolutions, and it entails "inciting people who have not yet revolted and exhort them to rebel against the rulers" (*khuruj 'ala al-hukkam*); this, he believed, should be part of a broader media campaign that should be carefully orchestrated and void of any apparent differences among jihadis.[208] The other strategy concerns Afghanistan, and it entails continuing to evoke the obligation of jihad there. In his mind, Muslims elsewhere regained their confidence and courage to revolt against their rulers thanks to the jihadis, who, by fighting against the United States in Afghanistan, dragged it into a war of attrition and weakened it. Following his logic, the jihadis' bleeding of U.S. resources in Afghanistan lifted the "coercive pressure" that the United States exercised elsewhere; this, in turn, allowed people previously scared and overwhelmed by the United States to rebel against its "agents," meaning their corrupt rulers.[209]

Notwithstanding the importance of jihad in Afghanistan, there was no doubt in Bin Ladin's mind that the "greatest obligation" incumbent upon jihadis during this phase is to "guide and advise" (*tawjih wa-irshad*) the *umma*, which would involve the clarification of fundamental Islamic concepts (*mafahim islamiyya*). This task "ought to occupy the largest share of our efforts";[210] more specifically, this entails "calling upon all those with literary capabilities, gifted with rhetorical eloquence be it prose or poetry to be delivered as audio, visual or in written [statements]."[211] In his guidance to `Atiyya, Bin Ladin asked him to remind the "brothers" in the region undergoing revolutions to be patient and warn them against entering into conflicts with Islamic parties. These parties, he suspected, will likely form governments in these countries and "our obligation during this period is to focus on *da`wa* among Muslims and win supporters by spreading proper understanding [of Islam]."[212]

`Atiyya had some different plans with respect to countries undergoing revolutions. He thought that it would be a good idea to send some of the "competent brothers" to their home countries to take part in the events and liaise with Islamic forces. Bin Ladin was more cautious, urging careful consideration, especially as to whether a safe route may be arranged for them. As to those who are too eager to go, he advised `Atiyya that their decision should be respected as long as they take as much care as possible as to their safety.[213]

---

[208] SOCOM-2012-0000010, 3.
[209] Ibid., 2.
[210] Ibid.
[211] Ibid., 3.
[212] Ibid., 4.
[213] Ibid., 7.

Bin Ladin made an ambiguous but intriguing reference in relation to Saudi Arabia. It appears that the Arab Spring caused some in Saudi Arabia to worry as to whether Bin Ladin might call on Saudis to revolt. A certain "Sahib al-Tayyib" from Saudi Arabia sent a letter to 'Atiyya to be shared with Bin Ladin, but its purpose is not explicit. Bin Ladin's guess was that scholars who are either connected to the Saudi regime or who themselves believe in the importance of stability in the Saudi kingdom and the Gulf region warned al-Tayyib about the danger of stirring up (*ithara*) the situation in Saudi Arabia so that he may pass on this warning to "us." Bin Ladin surmised that al-Tayyib was hinting too at the importance of stability in Saudi Arabia.[214] If he had a chance to call on people to revolt as he advised 'Atiyya, it is unlikely that he would have spared the people of the Saudi kingdom from his statements.

Bin Ladin's only public audio statement in response to the Arab Spring, released after his death, echoed some of the sentiments he expressed in his letter to 'Atiyya. It is somewhat of a paradigm shift, as he did not designate the movers of the Arab Spring as *mujahidun*; instead, they are "free revolutionaries" (*thuwaar ahrar*) and they are engaged in a liberation (*tahrir*) enterprise. He viewed this as an event like no other event: "*hadath tarikhi 'azim*" (a great historical event). "With the fall of the tyrant," he proudly continued, "the meanings of submissiveness (*dhilla*), servility (*khunu*), fear and restraint (*ihjam*) have [also] fallen," and the "meanings of freedom, dignity, courage and audacity (*iqdam*) have arisen."[215]

Within a week of his letter in response to the Arab Spring, Bin Ladin was killed. A month later, Ayman al-Zawahiri was announced as his successor. Al-Zawahiri is conspicuously distant from people in Bin Ladin's immediate circle. One of the documents consists of an edited copy of al-Zawahiri's fourth statement in response to events in Egypt; the edits are reflected in highlighted passages and bold fonts. It is not clear if Bin Ladin did the editing, but whoever did had solid grammatical foundations and prefered a self-effacing writing style. The edits were not included in al-Zawahiri's final speech which was released in a video on 4 March 2011, on jihadi forums.[216]

---

[214] Ibid., 6. If Sahib al-Tayyib is one of the unrecognizable personalities in the 17 documents, he could be the "middleman" who sent a letter to 'Atiyya in 2006, or the person who sent Bin Ladin the critical letter in 2006 – but unlikely; or very possibly the mysterious Abu Zifr/Zafr. It is interesting to note that in this instance, Bin Ladin slipped and used the term "al-mamlaka" (kingdom) instead of "Jazirat al-'Arab."

[215] Usama bin Ladin, "ila Ummati al-Muslima" (CTC Library).

[216] SOCOM-2012-0000013, 5. Of the 12 proposed corrections, only one appears in al-Zawahiri's speech ("*muwalin*" - *tanwin bi al-kasr* instead of "*muwalun*" - *tanwin bi al-damma*). This is an obvious grammatical error and the type that any native speaker would automatically correct when reading. It cannot therefore

Beyond the presence of this statement by al-Zawahiri in the documents, Bin Ladin referred to him (as "Abu Muhammad") in a number of places, but the references do not reflect that he was consulting him in the same manner he did with 'Atiyya. If the documents are representative of Bin Ladin's correspondence pattern and his immediate circle over the years, then 'Atiyya must have been his closest associate. Of the 17 documents, eight can be ascertained to have either been authored by or addressed to 'Atiyya. Not only does he seem to have acted as Bin Ladin's conduit, but it is also possible that he exercised more control than he was authorized. In one of the letters, for example, Bin Ladin appeared frustrated that the audio or visual recordings he was sending to 'Atiyya were either being delayed or not being released at all.[217]

Will there be another "Bin Ladin"? If Bin Ladin's instructions are closely followed, then the world might hear from Hamza bin Ladin, if he is still alive.[218] Bin Ladin intended for his son Hamza — who was released by the Iranians — to go to Qatar to pursue studies in religious sciences and preach to the *umma* the message of jihad. Unlike Arab rulers whom he abhors, Bin Ladin could not be accused of nepotism, and he certainly did not intend for his son to monopolize the right to preach jihadi discourse. Bin Ladin singled out Hamza not out of favoritism, but for "legal" convenience. Unlike many jihadi leaders — including some of Hamza's brothers — who are on the run and whose public statements are therefore constrained by their limited movement,[219] Bin Ladin reasoned that his son Hamza might be able to spread the message as a free man. Hamza was imprisoned while he was still a child and it would be legally difficult to indict him of

---

be viewed as evidence that Bin Ladin's edits, if they were his, ever reached al-Zawahiri. Given that the remaining grammatical errors were included in the speech, it suggests that this document with edits either did not reach al-Zawahiri in time or was never sent. For a version of the video, see: http://www.youtube.com/watch?v=XWOu4Eb3pP4 (accessed 30 April 2012).

[217] SOCOM-2012-0000003, 3.

[218] There were conflicting reports on the status of Bin Ladin's sons following the raid. Some have reported that Hamza possibly escaped. See Muna Khan, "Hamza Bin Laden, 'Crown Prince of Terror,' May Have 'Escaped' After US Raid in Pakistan," al-Arabiya, 11 May 2011.

[219] Sa'd bin Ladin was likely the son most involved in al-Qa'ida, but he is believed to have been killed in a U.S. drone strike in winter 2009. See Joby Warrick, "One of Osama Bin Laden's Sons Reported Dead After CIA Missile Strike," Washington Post, 24 July 2009. The documents confirm his death. Another son, Khalid bin Ladin, was living with his father in the Abbottabad compound and was reportedly killed in the raid. See Muna Khan, "Hamza Bin Laden, 'Crown Prince of Terror,' May Have 'Escaped' After US Raid in Pakistan," al-Arabiya.

any crimes.[220] Hamza, Bin Ladin assured, "is of the jihadis; he shares their ideas and their sorrows."[221]

Conclusion

On the basis of the 17 declassified documents, Bin Ladin was not, as many thought, the puppet master pulling the strings that set in motion jihadi groups around the world. Far from being pleased with the actions of regional jihadi groups claiming affiliation with or acting in the name of al-Qa'ida, Bin Ladin was burdened by what he saw as their incompetence. Their lack of political acumen to win public support along with their indiscriminate attacks resulting in the deaths of many Muslims is a subject that dominates Bin Ladin's private letters composed in recent years.

The American public might be surprised to learn that Bin Ladin was unimpressed by the recent trend of American populist jihad. For example, he did not hold the American jihadi citizen Anwar al-'Awlaqi (killed by a drone strike in Yemen in 2011) in great esteem; Bin Ladin was not even inspired by *Inspire*, AQAP's English-language magazine designed to appeal to Muslim Americans to launch random attacks in the United States. He warned of its "dangerous consequences," presumably due to its tasteless content and no doubt to the poor planning of the operations it promotes.[222]

In comparison to regional jihadi groups, Bin Ladin comes across as an outmoded jihadi. In contrast to their indiscriminate jihad, he was more interested in carefully planned operations. In view of the recent marketing of "lone wolf" operations as "New Age" jihad, Bin Ladin instead urged methodical planning of suicide operations. He asked 'Atiyya to write to regional "brothers" warning them "not to send a single brother on a suicide *fida'iyya* operation (`amaliyya fida'iyya*); they should send at least two...we tested this (i.e., sending a single brother) in many operations and their percentage of success was low due to psychological factors that affect the [designated] brother in such a situation."[223] It is noteworthy that Bin Ladin used a secular political expression to describe suicide operations rather than the common religious expression "martyrdom operation" (`amaliyya istishhadiyya*) typical of jihadi discourse. The regional groups' eagerness to declare "Islamic states" in their regions was moderated by Bin Ladin urging patience to first secure public support; while they aim to win the small short-term battles, his eyes were on a larger prize: defeating the United States to undo what

---

[220] SOCOM-2012-0000019, 44.
[221] Ibid.
[222] SOCOM-2012-0000015, 9.
[223] SOCOM-2012-0000019, 35.

he believed to be "apostate" Muslim regimes and liberate his fellow Muslims. Bin Ladin knew well how to articulate publicly the grievances that he believed Muslims suffer at the hands of their regimes and Western countries. His private letters show that saving his fellow Muslims from the indiscriminate attacks of his jihadi "brothers" weighed even more heavily on his mind.

Appendix

This appendix attempts to explain how some of the letters related to others, and in one instance it provides alternative interpretations of a specific letter. Additionally, the appendix includes the author, the recipient and the date of each letter. The conversion from the Hijri to the Gregorian calendar is inaccurate in some of the letters. If there is no summary after the basic information, then the letter does not appear to be directly related to another. This appendix is not meant to summarize each letter; for a brief summary of each of the 17 documents, see the summaries accompanying the documents.

SOCOM-2012-0000003
From: no name listed (assessed to be Usama bin Ladin)
To: Shaykh Mahmud
Date: Thursday, 17 Ramadan, 1431 (26 August 2010)

SOCOM-2012-0000004
From: no name listed (assessed to be Adam Gadahn)
To: unknown
Date: post-January 2011

The letter does not explicitly state who is the author or to whom it is addressed. Since the author remarked that the American television channel ABC broadcast a part of a statement he gave on the fourth anniversary of 9/11, this suggests that it was authored by Adam Gadahn who did indeed release a statement then, part of which was broadcast on ABC. The letter is unlikely to have been addressed to Usama bin Ladin since the author referred to him in the third person. It is also not dated, but it must have been authored either in January 2011 or soon thereafter since he referred to the resignation of Octavia Nasr from CNN in July 2010 (he erroneously stated MSNBC) and that of Keith Olbermann from MSNBC on 21 January 2011. The letter is in essence a response to many of the requests/queries that Bin Ladin made in his letter to `Atiyya dated October 2010 (SOCOM-2012-0000015), particularly those concerning a media strategy for the ten-year anniversary of 9/11. It is possible that `Atiyya shared SOCOM-2012-0000015 with Gadahn and this letter by Gadahn addressed questions raised in SOCOM-2012-0000015.

SOCOM-2012-0000005
From: Usama bin Ladin
To: Mukhtar Abu al-Zubayr
Date: Friday, 26 Sha`ban, 1431 (6 August 2010)

SOCOM-2012-0000006
From: unknown
To: Azmarai
Date: 6 Muharram [1432] (c. 11/12 December 2010)

The letter is addressed to "the honorable brother Azmarai," not Zamarai — the other name Bin Ladin used as his signature. The only other instance Azmarai is used in the documents is not by Bin Ladin, but by `Atiyya in his 2009 letter to Bin Ladin (SOCOM-2012-0000012). It should be noted that Bin Ladin is normally addressed as "shaykh," not as "brother" as the author of this letter addressed Azmarai. Below are two different interpretations of this letter.

First Interpretation
The letter may have been addressed to Zamarai/Bin Ladin, and Azmarai is simply a typo. Since it referred to the "brothers in Somalia," urging reconsideration of Bin Ladin's decision not to declare publicly a union with them, it can safely be dated as having been composed post Bin Ladin's letter to Abu al-Zubayr dated August 2010 (SOCOM-2012-0000005). Therefore the Hijri date of 6 Muharram should be in 1432, which would make it c. 11/12 December 2010.

This letter suggested that Bin Ladin's position with respect to rejecting formal mergers with regional jihadi groups was subject to internal criticism. Instead of seeing it as a sign of "God's grace" and a testament to al-Qa`ida's growth, Bin Ladin was virtually accused of "being burdened by this expansive body."

Who might this author be? As noted in this report, the only regional jihadi group that Bin Ladin publicly admitted into the fold is al-Qa`ida in Mesopotamia (AQI) back in December 2004. All other groups that were publicly admitted were announced by Ayman al-Zawahiri, who recently admitted al-Shabab into the fold in February 2012. Was the author al-Zawahiri? It is difficult to assert, but given his disposition towards expanding al-Qa`ida through mergers, it is possible that it was him. If so, al-Zawahiri did not share Bin Ladin's strategic vision with respect to al-Qa`ida's relations with the affiliates; moreover, unless Bin Ladin changed his mind about al-Shabab, then the February decision to admit the group in the fold would not have been blessed by Bin Ladin if he was still alive. Following the same logic, one also has to wonder whether al-Zawahiri acted on behalf of Bin Ladin or against his directives when he publicly admitted other groups into al-Qa`ida. If al-Zawahiri was doing so against Bin Ladin's directives, then Bin Ladin did not have a firm grip on al-Qa`ida itself, let alone its so-called affiliates. Given that the documents show that Bin Ladin would not publicly denounce groups like AQI/ISI, al-Zawahiri might have assumed that Bin Ladin would not publicly refute him.

Second Interpretation
The letter may not have been addressed to Bin Ladin and "Azmarai" is not a typo but perhaps a code indicating that it was not addressed to Bin Ladin, but about Bin Ladin. Several reasons could justify this alternative reading.

-   As noted earlier, Bin Ladin is addressed as "shaykh," not as "brother," as this letter does.
-   The author was cryptic, referring to the "letter of our friend" (*risalat sahibina*), before switching from the singular when he referred to this "friend" to the plural when he referred to the "brothers" even though the two are meant to refer to the same person or group. The first reference to "brothers" cannot be to the "brothers in Somalia" since the first "brothers" referred to those who were fearful of al-Qa`ida's growth; Bin Ladin's letter to Abu al-Zubayr showed that al-Shabab was seeking union with al-Qa`ida. Thus, the "brothers" cannot be seeking this union and at the same time fearing it.
-   The author of this letter was explicitly critical of the pursuit of "construction and development," which Bin Ladin explicitly outlined in his letter to Abu al-Zubayr. Emphasis on "construction and development" is atypical al-Qa`ida discourse, and his own letters show that Bin Ladin was starting to emphasize it at least for Somalia. Yet the author referred to those who wished to pursue this path of "construction and development" in the third person plural. If he was addressing Bin Ladin directly, why did he not use the second person singular or plural? More than likely, the switch from singular to plural and from third person to second person plural was to make the message all the more cryptic.
-   The reference to those satisfied with people seeking them but not wanting to go beyond that may well be a remark about Bin Ladin, who was reluctant to admit groups in al-Qa`ida's fold as the letter to Abu al-Zubayr suggests. The reference urging "you" (in the plural) "to reconsider your decision" is a reference to the recipient who could in turn exert influence on Bin Ladin to change his mind.
-   Finally, this is the only letter whose author requested that its recipient destroy it after reading it. If it was addressed to Bin Ladin, why would the author be concerned?

If this letter served as a criticism of Bin Ladin behind his back, it is still possible that Ayman al-Zawahiri authored it for the same reasons indicated above. But one might justifiably ask why it should be in his electronic files? One possible explanation is that its recipient decided to share it with Bin Ladin in view of its seriousness and/or out of loyalty. Alternatively, it may have been on the thumb drive of an operative, perhaps `Atiyya, who deleted it (as the author explicitly requested) and used the same thumb drive to deliver different letters to Bin Ladin.

SOCOM-2012-0000007
From: Mahmud al-Hasan (`Atiyyatullah) and Abu Yahya al-Libi
To: Hakimullah Mehsud
Date: 27 Dhu al-Hijja (3 December 2010)

SOCOM-2012-0000008
From: Jaysh al-Islam in Gaza
To: `Atiyya/Shaykh Mahmud
Forwarded to: `Abd al-Hamid (and later forwarded to Usama bin Ladin)
Date: Shawwal 1427 (October-November 2006)

SOCOM-2012-0000009
From: unknown
To: unknown
Date: unknown

SOCOM-2012-0000010
From: Abu `Abdallah (Usama bin Ladin)
To: Shaykh Mahmud/`Atiyya
Date: Monday, 22 Jumadi al-Awwal 1432 (25 April 2011)

SOCOM-2012-0000011
From: unknown (likely of Egyptian origin)
To: `Adnan (Hafiz Sultan)
Date: 9 Rabi` al-Awwal (28 March 2007)

SOCOM-2012-0000012
From: `Atiyya
To: Honorable Shaykh (assessed to be Usama bin Ladin or another senior leader)
Date: Thursday, 11 June 2009

SOCOM-2012-0000013
From: unknown
To: unknown
Date: unknown
Publicly available document – a public statement by Ayman al-Zawahiri

SOCOM-2012-0000014
From: unknown (intermediary between `Atiyya and Saudi religious scholars)
To: `Atiyya
Forwarded to: Usama bin Ladin
Date: Early 2007

SOCOM-2012-0000015
From: Zamarai (Usama bin Ladin)
To: Shaykh Mahmud
Date: Wednesday, 13 Dhu al-Qidah, 1431 (20 October 2010)

SOCOM-2012-0000016
From: no name listed (assessed to be either Usama bin Ladin and/or `Atiyya)
To: Abu Basir (Nasir al-Wuhayshi)
Date: assessed to be post October 2010 (see notes below)

SOCOM-2012-0000017
From: no name listed (assessed to be Usama bin Ladin)
To: unknown
Date: unknown

It may be helpful to approach the above three documents in terms of their possible relations to one another in the context of the following: SOCOM-2012-0000015, authored by Bin Ladin, noted on page five that he was enclosing a file consisting of parts of a letter that he would like `Atiyya to edit for the purpose of sending to Abu Basir (Nasir al-Wuhayshi), the leader of AQAP. He indicated that `Atiyya is better placed than him to draft it because he knows the "brothers" there (in Yemen). He also asked him to share the final format of the letter. SOCOM-2012-0000017 consists of many paragraphs and notes that do not form an internally coherent essay/letter. Some of these are identical to paragraphs included in the letter to Abu Basir (SOCOM-2012-0000013). It is therefore possible that SOCOM-2012-0000017 was the draft that Bin Ladin enclosed to `Atiyya; in turn, `Atiyya used parts of SOCOM-2012-0000017 and transformed them into a coherent letter to Abu Basir, and this coherent letter is SOCOM-2012-0000016 – which is not signed – to share with Bin Ladin before sending. It is not clear whether Bin Ladin wanted `Atiyya to sign it in his or Bin Ladin's name.

SOCOM-2012-0000018
From: unknown based in Riyadh
To: Honorable Shaykh (assessed to be Usama bin Ladin)
Date: 08/20/1427 (c. 12-14 September 2006)

SOCOM-2012-0000019
From: no name listed (assessed to be Usama bin Ladin)
To: Shaykh Mahmud
Date: unknown

The content of the letter makes it evident that it is authored by Bin Ladin. The letter is not dated, but its author refers to a report, "Nisa' al-Qa`ida," on al-Arabiya, dated 4 July 2010. The letter then had to have been composed post 4 July 2010 but before 20 October 2010 because parts of SOCOM-2012-0000015 (dated 20 October 2010) follow up on issues raised in SOCOM-2012-0000019.